Lean Development and Innovation

Hitting the Market with the Right Products at the Right Time

T0384028

Lean Development and Innovation

Hitting the Market with the Right Products at the Right Time

By
Luciano Attolico

Routledge
Taylor & Francis Group

A PRODUCTIVITY PRESS BOOK

First edition published in 2019

by Routledge/Productivity Press
711 Third Avenue New York, NY 10017, USA
2 Park Square, Milton Park, Abingdon, Oxon OX14 4RN, UK

© 2019 by Luciano Attolico
Routledge/Productivity Press is an imprint of Taylor & Francis Group, an Informa business

No claim to original U.S. Government works

Printed on acid-free paper

International Standard Book Number-13: 978-1-138-48183-1 (Hardback)
International Standard Book Number-13: 978-1-138-48181-7 (Paperback)
International Standard Book Number-13: 978-1-351-05959-6 (eBook)

Library of Congress Cataloging-in-Publication Data

Names: Attolico, Luciano, author.
Title: Lean development and innovation : hitting the market with the right products at the right time / Luciano Attolico.
Description: New York, NY : Routledge, 2018. | Includes bibliographical references and index.
Identifiers: LCCN 2018021197 (print) | LCCN 2018021979 (ebook) | ISBN 9781351059596 (e-Book) | ISBN 9781138481817 (pbk. : alk. paper) | ISBN 9781138481831 (hardback : alk. paper)
Subjects: LCSH: New products. | Lean manufacturing. | Technological innovations.
Classification: LCC TS170 (ebook) | LCC TS170 .A88 2018 (print) | DDC 658.5/75--dc23
LC record available at https://lccn.loc.gov/2018021197

**Visit the Taylor & Francis Web site at
http://www.taylorandfrancis.com**

Contents

Foreword

My original study of Japanese automakers back in 1983 focused on supplier involvement in product development, focused on Toyota, Mazda, and Nissan. All three had similar approaches and were vastly different from American automakers at the time. The difference simply was one of working with trusted partners in Japan from the earliest stages of concept development to Americans controlling the design internally and treating suppliers as vendors shopping their wares and competing on price. It was clear even then that Toyota had a more defined and sophisticated approach to product development than the other two Japanese companies and that led to me delving more deeply into Toyota's system with associates and students, leading ultimately to *The Toyota Product Development System* with Jim Morgan (Productivity Press, 2006). At a high level, what we learned was that Toyota effectively integrated people, processes, and technology with highly focused product development projects supporting long-term strategic plans. The emphasis was on the people—developing them technically, developing their way of working as teams, developing leaders able to get people aligned toward common objectives, challenging them to perform at exceptionally high levels, and treating outside partners as integral parts of the team. We argued that Toyota's product development system was one manifestation of the broader principles I documented in *The Toyota Way*. These started with a philosophy of thinking long-term and investing in the future, developing Lean processes to design in quality from the start, and developing people and partners to rigorously solve problems and turn what they learned into a knowledge database for the future.

At the time of our book on product development, there was relatively little Lean activity in manufacturing organizations beyond the shop floor. In fact, we argued that starting Lean in the core operations for learning and immediately visible results was an effective strategy. Since then, companies have been steadily moving upstream and recognizing that the greatest opportunity to impact long term cost, quality, and customer satisfaction is in Lean Product Development (LPD)—or the conception of whatever your product or service is. LPD consulting has become a cottage industry and extended to other areas such as agile software development. As consultants developed their packages and companies wanted something neat and tidy to purchase, LPD too often became a toolkit to be implemented like a new piece of software.

In parallel with writing books with colleagues, I also have a network of associates who consult for a living attempting to develop in organizations the philosophy and culture we have learned from observing Toyota. The Toyota Way principles form the backbone of our approach. One of my best consultants, John Drogosz, PhD, has worked particularly intensively on LPD for almost a decade and one of our clients was Siemens VDO (the automotive division) that had embarked on a transformation to LPD. In the course of that work, John met Luciano, the author of this book, who at the time was a manufacturing engineering manager for Siemens VDO in Pisa. He took our courses through the University of Michigan on Lean and was one of the bright, rising stars at Siemens who actually practiced what he learned. Luciano later left Siemens VDO, which was sold off, and has since been working as a Lean consultant collaborating with John on several projects. John describes Luciano by saying he is "very passionate about Lean and clearly knows that it is not about the tools, but more about the culture."

This is the key lesson we learned from Toyota and one few people seem to be able to deeply understand. Part I of Luciano's book is the foundation of LPD and the most important insight: "Lean innovation and long-term vision." There is a lot of insight in this simple combination of ideas. Too many people think Lean is the simple application of tools to eliminate waste and ultimately standardize the process so it is mistake proof. Applied to product development, this implies that engineers begin to function as mindless robots. Nothing could be further from the truth. What we learned from Toyota is the key principle of "challenge," which is to face the uncertainty of the future environment with confidence and determination to discover new solutions to solve customer problems. Since product development is work done today for future products, it must be future oriented, using innovation to solve problems anticipated in the future—a lofty and challenging goal indeed. This requires a long-term orientation to invest today for benefits that may not be achieved for years into the future. In fact, the original project which led to the first Prius was an investment that would not really pay off for more than a decade—developing a car for the 21st century.

So what does creative innovation have to do with standardization and Lean processes? The answer starts with your view of how innovation occurs. If the vision is of the brilliant individual who, unencumbered by any rules or bureaucracy, hangs out in the lab waiting for moments of insight, then the last thing you want is to impose standards and a particular process on the creative people. In fact, in Toyota there is relatively little semblance of Lean in the design studios, where artists sketch many alternative designs for future cars.

On the other hand, Toyota views most innovation as coming from teams of people who have deep knowledge in their specialty, working together toward a common, defined, challenging objective. It happens in stages through many small innovative ideas and a few big ones. In the development of automobiles, a complex system which involves thousands of parts coming together and which ultimately must be manufactured with high quality at low cost, there is a tremendous need for communication and coordination across many different people with different knowledge bases…and there are clear timelines for product launch.

Even in the case of the Prius, in which the vision was a car for the 21st century and started with a broad concept more than ten years before the 21st century, Toyota used an organized process with clear timelines. The stages were the blue sky concept, which led to a description of the vehicle and a full-scale drawing; the development of a concept vehicle for auto shows; and finally the development of the first production version of the Prius. Getting the vision right upfront was very important, in this case a fuel-efficient, environmentally friendly vehicle that felt spacious for an entire family. By the time of the development of the first production vehicle it was all hands on deck meeting challenging timelines to be the first mass produced hybrid on the market. It required vision, strong leadership, dedicated engineers solving problem after problem, strong communication across many departments from sales to purchasing to manufacturing to many engineering specialties, and a long-term vision. The significance of the long-term vision was that Toyota did not expect to have a blockbuster product on the first try that made buckets of profits. In fact, the first-generation Prius was primarily for learning—to be improved on in the second generation and so on. Learning about the core technologies, like high-performance batteries, and improving on how these core technologies were designed and manufactured was as important as sales—developing the capability to be prepared to face the challenges of the 21st century.

So let's return to LPD. When you have a complex system that involves coordination and communication of many people in many specialties, you

need well-defined processes, well-defined timelines, clear roles and responsibilities, and strong leadership from a chief architect—which Toyota calls
a "chief engineer." You also need a way to learn over time, so Toyota has
highly developed knowledge databases owned and updated by engineers
with deep technical knowledge in each specialty area. You also need engineers with the social skills to communicate, listen carefully to new ideas,
consider all disconfirming data, and develop integrative solutions that fit
many points of view, such as sales, purchasing, manufacturing, safety, cost,
quality, and more.

The organized system that brings this together is what we describe as
LPD. The underlying philosophy of LPD is that it requires building a strong
culture, and the specific tools used and human resource practices need to be
evolved in each organization over time. So for example, taking an organization with a culture in which professionals do not work effectively in teams or
across functions, do not share knowledge with others or capture it over time,
do not think upstream about the implications of decisions for downstream,
do not plan effectively so that deviations from the plan become the norm,
and generally are working to survive chaos every day will not benefit greatly
from a few tools such as a big room to meet in (Obeya) or problem-solving
forms to fill out (A3). Developing the culture, the deep expertise, the teamwork, the strategic focus, and the ability to deal passionately with uncertainty
and solve difficult problems all require leadership that is patient, thinking
long-term, and has as a top priority the development of people and culture.

Luciano has learned this in the only way possible either as manager or
as consultant and trainer: by studying and then immediately doing and then
studying some more and doing some more. This iterative learning process
deepens your understanding of how to create a system of people, processes,
and technology that can lead your company into the future with products
that truly solve customer's problems. This is the path to becoming a market
leader and an excellent company. Please take this opportunity to learn from
Luciano's journey about the power of Lean thinking in innovation and product development.

Jeffrey K. Liker, PhD

*Professor, Industrial and Operations Engineering, University of Michigan
Author of* The Toyota Way *and co-author of* The Toyota Product
Development System

Preface

My passion has been to build an enduring company where people were motivated to make great products. Everything else was secondary. Sure, it was great to make a profit, because that was what allowed you to make great products. But the products, not the profits, were the motivation. […] People don't know what they want until you show it to them. That's why I never rely on market research. Our task is to read things that are not yet on the page.

Steve Jobs

A few years ago, while reminiscing with my Canadian business partner and good friend John Drogosz, I realized that I had actually begun to implement Lean Thinking long before I even graduated or gained work experience in a multinational company.

I was fifteen at the time, and worked for a restaurant chain where I was responsible for making sandwiches. The production center distributed its perishable products to eighteen bars and restaurants dotted around an exposition and trade fair venue. The biggest problem was supplying them with the right quantities, while always trying to deliver the highest quality product.

Without knowing anything about Lean Production, Lean Supply Chain, or Just in Time, we set up a service plan with min/max inventory levels based on the previous year's sales. Then, armed with bikes and full/empty containers, we continually replenished the bars and restaurants as soon as they consumed their sandwiches.

A few years later, I was to discover that I had actually applied, to the letter, a system called "Kanban," a basic technique of one of the pillars of Lean Production: "Just in Time."

After my university years, armed with a degree in mechanical engineering and the temptation to pursue an academic career as a researcher, I realized that I got more enjoyment out of applying certain theories than studying them. Not by chance I found myself, in 1995, in my first job as an engineer, handling the Just in Time principles at Magneti Marelli, a Fiat Chrysler Automobiles Group company. From making sandwiches to a "white collar" job was a huge step, but the experience in the field had already begun earlier. However, the real breakthrough came when I began working beside Masaaky Yutani, an experienced Japanese mentor, formerly with Toyota. I listened, learned, and began to experiment with applying the Toyota Production System methods and principles, with a person who had lived them for years.

After Magneti Marelli, I had my first experience as a consultant, and worked for almost three years for a well-known international consulting company where I was involved in industrial streamlining projects. Notably, I worked on a project team in charge of the merger of Case and New Holland operations between Italy, the United States, France, and Germany.

Another step came in 2003, and it was to have major consequences for me. I began handling the development of new products and processes at Siemens VDO Automotive, where I met John Drogosz and Jeffrey Liker.* I was part of the launch team of the Lean Transformation program, and early on the company's senior management decided we needed help to guide us through our Lean journey and called on the services of one of the foremost authorities on the Toyota Production System and Lean thinking, Jeffrey Liker.

After personally meeting Jeffrey Liker and having read his books, I was struck by the fact that this man not only talked about the Lean theories, but he had also helped put them into practice in more than twenty years of activity with a group of people selected in the United States to promote the Toyota Way model.

Toyota has gradually built an entire system from scratch. They did not "copy and paste," but rather created it within its specific context that increased the technical and managerial skills of the people to create the right technical and social model fitting the Toyota Way principles.

---

* Jeffrey Liker, a professor at the University of Michigan and author of several bestsellers, including: *The Toyota Way, The Toyota Product Development System*, and many others. In the bibliography is the complete list of texts that I have used as references in this book.

Jeffrey Liker, having seen the Toyota Way in Japan and the United States, internalized the technical and social model, so much so that he was able to describe, recount, and teach it to other companies, as well as the neo-Toyota Americans. John Drogosz worked alongside Jeffrey Liker for over fifteen years and contributed personally to both the writing of some of his books and the business applications of the Lean model. During my time at Siemens VDO Automotive, we created a training program and specific applications that achieved significant results. Above all for me, it contributed to a profound evolution in the way I conceived and applied the Lean principles I had already known for more than a decade.

In my career, therefore, it was inevitable that I would find myself in Japan in late 2004, to visit and study the best Japanese companies, including Toyota, Honda, Sony, Bosch Japan, Omron, and Daikin. The experience was so enlightening that I decided to leave Siemens VDO Automotive a few years later, in December 2007, to continue to work full time as a researcher, consultant, and trainer in the areas that, from the beginning of my career, I have never stopped cultivating in my different jobs: Lean Thinking and Innovation.

Since that time, I have continued to combine the experiences of my American colleagues with mine and those of the group of people who are now part of Lenovys, the consulting firm I founded in 2009.

Lenovys has been ranked in April 2017 by Financial Times among Europe's one-thousand fastest growing companies, which have achieved the highest percentage growth in revenues between 2012 and 2015, according to the data of an independent extensive research that covered thirty-four countries of the European continent focused only on companies with organic, internally stimulated growth. Lenovys' clients in these years have been many and have covered many different industries. Some of them are: Continental, Lamborghini, Roche, Sacmi, Natuzzi, Nestlè, Heineken, Tetra Pak, Campari, Danieli, Honda, Johnson Electric, Laika, Lavazza, Lundbeck, Mahle, Telecom, Solvay, Lucart, and many others. Today Lenovys is the Italian partner of Liker Lean Advisor, LLC, the successful consulting firm of Jeffrey Liker that works in product and process innovation for major global companies such as Caterpillar, Herman Miller, Harley-Davidson, Peugeot, Hertz, GM, Areva, Schlumberger, and Siemens. Thanks to Jeff and John and their valuable contribution I developed with my team all the Lenovys know-how, including the "Impact Innovation" and the Lean Lifestyle® frameworks, which are explained and referred to extensively in the pages that follow.

Why this book, then? Another book on Lean Management?

No. I don't want to add another theoretical work to the many excellent books already available on the market.

I have worked for more than twenty years with Italian, European, and U.S. companies—small, medium-sized, and multinational—and what I want to do in this book is to condense that experience so as to provide some ideas for concrete reflection.

I have placed the social and human aspects of the corporate world at the center of my work and approach. This is the intangible body of know-how possessed by individuals, which is not deposited in written or formalized processes, but often determines the success or failure of a company and of everyone operating in it. The results achieved by a company are largely determined by the products and services offered to customers. Acquiring greater effectiveness in the research and development (R & D) process, from the early phases in the life of a product through its market launch, makes it possible to gain a competitive edge over the competitors and to ensure enduring prosperity.

In this book, I have focused on this phase, vital for every company but often ignored in favor of more operative phases, such as production, logistics, sales, and many others. These phases undoubtedly drain energy, attention, and company costs, but often these are the effects and not the causes of a process that began much earlier: when the product was conceived, when decisions were taken, too many times with little thought, but drastically influencing, for better or worse, the whole lifecycle of the product itself.

I hope you will find ideas for comparison, for reflection, and for putting into practice the different perspectives arising from direct experience over the years of working side by side with hundreds of businessmen and businesswomen.

Every company I have worked with has taught me something or helped me see a winning strategy, and I have come to realize that a level of systemic abstraction and a formalization of winning models is possible.

In the following pages, you will discover how it is possible to effect major changes in a company's life thanks to the application of "Lean thinking" in the development of new products and services. Concrete lessons can be learned from many success stories of companies that have overcome difficult periods and major challenges thanks to the ability to innovate with new methodologies and, above all, with different mental attitudes.

By the time you reach the end of the book, you will be "trained" to quickly recognize the areas of waste that exist in companies, or even in our own personal lives. You will be able to distinguish activities on the basis of the level of added value they bring to a product. You will learn to "wear the spectacles" that show us the reality of a company or of an individual in a clearer light, enabling a better understanding of how the concept of value can make the difference between success and the status quo in everyday life.

My aim in this book is to question a number of "paradigms" that we have perhaps become accustomed to over the years. You will discover, in fact, how some companies have managed to drastically reduce the time required to develop their products, and to whittle down costs while increasing value.

Besides the many examples drawn from different national and international contexts, the book features seven case studies of companies that were or are Lenovys and Likers Lean Advisors clients, focusing on innovation and product development projects: Sacmi, Laika, Continental, Natuzzi, Lamborghini, and Peugeot Citroën. The cases are examined in detail, and from each of them, I believe, you will be able to gather valuable ideas for your own projects.

The book is organized into the following chapters.

Chapter 1—Lean Product-Process Innovation and Long-Term Thinking. When value innovation and winning products make the difference for the long-term success of companies.

Chapter 2—Processes: The Way We Work to Add Value. The importance of defining processes within a company in order to activate improvement at all levels, not to accumulate paper in dusty files containing often forgotten procedures, but to create empowering new habits for individuals and groups.

Chapter 3—People: The Engine for Creativity at the Heart of Long-Term Success. The irreplaceable protagonists of any company. Like Lean Leadership, responsibilization, awareness, sharing, balancing of competences, and learning methods can make the difference between a "leader" company and a "follower." The importance of individual growth for achieving company success.

Chapter 4—Tools for a Lean and Innovative Company. The importance of adopting the right tools and placing them in the right hands and at the service of the right processes, without ever taking a bazooka to kill a fly and without ever putting the tools themselves before the processes and the people.

Chapter 5—Companies That Have Successfully Streamlined and Innovated Their Product Development. A hundred pages devoted to seven cases where Lean Innovation and Product Development principles have been successfully applied in developing new products and processes, hinging on the energy and abilities of the people who drove the change.

Appendix—Modularity: The Way to Reduce the Total Product Costs While Drastically Increasing the Industrial Flexibility. A final chapter that focuses on a vital technique for all the companies aiming to implement product platform strategies, to reduce their industrial complexity, to increase the responsiveness to the market, to reduce the full cost of their products, and to gain flexibility along the entire supply chain.

Furthermore, it is possible to learn more about the topics and carry out many other resources on the web through the links you will find at the end of each chapter.

I hope your journey will benefit from this book.

Good Reading.

Luciano Attolico
CEO and Founder, Lenovys

Acknowledgments

I would like to thank all the people who contributed to the birth of this book, apologizing in advance to all those who I have not mentioned.

A special thanks to Jeffrey Liker, professor of Industrial and Operations Engineering at the University of Michigan, author of *The Toyota Way*, and co-author of *The Toyota Product Development System*, who deeply inspired me with his teachings and his works: thanks for his contributions and for the trust placed in me.

I am grateful to my friend John Drogosz who, with his generous mentoring, his motivation, and his unreserved support, has guided me and my team in our professional growth and who has contributed to the drafting of the Peugeot Citroën business case.

When I think of my friend and sensei Gianluigi Bielli, I am convinced that, without his constant and tireless support over the last years, I would not be where I am today; a huge thank you also for having enriched this volume with the writing of the Appendix on modularity.

Tommaso Massei, with his intuitions, his contributions, and his enthusiasm, has been crucial in giving the final inputs to the writing of this book. The adventure of the last years would not have been the same without my friend and colleague Leo Tuscano, with whom I shared hundreds of reflections and discoveries: thank you for your unceasing help on all fronts. A big thank you to Simone Bielli, Giuseppe Patania, Federico Loffredo, and Emanuela Frasca for their continuous support and for the precious revisions of texts.

I thank Pietro Cassani of Sacmi for having believed in Lenovys from the very beginning and Mauro Ferri, Agnese Peliconi, Emanuele Ceroni, Davide Baldisserri, and Marco Salieri for their contributions to the cases exposed.

Thanks to Luciano De Oto of Lamborghini for sharing the processes and tools of a company that makes the whole world dream.

I appreciate the courage and support of Jan De Haas of Laika, whom I thank very much together with Roberto Viciani, Ennio Frullano, and Francesco Gabrielli for sharing their Motorhome project. Thanks to the whole Laika team for the work done together in recent years: Filippo Masini, Elisa Brettoni, Enrico Ciacci, Paolo Bisanzi, Monica Rigacci, Simone Mazzuoli, and Giuseppe Lovino, along with the rest of the team.

A sincere thanks to Alberto Marinai, Riccardo Toncelli, Fabio Sarri, and Marco Fiaschi of Continental for their contributions and for having agreed to disclose the business case presented.

Special thanks to the PSA Peugeot Citroën team for sharing their experience on the Set-Based Concurrent Engineering. Thanks also to Olivier Souliè of the PSA Excellence group for sharing his insights and collaboration in providing the contents of the case presented in this book.

A big thank you to Pasquale Natuzzi, source of vision, tenacity, and courage for all of us, Filippo Petrera, Antonio Cavallera, Michele Colucci, Domenico Ricchiuti, Antonio Paparella, Livio Mottola, Antonio Ventricelli, and the whole Natuzzi team for their work and contribution to the project.

Without the trust and support of my Italian editor Hoepli, mainly in the person of Andrea Sparacino, this book probably would not have come to light as you see it today. And a big thanks to Michael Sinocchi, Productivity Press, for trusting and supporting me in the completely updated and revised English edition of this book.

Thanks to all my clients and my collaborators for their mutual trust and for the journey done together. Thanks to the many hundreds of people who have attended my Seminars, Executive Masters, and Workshops in these years.

Thanks to my family and friends who have supported me despite the long distances and the frequent absences.

Thanks to my wonderful wife Francesca, for her tireless support and for always being close to me even in difficult moments. A final thought, full of love, for my child Amedeo, who has been enlightening my life since his birth.

Author

After a Master's Degree with honors in Mechanical Engineering, Luciano started his professional career in Magneti Marelli, which is nowadays part of the FCA Group. He was responsible for the production launch of an electro-oleo dynamic system for mechanical gear shift, used by Mercedes, Ferrari, and Renault vehicles.

He moved to Siemens as Industrial Engineering Director and later as Advanced Technology Development of the Automotive Powertrain Business Unit. He was responsible for the development of production technologies and systems, as well as for the production launch of new production systems for BMW, Mercedes, Audi, and Porsche, coordinating offices and plants in the United States, Germany, France, Italy, and China.

In these industrial experiences he led many international Lean projects with mentors such as Masaaki Yutani, former Toyota sensei, Hiroshi Moriwaki, Jeffrey Liker, and John Drogosz. While working as manager, Luciano completed his specialization courses of the University of Michigan in Lean Manufacturing and Lean Product and Process Development.

Luciano is co-founder and CEO since 2009 of Lenovys, a primary European research, Lean consultancy, and training firm based in Italy that focuses on Lean Leadership and Innovation. Lenovys was recognized in 2017 by the Financial Times as one of the Europe's Fastest Growing Companies, a special ranking called "FT 1000" that includes the top one-thousand independent European Companies with the highest rate of innovation and organic growth. Together with his team, Luciano Attolico has supported relevant companies in their Lean Transformation and training projects, such as Lavazza, Sacmi, Continental, Roche, Lamborghini, Heineken, Tetra Pak, MAHLE, CNH, Frigoglass, Natuzzi, Campari, Streparava, Ideal Standard, Lucchini RS, DeWalt, Whirlpool, Leroy Merlin, and many others.

Luciano has developed the Lean Lifestyle® approach, a management framework that aims to achieve the Lean Thinking as a Lifestyle. Its ultimate goal is to get more value with less stress and waste of people energy, bringing at the same time well-being and high performance in the company.

Presently, Luciano is actively engaged as a keynote speaker in the fields of Lean Leadership, Innovation, Human Energy, and Change Management, bringing his long experience, his personal philosophy focused on human value and on the continuous research to achieve more results with less efforts and higher well-being.

Luciano is author of the Italian best-selling book on Lean Innovation, *Innovazione Lean* (Hoepli, 2012); co-author with Jeffrey Liker of *Toyota Way. I 14 principi per la rinascita del sistema industriale italiano* (Hoepli, 2014), a special Italian edition of the classic Liker's book; and editor for the Italian edition of *Toyota Way per la Lean Leadership* by Jeffrey Liker and Gary Convis (Hoepli, 2015).

Chapter 1

Lean Product-Process Innovation and Long-Term Thinking

We often underestimate the impact that innovation in the products or services we provide to our customers has on the long-term prosperity of any business. In fact, no amount of operational excellence will compensate for a poorly designed and thought through value offering to the customer. We are simply putting a well-made and executed, but unappealing or unuseful, product or service up for sale. This chapter discusses the links between innovation, product development, and business strategy. When companies focus on the beating heart of their business, that is, the set of products and services they offer, they are better able to devote their scarce resources to the things that can really make a difference to their customers. Through the years of the Great Recession and its aftermath, too many companies saw their only way to survival as cost reduction often gutting the innovation engine that was the key to their future. What those that could afford it should have been doing is using the downtime to apply the principles of Lean thinking to the development and innovation process to have a true competitive advantage when the dust settled and the economy began to recover.

1.1 A Strategic Question: Excellence in the Long-Term or Mediocrity in the Short-Term?

> He that does not foresee things in the distant future, exposes himself to unhappiness in the near future.
>
> **Confucius**

Is it possible to generate profits and prosper over a long time, in today's capitalist world, by setting targets that are not exclusively short-term "for profit" targets?

If we look at what great companies have been able to do, we realize that not only is it possible, but also that it is the only way to guarantee success in the long run.

For high-performing companies, the long-term strategies and their competitive advantages acquired over time always seem to take priority over short-term gains. These companies are inspired by the dreams of their visionary leaders. Companies that come to mind include Google, Apple, Microsoft, Walt Disney, and Cirque du Soleil. In Italy, we can point out to Luxottica, Diesel, Ferrari, and Lamborghini.

In the book *The Toyota Way* by Jeffrey Liker, we discover that the first of the fourteen management principles that enabled Toyota to produce the industrial miracle it is today is precisely this: *the actions that lead to greater long-term benefits should always be placed before those that yield modest short-term gains.*[1]

The Japanese giant has shown how it is possible to align the goals of nearly 250,000 people to something greater than simply "making a quick buck this quarter." Their strategic mission is to create value for the customer, society, and the economy through their products and services. Irrespective of the many fine words, it is amazing to witness the commitment of their people to this strategic objective, translated into everyday activities aimed at increasing the value of their products and the relentless effort to eliminate waste. The deep and tangible conviction is that, without a doubt, by living this principle it is possible to achieve higher profits over time.

Sometimes we are asked: Why haven't American companies replicated Toyota's successes, in spite of being familiar with their model since the 1980s? General Motors had a chance to experience it firsthand starting in 1984 when they launched a fifty-fifty joint venture with Toyota in California called NUMMI.

In fact, this is a paradox, because it is essentially thanks to American and British scholars like Jim Womack and Daniel Jones, who were funded by American companies to study the Toyota model and disseminate knowledge of it,[2] that we came to know the Toyota model.

It was not the Toyota people who were marketing themselves, but in fact the Americans and the British who gave the best possible visibility and promotion of the Lean model that, since the fifties, has revolutionized their way of doing business, teaching the world to achieve more with far fewer resources. Theoretically, the Americans should have known exactly what to do to achieve the same benefits, but one of the things that led the major American automakers to the brink of (or actual) bankruptcy was their inability to break away from short-term thinking. For example, it is interesting that General Motors originally viewed NUMMI as having two purposes: One was to learn how to make small, fuel-efficient cars profitably (which at the time they were unable to do) and the other was to learn the Toyota Production System (TPS). In reality, they simply used NUMMI as a way to get Toyota to run a plant that could build small cars profitably with GM nameplates on them. Almost nothing about TPS was learned by GM and they did not learn much about developing and making profitable small cars by simply letting Toyota do it. The short-term benefit of the profitable, high-quality cars coming out of the plant seemed enough for GM, while Toyota intensely was studying and learning how to bring TPS to American culture so they could spread this know-how as they launched new overseas plants over the coming decades.

In most publicly traded companies, senior positions are typically filled by people motivated to focus on quarterly financial statements to show "gains," often from outside the company or even the industry. Success equates to satisfying shareholders. The focus on "quick wins" and a high degree of personnel rotation were clearly some of the contributors that led to a genuine long-term strategic dysfunction for those companies and it shows in the lengthy development of new products that are of little interest to customers.

Toyota's rise to prominence clearly shows how the value of a company can grow significantly over time, with a clear long-term strategic vision that drives daily activities. But, as we shall see, Toyota is not the only one. For these long-term thinking companies, when it comes to innovation and product development, we are referring to business strategies and not just tactics, as happens in many companies. These organizations prefer to spend more on product development and design, rather than resorting to having to spend hundreds of thousands of dollars in post-production fixes and "enhancements" after the fact.

Deciding to invest in better products and taking preventative measures from the beginning is a cultural trait of innovative Lean companies. Before techniques, even before the methods, the culture plays a crucial role in the way that a company approaches innovation. Focusing solely on short-term results can literally shift the future destiny of both companies and individuals. Lean innovators make a great effort to evaluate the real long-term impact of what they choose to do: the real risks to be taken, the real costs (short- and long-term) to bear, and the true benefits that will result for their customers and ultimately their bottom line.

In a 2006 article in the *Harvard Business Review,* Edmund Phelps[3] argues that the rate of innovation in Western companies, starting with those in the U.S., was on a path to dangerously low levels. Among the main causes of this according to Phelps is the lack of a strategic long-term vision. This lack of strategic vision from senior management and entrepreneurs is attributed to the increasing pressure from financial markets (institutional investors and security analysts) to constantly surpass profit quarterly growth goals. This is reinforced by "deviant" compensation mechanisms, such as large quantities of stock options, which tend to reward managers on the basis of the results obtained in relatively short time spans. The resulting shift toward the achievement of short-term goals results in important consequences that seriously affect business management. Companies decide, for example, on drastic reductions in spending on R & D, and do not invest in training and people development. The tendency is to overlook a whole series of key activities that will be fruitful well beyond the short-to-medium term. According to Phelps, failure to invest in innovation in the long run will deprive the U.S. economy of one of its key success factors, namely the ability of entrepreneurs to build new businesses, develop new products, create new markets, and establish themselves in new market niches. Phelps also points out that innovation cannot be created artificially, from the top down, or by central public organizations. Innovation comes from the bottom, stemming necessarily from a passion for the product, from the desire to realize ideas and the desire to make "real" money.[4]

It is not all dire news, as there are illuminating examples of companies doing the exact opposite including Apple, Harley-Davidson with its timeless motorcycle, and Schlumberger, the largest oil services company in the world. All these companies in diverse industries have something in common: they are making some far-sighted choices by maintaining or, in some cases, even increasing investment in product innovation and in R & D, instead of stopping and slowing everything, frightened by the winds of crisis. Even Boeing with all of its self-inflicted crises in the development and launch of its revolutionary Dreamliner has orders into the future far beyond production capacity that will help set the company up for long-term success.

It is in product development and innovation management where the real key to the long-term success of a company is hidden. Innovation can be the result of being truly strong or simply playing hard. Imagine two boxers in the ring. One boxer lands his blows in a powerful and precise way, while the other one, flustered, thrashes around, lashing out with frequent, poorly aimed punches. Who is likely to win the match?

This is exactly what happens every day in business!

1.2 Innovating to Achieve Success

> If I'd asked customers what they wanted, they would have said a faster horse.

> **Henry Ford**

For any business today, it is impossible to survive in the marketplace without continuously innovating products and services. Everything we produce will sooner or later be made by someone else at a lower cost and probably of the same or better quality. This "rule" is now true in virtually every industry. The meaning of innovation is commonly understood as something extraordinary, outside the scope of what we encounter daily. Generally, it is something that has a long gestation period, typically within a few groups of dedicated people, before it sees the light of day. This is certainly a type of innovation, but isn't the innovation required to create the next-generation iPhone—making it faster, lighter, with a better camera, and a higher resolution screen? In Toyota, they say the two products that take the highest level of engineering is the newest Lexus which always requires some breakthrough technology that has not been in a vehicle before and the Corolla which requires packaging more features into a lighter weight vehicle at a low cost.

If we analyze what leads companies to continually bring to market new products that build market share we find that it is impossible to separate the innovative process from the people and culture of the company. In fact, the process is the thinking of people and teamwork to share thoughts and build on new ideas.

On occasion the lone inventor will have a eureka moment, but companies that renew themselves continually depend on a certain type of leadership, an environment that supports teamwork and creativity, and a lot of trial and error. In other words, innovation is the result of a widespread mentality and culture of continuous improvement and not just *the stroke of genius* of one or a few people.

To better understand this statement, let's analyze more deeply the various types of innovation in a company, taken from our framework *"Impact Innovation"*:

1. *Product Innovation*
   This is the most frequently discussed type of innovation which includes:
   a. *Incremental improvements of existing products*: These are modifications of older products with some improvements such as improved performance, updated styling, or added features. This is often used to help maintain the competitiveness of a product and keep existing customers.
   b. *Introduction of new generation products*: Replacing or significantly improving the value proposition of existing products. In this case, it is a major redesign changing the appearance, function, or cost of the product. In this case, it is not just about keeping existing customers but trying to "steal" customers from other product segments or the competition.
   c. *Introduction of "out of the box" products that did not exist before*: These products are created to meet unfulfilled customer needs which can lead to the creation of new markets.
2. *Commercial innovation/extension of the perception of value*
   How products are presented and delivered is another area of innovation:
   a. *Marketing, promotion, and communication of products*: Using creative means through this channel increases the perceived value of the products or makes them stand out in comparison to other similar products. As an example, think of those advertising campaigns that leave the jingle stuck in your head for hours after you saw the advertisement.
   b. *Extension of the experience of value linked to the product*: Pulling the customer toward the product or service to have them see or feel the value firsthand. Consider the case of the Apple Store, where the

potential customer becomes a user who can experience products, service, and culture before actually owning them. Another example is Toyota's attempt to attract younger buyers to Lexus by changing the look of the dealership including adding a café.

3. *Innovation of processes/tools for the manufacturing of products*
   Many of these types of innovation may not be directly seen by the customer but nonetheless help drive value behind the scenes.
   a. *Incremental improvements to existing operational processes:* Reduction of elements that do not add value for the end customer and increases efficiency in terms of cost and use of resources. Examples would include the kitting/packing operations at Amazon.
   b. *Introduction of new processes or operating methods:* These typically employ radical product innovations from other sectors such as new machines, new technologies, new measuring devices, etc. An example would be Fed Ex's state-of-the-art sorting system that enables their overnight delivery service.

4. *Innovation in the company to support people*
   While innovation comes from people, innovations can also come about in ways to enable creativity. Some forms of people innovation include:
   a. *Creation of social and organizational conditions* that foster the identification and adoption of innovation in the company's product and process.
   b. *Leadership and cultural evolution of the individuals:* investments in developing people and culture to enhance internal expertise, motivation, and spur creativity.

Unfortunately, innovation alone does not guarantee success. Many companies have invested in new products and services and not seen sales materialize or gain a solid return on their investments. For example, in 2000 Procter & Gamble found that only 15% of its innovation projects met the turnover and profit target. By reviewing and improving the company's entire innovation system, incredible results were achieved. The company created a structured plan in which the principles of Lean Thinking were gradually introduced along with a reorganization of the entire Research and Development group to enable innovation to thrive. In ten years, the success rate, i.e., innovations that met and exceeded the target profit and turnover, rose by over 50%.[5]

1.3 From Lean Management to the Lean Development and Innovation System

> Those who are enamored of practice without science are like the sailor who gets into a ship without a rudder or compass and who can never be certain of where he is going. Practice must always be founded on sound theory.
>
> **Leonardo Da Vinci**

1.3.1 Lean Thinking

Lean thinking is, first and foremost, a different attitude in the individuals who work within an organization. It is an attitude that leads straight to the heart of things, to respond promptly to a clear need: Who is our "real" customer and how can we provide them value?

It can be an external or internal customer, our colleague or a boss we provide with a product or service. With Lean Thinking, we constantly question not only what value customers *exactly* expect from us, our products, and our services, but how we can continually increase it while at the same time reducing activities that do not add value. For this reason, applying the principles of Lean Thinking are vital to any innovation process.

From the Lean Thinking perspective, an activity can fall into one of three types:

- *An activity that the customer is willing to pay for* and therefore a *value-added activity* that is also recognizable by the end user; (Luciano's Japanese *sensei*,[6] Masaaky Yutani, added that in his opinion an activity is value-added when the end user is *happy* to pay you for it).
- *Activities that do not add value for the customer*, but that are deemed *necessary*. For example, an activity that meets legal and regulatory requirements. Despite being "auxiliary," they can be crucial to the company's ability to function.
- *A completely non-value activity*, i.e. pure waste, that the customer would never pay for and may even lead them to question their desire to purchase the product.

The starting point, in the spirit of Lean Thinking, is to see our activities through the eyes of the customer. Learning to recognize the value in our processes, and distinguishing them from the possible different forms of waste is our task.

To start wearing "Lean glasses" means completely changing the point of view of how things are done, managing to be "honest critics" of everything we do, beginning a journey that can take us a long way toward freeing up our time to do more innovative value-added tasks.

1.3.2 *Historical Background of Lean Thinking*

Lean thinking has its roots in Lean Manufacturing, the production model now known all over the world that originated with the Toyota Production System. It actually all started with Henry Ford and his moving assembly line, which became the model on which Toyota based its production system in the forties, "a continuously moving line is a continuous flow of material," which is the ideal of the Toyota Production System (TPS). It then follows that anything that blocks or slows down the flow of material is waste. Unfortunately, the Ford Motor Company did not continue its commitment to the original vision of Henry Ford. At its largest factory along the River Rouge, near Detroit, Michigan, one of the largest complexes of the manufacturing era, the focus was shifted from the flow of material to the objective of making as many parts as possible to keep the machines constantly running, whether the downstream processes were available or not. Inventory grew enormously as each machine worked on its own time cycle, regardless of the demands of the other processes. Ford made the mistake of turning the Rouge plant into a series of "process villages," disconnected islands full of semi-finished products waiting to be assembled into a final product. The fluctuations of market demand were absorbed by a production that forced the finished products into the sales network ("push" production). Flow production (as it was designed by Ford in 1914) was transformed into *mass production*.

Meanwhile, Toyota was developing the Lean manufacturing system that allowed it the flexibility to build to customer demand (the Toyota market was originally confined to Japan, which required small quantities of highly varied products) and to continually improve its products and processes.

Taiichi Ohno had the task of closing the huge productivity gap that divided Toyota from its American competitors—originally Ford was nine times as productive. He built from many ideas imported from those same American companies and with a long series of experiments he managed to develop what is now known as the Toyota Production System (TPS). One of Sakichi Toyoda's earliest innovations, when they were still making looms for weaving was the ability for the machine to detect defects and stop every time there was a quality problem. This became the basis for one of the key concepts of the Toyota Production System, *Jidoka* (stop when there is a problem in manual or automated processes and fix the problem). Ohno turned the idea of Kiichiro Toyoda into reality, established the second key concept of TPS: the *manufacturing pull system*, or *Just In Time*, which consists of "pulling" the entire production system according to the demands of the products as customers request them. Ultimately, this led to organizing the entire management of the materials, both internally and with the suppliers, on this principle of replenishing in small quantities each item according to actual consumption.

Toyota also recognized the importance of its people, who were not just viewed as low skilled workers, but were valued team members expected to participate in continuously improving processes. Another of Toyoda's key innovations (working with Shigeo Shingo) was to make production lines flexible to make multiple products by minimizing setup times between one product and another.

While TPS enabled Toyota to grow its sales, it was not until the early 1990s when the book *The Machine That Changed the World* was published that the global business community truly saw the power of TPS. It was from this book that the term Lean Manufacturing, or Lean Production originated, as Toyota was doing more with less of everything: less space, fewer people, less capital, and fewer warehouses.[7] For many years, Toyota closed with annual profits consistently higher than those of GM, Chrysler, and Ford combined. Toyota's market value in 2005 amounted to 177 billion dollars, exceeding the sum of the three great American companies (Ford, General Motors, and Chrysler) put together. The design and development of a new product requires twelve to eighteen months for Toyota, while the main American and European competitors take up to two to three years.[8] Even today Toyota, despite the unfortunate recall campaigns of 2010,[9] remains a beacon in the world for its market value, its profits, the very high quality of its products, its high productivity, its reduced cycle times, and high flexibility.

1.3.3 What Can We Learn from the Toyota Model?

This historical overview explains why the Toyota model has been so thoroughly studied and promoted throughout the world. I have also learned a great deal from this study, in fact, I have been deeply influenced by it, having worked under a Toyota *sensei*. What I tried to do is to understand the similarities between Toyota and other companies that have had similar excellent growth, even outside of the automotive industry. In my professional career, I have always tried to figure out how to apply, in different contexts, the models that are foreign to us in terms of their industrial culture and extraction.

For example, a fundamental concept very dear to Taiichi Ohno is the famous "circle of Ohno." It was an actual circle drawn on the floor inside the factory where he spent hours standing to observe what happened in the production department. He continued to watch and observe, hunting down all forms of possible waste. Unnecessary movements, unnecessary transport, scrap, redundant processes, products not shipped on time, excess inventory, people waiting for materials, and so on. His goal was to identify the causes of waste in production in order to reduce the time that elapses between the moment the order is received and when the product is shipped to the customer ultimately leading to payment for the product.

Accordingly, he classified what he saw in production, into seven *major forms of waste (+ one)*.

1. *Overproduction*: the worst waste of all, when you produce something that is not strictly required by any customers.
2. *Waiting*: for materials, information, orders, or anything else that impedes flow.
3. *Unnecessary processes*: redundant tasks, processes that are not strictly necessary that drain company resources without having a particular added value for the end customer.
4. *Scrap, reprocessing, and poor-quality products*: every time we produce semi-finished or finished products that need additional processing and resources to eliminate defects.
5. *Unnecessary transport*: transport from one area to another
6. *Inventory*: takes up space to store material waiting to be sold or shipped to the customer.
7. *Unnecessary movements*: any movement that does not directly transform material into value for the customer.
8. *Not using the full human potential at our disposal*: this type of waste was added by Jeffrey Liker a few years later as part of his early studies.

Ohno's focus was to break down all the waste to maximize *cash flow*, minimizing the time between receiving the order and delivery of the finished product in order to obtain new cash to be reinvested: this concept is fully adaptable to this day in all contexts, because in the end, it means asking a question that prevails over all the others: *How can we reduce the time materials, information, and resources that are present in our company?* The less time a product is in the system, the faster it can get to the customer (and the cash can be collected).

1.3.4 Wastes in Product and Innovation Processes

What regularly happens with improvement projects that are carried out in administration and new product development?

In the example in Figure 1.1, we see a typical flow of development activities of an automotive product, which is very similar to the product development flow of other industries. We move from the stage of conceptualizing the new product, where stages of marketing, modeling, styling, prototyping, and developing the production processes all come together, arriving at the tooling phase and the final production launch. The total time of most development projects ranges from eight months to two to three years, depending on the product complexity.

If we divide the typical development activities into activities that are value-adding for the end customer (dark areas in Figure 1.1) and the others that are non-value added (light areas in Figure 1.1), on average, less than

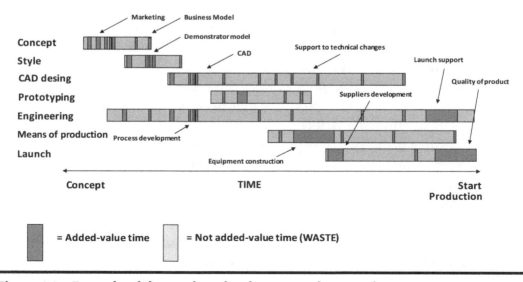

Figure 1.1 Example of the product development value map for a car company. (Source: Morgan J. and Liker J.K., *The Toyota Product Development System: Integrating People, Process, and Technology*, New York: Productivity Press, 2006.)

20% of the total time spent in product development in a typical company is devoted to value-added activities. So, if we look closely at the example, the reason we take so long on projects is not due to the dark blocks of activity, but rather the gray ones (i.e. wastes).

I don't know why, but we tend to focus more on improving activities in the dark area, value-added, that are generally already the smallest part compared to the whole.

Ironically, traditional improvements in product development in the past years have been focused on the dark blocks (value added activities). For example, companies have spent millions of dollars and thousands of hours have been spent on implementing new information technology (CAD stations, simulation, engineering change order systems, etc.). While these tools have clearly helped improve design quality and computational speed, they have had only a slight impact on the overall product development cycle time (see Figure 1.2).

However, many have stopped there. Consequently, nothing happens to reduce the number of days in which data is waiting between areas or the vast number of drawings that are re-done over and over again. Nothing is done to avoid wasting weeks churning over designs and validating them. If the goal is to reduce the total development time of a new product or service, then it is smarter (and cheaper) to attack 80% of the problem, the light parts, of waste, rather than the dark parts of Figure 1.1. With Lean product development, the focus is on attacking these wastes that are stopping us from getting our product to the market.

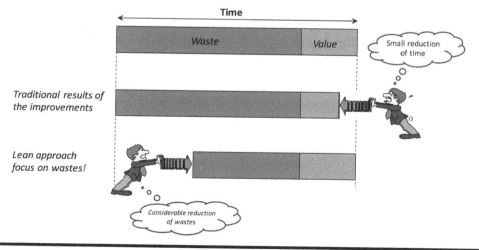

Figure 1.2 Example of the difference between the traditional approach and Lean approach to improving.

That being said, the goal is to improve the speed of the overall product development Value Stream and not necessarily the speed of each area. Sometimes it is possible to make significant improvements to products by spending only a few minutes more than usual, interacting upfront in the design phase. For example, during the design of a mechanical component, taking the time to draw an edge that is a little more rounded in order not to cause problems for those who handle that piece in the manufacturing facility or researching for a cheaper but equally functional material in order to reduce the cost. These examples illustrate how working upstream in design can eliminate unnecessary waste downstream in production.

Often thinking of attacking these problems is more difficult, more awkward, more complex, because it forces us to create interaction between technical aspects and social and behavioral aspects; one is forced to go much deeper to discover the causes of waste and this forces us to do a 360° turn to see waste within the company. So, learning to recognize waste and focusing on eliminating it is what will contribute the most to a company's success, especially when we learn to do it in the early stages of product development. In this way, we get the most value with the least overall effort.

When you make an improvement on a value-added activity, you achieve marginal improvement in the individual activities involved. For example, look at high-performance computers compared to the past and the use of email. While it is true that there has been an undeniable improvement in single activities that involve the use of the computer itself or the use of the email (fast processing and communication of individual data), we cannot say that the total flow activity involving PCs and email have seen significant improvements. In fact, in some cases, real communication between people within projects have even worsened.

Therefore, when measuring the benefits of an improvement we need to consider it in the context of the entire Value Stream. If we cannot measure the effects from the perspective of the Value Stream, the flow of value, from the idea of a product to when the customer is actually holding the quality product he expected in his hand, then it will also be more difficult to verify the successful reduction of waste.

From this point of view, any improvement activities leading to a reduction in overall product development time, such as reducing the number of iterations, the reworking of tooling, and the useless waiting, in design and administrative tasks should be encouraged. Certainly, the elimination of such waste has a tangible effect on *cash flow*, even though traditional accounting systems are often not designed to give immediate evidence of this; in the end, it will show up in either reduced development costs and/or product costs. Perhaps, more importantly, the product or service gets to the market sooner and hence generates revenue for the company sooner.

Therefore, by reducing the light blocks, the waste, there is a gain for the company with almost zero investment, except for the cost of the people who are involved in the critical review of their own processes and their habits.

While it is true that outside help can arrive to more quickly identify waste and lead the company toward possible solutions, in the form of mentoring and coaching, rather than traditional consultants, it is also true that the greatest effort is made by the people within the company. In these Lean projects, the consultant cannot replace the people who do the work everyday. However, outsiders can provide examples of other companies that have faced similar experiences and provide guidance and methods to help quickly bring out waste that is already present in the working group but not expressed or is buried by deep-seated habits or lack of initiative and leadership.

In fact, the success of a Lean journey depends, in part, on the choice of a good *sensei*—a mentor who is knowledgeable about Lean, has a long history of implementation, and someone who has the ability to change the people's way of thinking. This is the big difference, from the point of view of the business of traditional management consulting. Empowering customers by teaching them to be independent is, on the long-term, more important than providing the right solutions to the problems.

With a Lean approach, giving the attention to the customer must be the true focus of all those involved in the Value Stream and cannot simply be staffed out. Almost always, waste reduction is achieved with very simple tools and above all with changes in attitudes, ways of thinking, and habits by those involved in the process everyday.

1.4 Types of Waste in the Innovation Process

A wise man will make more opportunities than he finds.

Francis Bacon

How to recognize waste in the forest of endless meetings, without constructive conclusions, dependency on emails, attitudes of justification rather than solutions, good ideas that are untapped, knowledge distributed, or maintained by word of mouth and not structured?

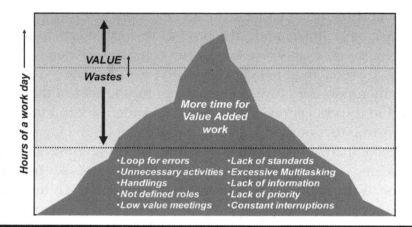

Figure 1.3 Most of our time is typically spent in wastes according to the Lean Thinking principles. Our main job should be distinguishing value added from waste.

You can summarize the causes of waste in major categories, just as Taiichi Ohno did by dividing into seven macro wastes the causes of lost productivity in a production environment. Over time, different approaches have expanded on the concept by combining the major categories of waste to product development and processes (Figure 1.3).

In their research, Morgan and Liker categorized waste into twelve items that are specific to the design and development environment. These include:

1. *Handoffs*

   Handling occurs when activities and responsibilities are transferred from one part to another, when we pass a "semi-intellectual" job from one person to another. This actually occurs many times and often without realizing it, when we pass the ball of responsibility from one person to another, when one person begins a job and another finishes it, when the right hand doesn't know what the left hand is doing, when a group task is confused with a lower level of responsibility and individual *ownership,* when a task is fragmented into too many subtasks, and loses the thread. Some of the causes of this type of waste are identified in poor communication, in poor interpretation of those giving and receiving information, in poor assessment of the full individual potential for overseeing the entire flow of a series of interconnected activities. This category of waste is comparable to unnecessary transport and unnecessary movements that occur during production.

2. *"External" Excess*

   Falling into this macro-category are all the effort and time spent collecting data that no one will use, data that no one reads, and reports used to 10-20%. The paradoxical thing is that this waste is often linked to its opposite: the data required is not available when it is needed, or it takes three times as long to find it amongst all the other unnecessary data.

3. *Waiting Times*

   Waiting for data, answers, decisions, and revisions, due to lack of capacity and resources (human and machine). We often confuse various kinds of waiting with the value-added process, such as every time we stop or slow down because of lack of control, too much information, complicated research, outdated information, incompatibility of information, or software incompatibilities. And also: communication errors, security issues, lack of direct access, reformatting, and the need for further information or knowledge.

4. *Redundant Tasks*

   For example, multiple inspections and checks, rushing, creation of unnecessary data and information, dissemination of information, too much customization, and too many iterations.

5. *Stop and Go*

   This occurs whenever an engineer, technician, or employee must reorient to a task. When you recommence a project several times it is like having multiple set-ups. This waste is what causes the greatest inurement and goes hand in hand with interruptions. It is often mistaken for a virtue, indeed there are those who boast of being capable of having dozens of projects going on at the same time. Whenever someone is forced to stop and restart, on average it takes about fifteen to twenty minutes to return to the level of intellectual energy and concentration that they had when they were interrupted.

6. *Transactions*

   This is time wasted in ancillary but necessary activities. For example, contracts, negotiations, meetings to work on various offers, complex contracts, supplier selection, scheduling resources, trade union activities, etc. These are all activities that force us to waste too much time when there is a lack of clear processes, clearly defined responsibilities, or mechanisms that do not delegate enough.

7. *Reinvention*

   Recreation or rediscovery of things that are already known. How often do we reinvent things invented by others? How often do we confuse creativity with reinventing something? Instead of worrying about inventing something that has not yet been invented we are content to reinvent something that has already been invented. Instead of starting from a higher level to create something of greater value, often we are witnessing reinvention.

8. *Lack of Discipline*

Being certified and using a wealth of procedures written on paper does not provide real discipline in operational processes. Can you imagine any sport, individual or team sports, without rules and particularly without the discipline to follow those same rules? What would happen to that athlete or that team? Beyond the legal aspect of the issue and then the penalty that might be applied, what would happen would certainly not help in terms of sports performance, as much as all the schemes are actually designed to maximize performance in the ongoing competition. Moving on to company dynamics, the lack of discipline causes variability in the output of a process to change the time and the people involved, as well as unpredictability of the length of the line-ups waiting at each center of intellectual work.

It is often assumed that the presence of procedures, or practices due to years of repetitions of the same behaviors, automatically mean real optimized processes and relative discipline in following them. So we are not talking about the external rules imposed, but the rules and regulations that arise from the inside with the purpose of increasing the performance of the individual and the group. It is well known that discipline and creativity are two sides of the same coin: the more teams and people learn to be disciplined and follow the rules of the game, the more natural space is found for creativity that adds value. Putting together discipline and creativity liberates vital energies because with the rules of the game you learn how to do certain things almost automatically and "routinely," and at the same time it frees up energies for those activities with high added value in the spaces appropriately destined for this purpose.

9. *Variability of Processes and Inputs*

Late delivery of information. Delivery that is too early. The variability of processes, activities, and the arrival of input are some of the main causes for long lines and long crossing times. This happens, for example, whenever there are changes of direction, changes in objectives, or disruptions to an ongoing project. This category of waste is the same that causes inter-operational stockpiling in production.

10. *Overuse of the System*

    Once you reach 80% use of a system, every little change has dramatic effects on crossing times and then the performance of that system. Imagine that you always have an agenda full of commitments with no gap between one commitment and the other. How likely is it that you can fulfill all the commitments on time, rather than in the case where you have an agenda with scheduled commitments and gaps between one commitment and another? Nobody pays attention to the fact that a system of human beings has a productivity rate that depends on the load it is bearing. Having a team employed at 60% or 90% of their saturation rate makes a vast difference in that same team's yield. It is essential to take this into account when managing projects. The calculation of the saturation capacity of the teams is extremely important when developing new products.

11. *Large Batches*

    Data "pushed" forward and not "pulled" by those who need it. The cycle time increases with the size of what we do, or the lot or batch, and the same is true of intellectual production. The waiting times become longer for the delivery of large quantities of data. We have a real surplus when we work "in large batches."

    For the designer, it means having the parcel of one hundred drawings to be processed before passing it to the next department, instead of doing one thing at a time. How many times do you have the feeling of going faster by doing several things at once? In fact, the fewer things one does in the fraction of time, the faster you go in the long run. The concept of the large batch is the same for humans as it is in the production system: the more things you put into the "processing tube," the slower you go, even if you have the illusion of going faster.

12. *Simultaneous or Concurrent Unsynchronized Activities*

    This is one of the most insidious forms of waste and often seems the right thing to do even if it is often the basis of a whole series of other forms of waste. Has it ever happened to you to not be called upon to make your contribution in a certain phase of the project, only to realize that when you are called on to make your contribution, either it is given no space or it leads to changes and reworking?
    Contemporary unsynchronized activities and discipline are comparable to the waiting periods and therefore every time we move in the office, whether in accordance with the production or not, we are faced with

Waste in Production	Waste in the office
Over-production	Creation of unnecessary data and information. Data "pushed" forward in the flow and not "pulled" from those who need it
Stock	Lack of control, too much information, complicated research, obsolete information
Transport	Incompatibility of information and software, communication failures, safety concerns
Unnecessary handling	Lack of direct access, reformatting
Waits	Late delivery of information, advance delivery that leads to rework
Defectiveness	Haste, lack of reviews, tests, verifications. Need for further information or additional knowledge
Redundant processes	Unnecessary mass production, excessive customization, too many iterations
Creativity of the people not enhanced	Not added-value stress, lack of well-being

Figure 1.4 Similarity between the seven capital wastes of Taiichi Ohno and the wastes found in the offices.

a waiting problem that a person or a department is forced to endure, because there is no synchronization between different parts of the system (Figure 1.4).

1.5 Process Kaizen in Non-Manufacturing Processes

If our only tool is a hammer, every problem looks like a nail.

Bill Gates

The Lean approach, although developed in Japan over fifty years ago, has been consolidated by the experience of thousands of companies and today continues to offer a valid structured improvement methodology. In reality, the overall process improvement approach is no different whether we are considering a repetitive manufacturing process with short cycle times or a non-routine, long cycle process like product development. A good starting point is to get a big picture view of the process to identify the big wastes and then systematically work toward solving the problems that prevent us from working more efficiently with shorter lead times. One tool that helps in

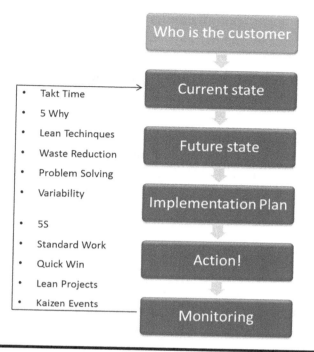

Figure 1.5 Typical flow of process kaizen.

viewing this big picture state, useful for manufacturing and product development, is *Value Stream Mapping*.

The Value Stream Map (VSM), also known as the "material and information flow map," makes it possible to somewhat crudely, but effectively, analyze the physical and information flows within any process. Figure 1.5 shows the major steps of the process. The departure point is always the customer after which we analyze what is happening today *(current state)* to identify the wastes. We then set aside the current state and all its constraints and think in an innovative way to define a new process without wastes referred to as the *future state*. The future state is then broken down to manageable pieces, or gaps between the current and future state, so that we can identify the root causes of these gaps, develop countermeasures, and action plans with accountability for improvement.[10]

While Value Stream Mapping and the subsequent process improvements are powerful, this in reality is the "easiest" part of the problem, the tip of the iceberg. Traveling all around the world, the finest consultants and managers may be able to provide the illusion of improvement and waste reduction, almost feeling themselves to be following the distant footsteps of Taiichi Ohno. But too many companies have more or less activated tactical improvements and "local" optimizations inspired by the good principles of Lean Manufacturing.

In the field of production, waste can be more easy to deal with because it is visible. In our offices, where often is spent the time of developers, managers and designers, on the contrary, it becomes more difficult because daily habit inures us to a huge range of large and small-scale waste.

Many times, the biggest part of the company iceberg, however, remains hidden below the surface. Just think of all the times we repeat a task, in which we repeat redundant gestures. Perhaps they are controls already performed by others, or when waiting for information that prevents us from fully carrying out our work or when we are interrupted in a task.

Interruptions are one of the biggest issues of the intellectual work: humans, like machines, are subject to the problem of set-up when they have to switch from one intellectual activity to another. It has been shown that, in office activity, the human being loses 40% to 60% of his/her efficiency due to the power of interruption and the devastating effect of multitasking. Now in our working days, it is increasingly easier to go from one interruption to another rather than from one task to another. The continuous interruptions are only one of the forms of waste that we try to eliminate in product development activity. Being aware of the motivations related to interruptions, or the other types of waste typical of intellectual activity means investing in "awareness of people" before technology and other substantial expenses. If, therefore, recognizing waste in production means careful observation of the physical world around us, learning to recognize waste in the office means learning to look at ourselves differently and learning to recognize waste that we become accustomed to every day, to then understand how such individual forms of waste concatenate with the waste of others.

1.5.1 Waste "Suffered" and Waste "Generated"

Sometimes inefficiency occurs due to the habits of working groups with whom we interact, but often we play a vital role in creating some of that waste.

Think of the above-mentioned interruptions. Think of when we superficially copy knowledge to people who are not essential, creating truly useless activities. Not worrying too much about other people's time reflects on how much we value our own personal time. Unfortunately, we are so inured to the waste that we no longer notice it and therefore, not only do we bear it, but we have also learned how to create it silently.

Sending on a "miscommunication," for example, is another fact that should make us think, as it will most likely be the trigger for a further waste of time related to the ease with which we initially created the ineffective communication. Having discipline and seeking forms of standardization in certain areas of our business does not mean losing creativity; instead, it means more space for creativity. And every time we touch upon all this waste, like reducing interruptions and reducing redundant things, we do just that, we remove some of the wastes in our individual and organizational processes. If this becomes common practice, then we will begin to notice that our project times will shorten inexorably. I think we are all obliged to try to figure out how to free up more space for our creative staff to give more value to ourselves and to our customers, both inside and outside the company.

1.6 Why Invest in a Lean Development and Innovation System?

> It is not the strongest of the species that survives, nor the most intelligent, but the one that is most responsive to change.
>
> **Charles Darwin**

The key word here is "system." Often, we witness excessive "personalization" of groups or departments, entrusting the burden (or the honor) to the resolution of some problems to a specific person working that shift. This often leads to finding ourselves repeatedly facing the same errors over and over again and feeling the same frustration time and time again. We are then forced to take on extra tasks ourselves to perpetually "fix" the problem or we need to rely on that one particular person who knows how to fix it. If we see this happening, clearly something is wrong with our product development system. In fact, there are two systems that interact in every company in this world: the individual and the company. One is made up of internal rules, habits, beliefs, and emotions. The other is made up of more or less written rules, policies, procedures, organization, processes, and tools (Figure 1.6).

The two systems have a strong impact on each other, creating a mutual interdependence. When you work on both systems to make them grow and to make them interact better with each other, you create the conditions in which solutions are found, ideas are put into practice, rather than just doing tasks that are transitional and impromptu, but are a solid ground in which to sow new ideas, new solutions to new problems, without retracing your own steps.[11]

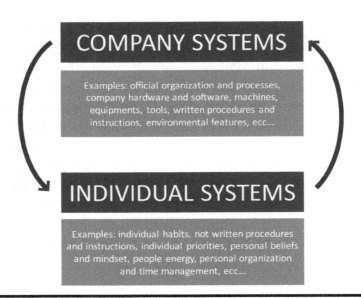

Figure 1.6 The difference between Individual and Company Systems. (Source: Andersen Consulting.)

Influence on the total cost of the product

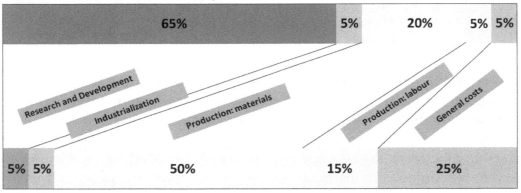

Impact on the total cost of the product

Figure 1.7 Influence on the costs of the product life cycle: about 70% of the total cost of a product is influenced by the phases of R & D and industrialization, although their incidence is approximately 10% of the total. (Source: *Lean Product Development Benchmark Report*, Boston, MA: Aberdeen Group, 2007.)

The opportunities for improvements in product and process innovation are well documented. If we consider the entire life cycle of a product or a service, the average costs that the company will sustain will be allocated as in the bottom row of Figure 1.7: about 5% will be costs of research and development of the product, 5% the cost of industrialization, 50% materials purchased, 15% labor costs, and finally about 25% indirect costs related to the product concerned.

This subdivision of budgets explains why most activities, to reduce costs and improve business, are typically focused on the areas of production, purchasing, and administration, rather than product development. In Lean Transformation programs too, the attention is often given to the areas with the greatest cost reduction opportunities. While clearly there is waste in those processes, some of it is actually generated further upstream in the product development processes.

What is puzzling is the almost complete indifference to a huge opportunity hidden in the heart of the product development of any company. In fact, approximately 70% of the total cost of most products (Figure 1.7) is predetermined in the development phase. So, while the cost of development of a product represents a very small amount when relative to the entire life of the product, most of the downstream costs are determined precisely at the stage of creating the design.

This evidence would logically lead us then to focus on the effectiveness of R & D, even if the ultimate goal is to reduce the cost of production, logistics, maintenance, etc. In other words, *focusing on simply cutting the cost of design for efficiency*, is risky and short-sighted because it is likely to increase our costs and reduce our viability as a company in the long term. Yet, focusing on the short-term is precisely what most organizations do.

This problem stems in part from the financial allocations of cost that sometimes inhibit us from being able to see the true total cost of a product throughout its life cycle. The principles of Lean Accounting can help us to reduce this risk. The traditional accounting systems are developed to support traditional production systems, and therefore poorly suited to a system that works on Lean principles. They provide reports and performance measures that are sometimes "distorted," in fact they force people to behave contrary to the Lean logic. A Lean Accounting system, however, is a set of principles and tools that allows you to align the language and have a consistent vision of the performance in a business managed by Lean logic, trying to reduce the transactions to the minimum necessary and properly supporting Value Stream accounting to eliminate waste throughout the course of the value chain.

In 2007, research conducted by the world-renowned Aberdeen Group on the product development methodologies quantified some the benefits experienced by companies applying Lean product development techniques,

Type of project	Advantage of the Best in Class companies *(in terms of reduced lead time)*
Minor revision of an existing product	14%
Major revision of an existing product	31%
New product, similar to an existing product (or a new product of the existing range)	25%
Completely new product (or new product range)	31%
Average	25%

Figure 1.8 Reduction of the development time of new products adopting the Lean principles. (Source: *Lean Product Development Benchmark Report*, Boston, MA: Aberdeen Group, 2007.)

demonstrating that, even outside the Toyota world, there are success stories of Lean product development methods that are changing company innovation methods.

As can be seen in Figure 1.8, the amount of reduction in total time of product development, where Lean Product Development methods have been adopted for a new product, stands at 31% less time. When, instead, an existing product is revisited, the advantages demonstrated are on the order of 14% less, leading on average to a 25% reduction measured and quantified through the sample of these four hundred companies. To this lead time advantage we must also add the product and financial ones: in fact, we can see the degree of achievement of the targets of the project shown in Figure 1.9.

Paradoxically, we find more advantages in developing a completely new product than remodeling an existing product because, with a remodeled product, we are more accustomed to waste, both technical and managerial, whereas when we challenge ourselves with a new product, we start from scratch and have more opportunities for real product and process innovation.

In conclusion: not only on-time launches, not only lower development and product costs, but also improved quality and a faster time to market. What may have sometimes sounded like a fairy tale from Toyota, has been

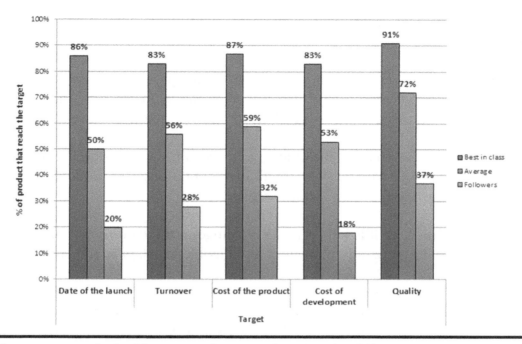

Figure 1.9 Level of achievement of project objectives for different companies.

shown to be valid for a statistically representative sample of other companies in a variety of industries. The world is changing and those who have success learn to innovate their products along with their processes and people. Lean Development is finally becoming a major focus of leading companies.

1.6.1 Integrating People, Processes, and Tools

Many companies have emulated the Lean transformations of Japanese companies, sometimes reaching and exceeding their performance in specific areas of production: spectacular examples of Kanban, beautiful "u"-shaped cells and 5S. All this, however, is often not enough to give companies prosperity and long-term success. There have been cases of companies that have become Lean Manufacturing models, but have found themselves on the brink of bankruptcy due to new product development programs always being late, projects over budget, and dissatisfied customers due to product problems. A business system based on Lean principles is something more complex than just production; it is a company that keeps its focus on the of highest quality for the end customers in the shortest time and with the minimum cost. Key to this vision are *robust products and processes*. The real breakthrough, the real quality leap, takes place when we care about:

- acquiring the stability that comes from robust products and processes;
- preparing the entire Value Stream tied to the product so that it can be manufactured and delivered at the highest quality and lowest total cost;
- committing to creating the culture to avoid further errors and continuously improve, whether we are talking about a physical product or whether we are talking about a service.

To make this leap it is key to make a change in the culture that develops people who are highly motivated and flexible to adapt to the continual change.

When you eliminate the marked division between the world of production and the world of the product, you begin to deal with the business as a system of joint development of products and processes that Morgan and Liker represent with a rather simple three-legged model, shown in Figure 1.10. If we want to have very high performance in a *product oriented* company, we must take the steps described below.

1. *Customer Value*: Define what you want to offer, distinguish yourself, and make yourself unique.
2. *Processes*: identify the standard, i.e. "rules of the game," determine where to add value and where to eliminate waste, to make the value flow according to standard and shared processes, thus ensuring flexibility and punctuality.
3. *People*: Make sure that the people involved in the development process are developed effectively. Identify gaps in skills and abilities, according to the defined processes. Organize a system that balances the specialized knowledge with the management side. Make the knowledge gained available to all.
4. *Tools*: After having taken the first three steps, verify that the tools and technologies are the right fit with the processes and people involved. That is, adapt the technology to the people, align the organization with simple visual systems, use robust systems to promote standardization and organization of knowledge. So, *technology and tools, yes, but in a way that helps people.* Not vice versa.

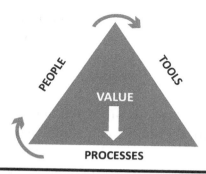

Figure 1.10 Scheme of the Lean system in the product development.

1.7 Each Situation Has Its Own Peculiarities

Maybe you are not responsible for the situation you are in, but you will be if you do nothing to change it.

Martin Luther King

Many times we have heard these phrases repeated:

"Japan is too different from us," "Culture, yes, the culture is not comparable," "The Americans are different too," "The Germans, yes, they were born with organization in their souls," "The company nearby, other leaders, those are real leaders, ours, no, I'm not a leader," "Here in our company, these concepts are not applicable, at least not for now..." and so on with the same content.

The culture of excuses becomes established in the language in many offices and in many departments of many companies. Each time, we begin by discussing this bad habit. We create a small working group, in a small pilot area and we give space to discovering the healthy desire, often dormant, to try to change a situation for the better using Lean techniques. This exercise offers unexpected stimuli for innovation.

This unconventional space helps get rid of ineffective habits repeated over the years of work, it provides an area that encourages people to apply new Lean methods, exhibit sounder problem-solving, and create enthusiasm for change. This is the first step toward typical experimentation and continuous improvement found in a Lean culture.

Once this *pilot phase* is underway, the tension is usually reduced because there is an awareness of being part of an "experiment," feeling oneself to be in a "neutral" zone in the company, where judgments and expectations have been temporarily suspended. It is similar to the practical simulations we do in all our Lean training sessions outside the company where participants concentrate with an unusual level of energy, combined with a healthy competitive spirit, that leads them to learn and demonstrate the effectiveness of methods that would otherwise perhaps take weeks or months to understand.

After the pilot phase, the results are evaluated, and then we try to figure out how to extend the benefits into other areas, by consolidating what we have just learned (techniques and habits). At the same time, we try to understand what did not work well in the first phase of experimentation and why, attempting to immediately implement the appropriate countermeasures. I am used to leading work sessions with my team, called *hansei* (Japanese), or *reflection* (English), to bring out both the positive and the negative aspects of the recent experience, to become aware of the causes, and to translate them into new operational steps that reinforce the strengths and reduce the effects of the weaknesses discovered. In Chapter 4, we will see the details of this technique.

The *expansion phase* is structured with the aim of aligning organizational, technical, and educational aspects, and above all redirecting the leadership so it can help grow the Lean culture throughout the company. At this point in the journey, coaching in Lean Leadership by the *sensei* aims to influence the mental attitude of management to help them drive the Lean Transformation into their groups.

Often at during the expansion phase, we happen to look back and laugh out loud thinking about when, at the beginning of the journey, someone said "yes, but here in our company it's different...," paradoxically revealing that indeed it was true. In every place, in every group, what happens is going to always be different. You learn that you cannot copy and paste other people's models, but rather you need to chart your own journey to challenge yourself to experiment with new ways to apply Lean thinking and to continuously learn and improve. This is how Lean Innovation will grow within an organization.

1.8 Summary of Key Points in Chapter 1

1. *Importance of long-term strategic vision* to pull daily activities. This is the antidote against short-term mechanisms that may in time cause the decline of an entire company and hinder risk-taking and innovation.

2. *Structured innovation* to drive perpetual growth. Looking at innovation from the point of view of products, services, processes, people, with a focus on customer value. When it becomes a widespread mentality in the company, opportunities at all levels are amplified.

3. *Lean thinking* to reduce waste across the entire value stream. From the teachings of Toyota to the adaptations to our situation, especially in intellectual activities, eliminating waste always leads to a reduction in costs. Vice versa, is not always the case. In particular, the focus on the reduction of the twelve wastes of intellectual activity brings benefits to both the company, in terms of productivity, and to people in terms of well-being and quality of life in the office.

4. *Systems approach* to ensure processes, people, and tools are mutually aligned to consistently deliver value rather than implementing individual techniques. So that neither innovation nor the waste reduction actions remain isolated wins, but rather become part of effective enterprise value stream.

5. *The real streamlining of the company*. Applying Lean Thinking to stimulate innovation in the development of new products and services can be a strategic weapon in the 21st century. The design stage influences about 70% of the total costs of a product and is the key driver of time to market. When you work in this area, the opportunities arising from it are far more fruitful and effective for the company than those in another area of a company.

Resources

https://www.lenovys.com/en/blog/airbnb
https://www.lenovys.com/en/blog/barilla/
https://www.lenovys.com/en/blog/5opportunities/
https://www.lenovys.com/en/blog/innovate-successfully/

Notes

1. Liker J.K., *The Toyota Way*, New York: McGraw Hill, 2004.
2. Womack J.P., Jones D.T., Roos, D., 1990.
3. Edmund S. Phelps won the Nobel Prize for Economics in 2006. He is currently the director of the Center on Capitalism and Society at Columbia University in New York.
4. Phelps E.S., Tilman L.M., 2010.
5. Brown B.B., Anthony S., 2011.

6. The *sensei* is a person of great experience who transmits knowledge within the company. In a Lean company, the figure of the *sensei* is a very important as part of the basic philosophy and culture. The *sensei* is similar to a coach or a mentor, external or internal, who teaches by example and through coaching.
7. Womack J.P., Jones D.T., Roos, D., 1990.
8. Morgan J., Liker J.K., 2006.
9. In this regard, see the official report at the NASA site (www. nasa. gov/topics/ nasalife/features/NESC-toyota-study.html) and refer to JK Liker's book, *Toyota Under Fire: Lessons for Turning Crisis into Opportunity,* New York: McGraw Hill, 2001.
10. The framework for this way of thinking about improvement is well defined in Mike Rother and John Shook, *Learning to See*, Cambridge, MA: Lean Enterprise Institute, 1999. This book uses a manufacturing case, but the principles apply equally well to an innovative engineering process.
11. Lenovys, the name of the company founded by Luciano, is an invented name, but terminologically, it is a portmanteau derived from the three key words mentioned: (Le) an In (Nov)ation S(ys)tem.

Chapter 2

Processes: The Way We Work to Add Value

Sometimes we lose time doing the same things over and over again. Often we see the recurrence of the same kinds of errors. The results of similar activities done by different people differ much more than we might expect. These are all signs of a lack of standardized processes. If we want to sustain and improve performance levels in a company, we must "design" and improve the way people conduct their work—from product development processes to the rules with which we organize knowledge in a company and keep it alive and easy to use. This part of the book looks at the key strategies for planning and managing a project from start to finish, drawing inspiration from the companies that have implemented the principles of Lean Thinking at the very heart of their business activity: the development of new products.

2.1 When Processes Are Real Solutions to Problems

Failures are divided into two classes—those who thought and never did, and those who did and never thought.

John Charles Salak

Before deciding which processes to adopt we need to think about what recurrent problems we want to solve.

Have you ever had to reconsider decisions that have already been made, or in a crisis make a quick decision because there is no time to put things off any further? Why does this happen?

A common cause of this is the lack of clearly defined processes, both global and individual processes. People are busy, maybe frantically busy, but they may be working on the wrong things at the wrong time and are not properly coordinated with others whose work is interdependent. Often when we lack a clear process we simply start to work on everything we can in parallel—a critical process error.

2.1.1 Do Many Things at the Same Time or Arrange Project Activities into a Sequenced Flow?

Should we start lots of things or a do things one at a time? How many times have you experienced such a dilemma? Perhaps you have experienced the stresses created by managers convinced that the best way to win time and earn money is to launch a disturbingly large number of projects and activities at the same time, all with maximum priority, and all with virtually the same deadline. And, a very tight deadline, of course. This *wishful thinking* is one of the main reasons for waste and inefficiency in office work. One thing is certain: the vast majority of projects that are launched inevitably end up being late or take much more effort than originally planned to get them done. And others will be, or should be, dropped. We know of a vehicle parts company that on investigation had over 160 R & D projects going on simultaneously without a strong rationale for any of them. In fact, their main customer for their core product was fed up with the outdated design and on the verge of dropping the supplier and there was no project to redesign that product.

Tasks that have been started and not finished, designs that are underway, and changes that come up create an enormous quantity of in-process work—in some ways not unlike building large quantities of inventory of parts that are not needed now and may never be needed.

When a new product is developed, the greater the number of in-process activities and the more the final output will be slowed down.

In the following pages, we will see what steps can be taken to counter this.

Another common issue is to see people literally throwing themselves into their development activities, in their own particular area of work, without having a clear overall vision of the final product, i.e. how it is going to be used by the customer, how the client will perceive it, where it will be used and why should the customer buy it versus our competitors' products. People run around trying to complete an assigned task or design or problem solve perceived issues, but often with little or no consideration about it will (or won't) add value to the customer.

How can we resolve these problems?

2.1.2 Pay Attention to Small Signals and Accumulate the Knowledge

Often we repeat the same errors time and time again without even realizing it. Solutions already found for past problems are forgotten, or the solutions already found by colleagues to problems sometimes are not even considered as a possible alternative due to a lack of understanding or trust. We do not give sufficient consideration to the value that can be generated by the exchange of experiences and viewpoints between people from different sites or departments. Instead, more frequently than not, people just happen to talk at lunch or by the coffee machine, and then only to complain about problems versus sharing solutions.

Frequently, no care is taken to make available, in a structured fashion, what has been learned along the way, so as to prevent the same problem happening again. Everyone holds on to their own "secrets," and often this tacit knowledge is so well guarded that we forget them ourselves, only then to find ourselves suddenly in the midst of a problem or conflict that makes us think "But I knew that," or sometimes exclaiming: "I told you so..."

Project teams from the same company who learn things that they don't then pass on, such as technical or project management errors, do not just highlight an inadequate exchange of knowledge within the company. They also reveal another cultural characteristic typical of Western companies, reflecting a psychosocial tendency of developed countries: the lack of attention given to capturing what is learned and incorporating it into a shared body of knowledge at the group and company level. Rather, we value the firefighters who swoop in to save the day with their "expertise."

In the Lean world, we are hungry for all the "small signals" of learnings, including the "oopses," "it's only a small thing," and "how did they do that so well" that are learned along the way of each project. If we are seriously concerned with making available to others everything that is learned, it clearly takes a conscious effort by everyone on the project team. Since innovation is the key to future success, then *the real competitive edge of a company is the capacity to learn faster than others.*

2.1.3 *Balancing and Synchronizing Work Loads from a Value Stream Perspective*

Another problem we see regularly is an imbalance in workloads between people and departments and over time. Generally, the majority of people we interact with are drowning in a pattern of "I don't even have time to look up to breathe and see where I'm going." Their workloads are 100%, and sometimes even more. In the same project, in some other office, someone else is waiting for the fruits of their labor to complete the next part of the job and typically ends up rushing to do it as they get the information late. Can you see any signs of waste in this scenario?

When we are working on a project that involves many people or work groups, the above scenario plays out on a daily basis. Every person or department is trying to optimize (or juggle) their work to get through the day. Unfortunately, often this does not provide the best flow for the Value Stream, and therefore causes the project to take more time and/or effort than is needed.

We will look in Section 2.5 at some methods for achieving a better flow of activities in projects. This is a delicate issue, and is often obstructed by managers obsessed by the saturation of resources of their department, or by individuals who concentrate on their own workload without paying attention to the overall result. Imagine, for example, what a designer does when faced with the task of producing some designs. If four drawings are required, the first thing that will be done, if he or she is parsimonious and attentive to the results, will be to level them according to the amount of time available. So, if it takes two hours to produce each one, the eight-hour working day will be divided into two-hour slots, one for each drawing. This, on a small scale, is an operation of leveling, but done only with a view to that individual person's workload and department. What is missing is consideration of who will receive those drawings, and which of the four is clearly identified as being needed before the others. In companies, this type of phenomenon occurs frequently: everyone saturates their people and then everyone tries to level their activities. Does this approach really level the flow of the product development Value Stream? Hardly!

Especially in innovation projects and in the development of new products and services, questions of this type are never sufficiently analyzed or discussed, in order to ensure the job is done in the least possible amount of time. If we spend more time managing the workload and flow, we can avoid several wastes such as waiting for work or generating more unplanned work caused by rework, modifications, or additions. Applying the concept of leveling correctly in product development starts by understanding who is pulling things forward and then aligning the whole cross-functional organization in order to optimize the schedule and costs of the entire project. Doing this will open up a world of opportunities that gives us an overall view of the entire Value Stream, which runs from beginning to end via the different participants in the project. For example, the design, checking, and validation areas are no longer isolated and are now balanced in a way that meets their downstream customers' needs.

When you see big jobs stacked up, your own or others, before assuming the problem is the scarcity of available resources, before thinking about adding resources, or, simply, resigning yourself to inevitable delay, try to observe the flow in its entirety—who is part of the internal client-supplier chain, where is the bottleneck, and what is the right sequence for ensuring that the final point of the chain can start moving and pull all the other links in the chain.

Only very rarely are you an independent single chain in a Value Stream for the products and processes you are creating together with your colleagues, suppliers, and clients. *A change in point of view, from that of the single chain to that of the Value Stream, will quickly lead you* to see the value of *putting into practice*, in a regular and standard way, *the flow of jobs through the various links in the chain.*

2.1.4 How Can We Ask for the Materials and Information That Are Needed When They Are Needed?

Another problem that can crop up in innovation projects relates to the supply of materials and information required during the project itself. Instead of having an organized plan for what is needed and when and triggering the order at the point it is needed, often a haphazard *Stop and Go* process occurs, with useless actions, wasted time for ourselves and others, lots of waiting for clarifications, and slow-downs, all with the conviction that the time saved at the beginning using a "head down, full steam ahead" approach always brings rewards. But this, unfortunately, only rarely happens.

2.1.5 Cause and Effect

Often it is not possible to see the effects of what we do, indeed at times, whole months can go by before we manage to see the effects of what we do (or do not do). This is true both in our private lives and in our working lives. So, when we do not cultivate the habit of associating waste with the effect it will have after two, four, or eight months, inevitably we lose sight of the damage associated with it. There is a full-fledged "oriental karma" effect. There will be short-term karmas, which produce an immediate effect, for example, a slap that hurts immediately, and long-term karmas, actions that have an effect on us, but which we do not see immediately. We do a series of things that will have an effect several months on, and in organizing our processes we need to take account of both short- and long-term effects of our actions on a project.

2.2 Make the Customer the Center of Attention: Concept Paper

> Don't take your eyes off the end.
>
> **Alessandro Manzoni**

Defining customer value is the first step to take before innovating to create and develop a new product or service. What exactly does the customer need and value? What do we want to present to the customer? Why are we doing the project?

Before anything else, it is worth visualizing exactly what is expected from the final product or service. Too frequently, superficial descriptions of value in the initial phases of a project are paid for dearly in the intermediate and final stages.

The less we know beforehand about the value that the product will have for the customer, the less easy it will be to distinguish waste from activities that add value. At the beginning of any project, then, it is fundamental to ask who the customer is and how we can solve important customer problems and please them. Note that the customer does not always know what they want. Henry Ford once quipped: "If I'd asked customers what they wanted, they would have said 'a faster horse'." Thinking creatively about what is possible, and really understanding how customers live their lives and what would help them and appeal to them requires going to the gemba. In this case, the gemba is where and under what conditions the product or service will be used.

Once the market, customers, and conditions of use are deeply understood they become requirements to be translated into concrete actions in order to obtain a product or service that is saleable to the customer. This process, illustrated in Figure 2.1, needs to be continually renewed during the early phases of the project to gradually bring into focus the true needs and to figure out how the project will deal with the trade-offs that will inevitably come up.

In other words, in development phases there is always a need to revisit the purpose and customer requirements cycling through implementation, control, and corrective action, following the Deming cycle:

Plan—Do—Check—Act[1]

This concept applies for all kinds of projects (Figure 2.2), ranging from those involving the customization of a product to ones involving strategic innovation or those in which innovation is limited to research projects.

In different types of projects, attention and focus will be directed toward certain aspects more than others, but the concept of value for the end customer, attempting to recognize what is added value and what is not, is critical in all contexts.

Drawing inspiration from the habits of a number of world-class companies, we have devised, and successfully used in many projects, a process for defining value for internal and external customers in the initial phase of a

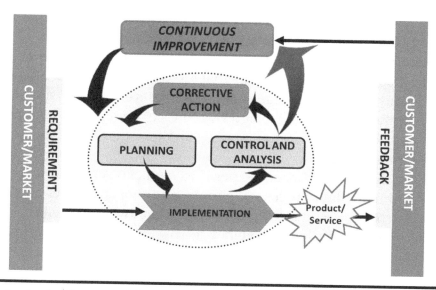

Figure 2.1   Logic diagram of the interaction between customer satisfaction and product development. (Source: Ulrich K. and Eppinger S.D., *Product Design and Development*, McGraw-Hill, 2004.)

	Customiz.	Strategic Innovation (technology push)	Limited innovation & re-integration (market pull)	Research	Products based on platform	Products with high incidence of process
Description	New products with slight variations compared to existing configurations	New technlogy, followed by the appropriate market	Market opportunity, followed by technologies to meet customer needs	Creation of a new concept of product or process	New product based on specific technological subsystem	Strong influence of the production process
Examples	Switches, engines, batteries, containers	Gore-tex waterproof clothing, tyvek bags	The majority of tools, furniture and sport items	New drilling technology with water and lasers	Consumer electronics, computers, printers, cars	Sneaks, cereals, chemical products, semiconductors
Focus	Product development process very structured. Aggressive target market	Adapting technology to market. Innovation product and process development methods	Development speed. Strong leverage on suppliers	Need to collect data, trade-off curves, analyze their applicability	Technologic platform, modularity, reduction in the variety	Imperative to develop product and process simultaneously at the earliest stages

Figure 2.2 Synthetic table of the various types of product development. (Source: Liker J.K., *The Toyota Way: Fourteen Management Secrets from the World's Greatest Manufacturer*, McGraw-Hill, 2004.)

project, particularly from Toyota. This process is laid down in a document called the *Concept Paper*. The term Concept Paper originally came from the initial project document created by Chief Engineers at Toyota to succinctly define their vision for the end product from the customer's point of view as well as critical specifications that are not negotiable. It also includes milestones and timing, cost targets, and other relevant targets such as fuel economy and weight. It is presented by the chief engineer in a large meeting to all key participants, including key suppliers, that launches the product development program.

The main aim of the Concept Paper is to explicitly state the voice of the customer and help align processes, people, and tools before commencing any project activity. Getting down on paper what awaits us before beginning to develop the product, through a structured process of sharing, might appear to be similar to many other documents generated at other companies by marketing or project leads. However, we will see that it is more than a document. It can help the project team to tap into the social dimension of the process of sharing, articulating, and building consensus on the key points necessary for clarifying customer needs.

2.2.1 Forming the Project Team and a Sample Concept Paper Format

Whatever it is called in a given company, each project's Concept Paper needs to contain clear information about the target customer, the product vision, key product characteristics, who does what, who will lead the project, who will sponsor it, who is part of the core team, and who is part of the broader team. In some organizations that follow Toyota's chief engineer system, this is only signed by the chief engineer. In other cases, it will function as a team charger and all key stakeholders will need to be in involved and agree about the description of the project, its purpose, the main objectives, the time scale, the key trade-offs, the main known risks, and the mitigation plans. This will then have to be formally approved by all stakeholders via signatures. Thus far, there is nothing new here, for well-organized companies.

But this is just the tip of the iceberg: what is different from a conventional approach is not the use of the format. The difference is in the way a company uses the process well, namely, in what lies behind the scenes, in what cannot be seen, which is the work involved in preparing the document. For more complex projects, the process may take many months—the process of sharing, and the in-depth analysis of the questions we are forced to ask step by step, if we are truly using a structured process. Welcome to the world of real processes, where *what we do and say every day counts much more than what is written down in some text or other.*

2.2.2 Who Guides the Process?

The first question that needs to be answered, before embarking on a project, regards the owner of the project. The chosen person must be able to deliver the value to the customer while fighting to reduce waste in the Value Stream as described in the previous chapter. In some companies this person is called the Chief Engineer, to indicate the profile that covers the responsibilities both of a Project Manager and those of a genuine system integrator. This person will deal with management issues on the one hand, while on the other he or she will have to integrate the technical parts of the product-system that need to be developed.

To get a better understanding of why it is best to have a single leader, let's consider a number of factors fundamental to a project's success. Generally, a product is the result of the contribution and point of view of many people in a company. Questions, opinions, and answers are bantered about the organization, which are not always shared or vetted by the various contributors to the project.

Marketing people, for example, ask questions and come up with answers. The designer does the same thing, and the manufacturing representatives continue after them to ask further questions and to find their own answers. But what we see too rarely in many projects is that there are "community" moments, during which questions are raised and tackled together at the root, with a shared response that takes account of a multiplicity of needs. To be effective, someone needs to be the focal point and drive the team to decision or ultimately make the decision themselves.

2.2.3 *Product and Market History*

Before describing where we want to go with the product, it is always a good idea to think about what has already been done up until now in the marketplace with our product and our competitors' products. This will help us to better understand the characteristics of the current product in relation to its market history and the reasons that are now prompting us to think of a new product line.

In this phase, *it is important to clearly define the link that exists between the nascent product and the company's strategy.*

2.2.4 *Who Will Use Our Products?*

We need to ask who our targeted customers will be and how will they use the innovative product or service we are proposing to deliver to the marketplace. Often, to answer these questions we need to get close to the end users to gain firsthand knowledge of what they desire.

This phase is clearly very important to be clear about what the added value will be for each of our customers. Frequently these questions seem rather trite, and are quickly passed over, the assumption being that we already know the answers. In the best of cases, just a small proportion of companies come up with answers, and there is a tendency to forget that the same questions can yield different answers according to the different points of view of possible end customers.

The value of a product can only be defined from the point of view of the end client. It is necessary to understand the real needs of the client, so as to supply a specific product and/or service capable of satisfying consumer needs at a given time and for a given price. Only when this step has been taken can the identified needs be matched with the company's capabilities to respond to them.

When we lead workshops in companies, with the aim of drawing up the Concept Paper together at the beginning of a new project, we often end up taking on the role of moderator and facilitator in what are sometimes quite heated discussions. The same questions often elicit different responses from people belonging to different departments sitting around the same table. Who is right? Through guided discussion, it emerges clearly that there is not a single, exhaustive answer to the same question. Each group is listening to the customer and seeing them from a different perspective. Making the effort to interpret the answers from customers, and above all, *to align all the answers before commencing the project* becomes critical to the success of any project. Otherwise, the unresolved problems and conflicts will continue to lurk beneath the surface, ready to reemerge and generate a churn of waste further down the line in later phases of the project.

2.2.5 *Classification of Product Features*

Questions regarding the requirements and functions desired by the customer should be a healthy debate early on about which features of the product are *musts*, those whose absence would not be tolerated by the client. This set of features must include the ones that are necessary to make the product indispensable and unique for the customer who buys it. Arguably, these are the distinguishing features, if done well, that give a company its strategic advantage over its competition. On the other hand, other features may be considered *nice to have,* but which the client could do without if needed. Clearly, the project should strive to deliver as many nice-to-haves as is feasible to gain goodwill with the customer. However, the trade-offs for the nice-to-haves should always be weighed with the risks to the project. If consensus is not done early on in the project to prioritize the features, this can lead to over or under engineering the product for the desired customers. This will result in waste of company time and resources, and extra costs—because the failure to establish priorities at the beginning can give rise to conflicts in later stages of the project or worse, if left unresolved, can lead to lost sales by not delivering the right product to the right customer at the right time at the right cost. Mutual understanding and alignment, prior to full project launch, about the *must* features, the *nice to have* ones, and those which should actually be excluded from the product or service, the *must nots,* is very important in order to prevent future conflicts in the project itself.

2.2.6 How Can We Understand What the Customer Wants?

When Luciano worked for a strategic consulting company, his desk was often piled high with huge folders containing market surveys designed to analyze and explain customers' new needs, which had to be satisfied at all costs. They contained an incredible amount of data and analyses of virtual needs, which often ended up substituting understanding in the field of what the real needs and problems of the customer might be.

In some Japanese and American companies, we discovered a happy return to pragmatic common sense. In Toyota, they talk about *Genchi Gembutsu* (in the United States, *Go and See*) as a fundamental principle of Lean thinking. "Go, see, and touch"—as an antidote to too many words, even when dealing with unknown or intangible characteristics that are hard to describe.

This concept holds true for the whole customer and supply chain involved in developing a new product. Some of the innovative features introduced in Toyota cars in the American market stem from such an approach, which was put into practice directly by their chief engineers. Some went to see how drivers parked their minivans at the school entrance, what they really did with their vehicles, how they opened the car doors, and what their most frequent actions were. Others went driving for a whole week in the United States and Canada to see firsthand what difficulties drivers face when there are rapid temperature changes, impossible road gradients, and long stretches without any gasoline or rest services. These are all things that are hard to appreciate with a marketing survey or a written interpretation of needs by someone in the business or marketing department.

Often customers themselves do not know they have a certain need, and would not even be able to put it into words. So, a return to the root of things, the *"Go & See," enables us to interpret needs from the customer's point of view*, as it would never be possible by pouring over reams of data and paper. Going back to "seeing for yourself" is something that even well-researched papers will never be able to replace. So, while many companies go through the motions of capturing requirements to varying degrees of completeness and clarity, what is almost always missing is an overall picture of the real processes and habits that underly the development of a good Concept Paper: the process of identifying the customer's needs firsthand, the process of sharing, consensus-building, and alignment within the company itself.

In this phase of the projects, the project leader/chief engineer should be "obliged" to go out into the field, to get to know his or her clients, trying to really understand both the poorly satisfied needs of current products, the strengths and weaknesses of the competition, and any new needs that might be satisfied with a new product in the marketplace. Without this necessary step, it is impossible to ensure that we are pointing our resources in the right direction to provide the right product features to the customer.

2.2.7 Radical Sharing

There is a process, which the Japanese call *nemawashi*, based on the metaphor of cultivating the roots of the tree, which refers to going person by person to get consensus on an idea. You can readily imagine that as moving a tree from one spot to another: it is necessary to extract the roots, prepare the terrain, organize appropriate transportation and conveying, and to take care when handling the tree. If these actions are not performed with due care, the risk of the tree dying off is very high. Doesn't the good preparation of a project, so it can be accepted in all the groups within the company, taking into account internal constraints, while best meeting the customer's needs, deserve the same attention upfront that can be found in the Japanese concept of *nemawashi*?

Besides customers outside the company, the Concept Paper must make an effort to embrace the needs of the in-house clients as well. The Chief Engineer has to go and see what the needs are firsthand, talking to the people involved, such as the designers, the production engineers, and the assembly-line workers, in order to understand what their problems are and to translate them into a document that might, in formal terms, look very similar to many others, but that in actual form becomes an accurate and coherent snapshot of the world of needs, internal and external, that have to be satisfied.

2.2.8 The Importance of a Single Unified Vision

The Concept Paper is most likely to be coherent and effective if written by a single person. Even great books tend to be written by one person. If there are several authors, one is the primary author who integrates the ideas of the others. In companies, too frequently, a product or a service requirement are written in various parts by several "co-authors" including the marketing, design, commercial, logistics, and production departments. While all the aforementioned groups are experts and provide very insightful contributions, what is often missing is the integration of these chapters into a single product view. The role of the integrator—the Chief Engineer, Project Leader, Team Leader, Project Manager, or whatever else it might be called—has, through the Concept Paper, the task of producing a single photograph of the target value for the client: the final story. The global vision of the integrator is extremely important because he or she is the one who ensures the "paternity" of the product, which is much more than just the bureaucratic management of the project. This figure moves forward from just the traditional role of project management and becomes the real parent of the product, the person who really knows how the end client will use it, who will guide the product through the development, and who manages, with that single clear photograph—the Concept Paper—to represent an overall vision the team needs to achieve. This person must possess both management skills and technical knowledge of the product to be launched, so that the activities are carried out well and with minimal waste. He or she must also be capable of retaining the right degree of flexibility with regard to the objectives themselves, because if they are too rigid they might impede the innovative new solutions, just as overly "soft" objectives might not give due value to the potential of the product. An excellent integrator assigned from the beginning and who will carry the product to the market undoubtedly makes a significant difference in the success of the entire project.

2.2.9 One Product or a Family of Products? The Right Choice Could Bring Big Benefits (and) Savings

During the elaboration of the Concept Paper for the new product or service, it is a good idea to understand whether the product we are thinking about will be a single item or the offspring of a platform, or if it will be the brother or sister of another product. This analysis at the beginning of the development phase is very important because lots of opportunities can be exploited that would otherwise remain buried by our habit not to do such analysis. We have often seen this methodological step done hastily and badly, or even skipped altogether. We have seen companies forget or not consider the fact that a model might be developed today and, in the space of just six months or a year, another "variant" of the first one then has to be developed which, unless it is just a case of making additions or simple variants, can lead to lots of inefficiency and waste. Asking what options might be requested or made available for the customer, and what additional modules might be necessary, may put us in a position to develop a full-blown platform with optional modules that can ultimately provide a variety of choices from the point of view of the end client, with a minimum effort if the platform itself is designed well at the start of the project.[2] Understanding if the product is the first of a line of future products or not can radically alter its architecture and lead to a modification of the way the project itself will be managed.

In one of Luciano's projects, a discussion was going on one day about the shape and attachment method for some functional-aesthetic covers for a complex piece of industrial machinery. The group of technicians of the cover supplier, together with a client's mechanical designer, were working on a solution for a single machine model, for which production was due to commence a few months later. Luciano decided to interrupt their discussion by asking a few simple questions. To what extent could those covers be reused for future models? How easily replicable would the attachment solution be? Were the molds for the production of the covers sufficient for the production of other models as well? At first, this battery of questions upset them. The immediate response, as in many other cases, was that there was no time to think about such matters. But, after moving beyond this stock answer, the group changed focus radically, and in the end it was even decided to slightly increase the number of components for the model, but with the effect of reducing the total number of components for the whole product family, given that the covers were in fact going to be reused. It involved a slight increase in the cost of that model, but a significant reduction in the cost of the whole product family: from the total number of components required to the cost for the supplier of producing the dies, the time employed by the designers and technicians, the cost savings of future development, and in logistical and maintenance costs. When the focus was shifted from what we will need to do in six months or a year's time to the long-term view, even if it may not be currently considered urgent, technical innovations can be unleashed leading to great cost reductions over the whole value chain.

Doing things well takes as long as doing things badly, but a great deal of time and money is saved afterward.

2.2.10 How Can We Standardize the Use of Product Components to Reduce the Final Cost?

The same kind of consideration is needed for every question of which components of the product-system can remain fixed and which should not. This is extremely important in order to ensure that the parts themselves are well designed. It should be borne in mind that the cost of a product will always be made "heavier" by the following three factors.

1. The single piece cost: this is the closest relation to the conventional cost of the product. Materials and direct expenses for obtaining the single part.
2. The cost of management: costs associated with the administrative management of the part, ranging from purchasing to logistics, from the person who has to manage the bill of materials to the one responsible for storing data, specifications, and designs. These costs often end up being lumped together under overhead, thereby hiding them from where they were generated.
3. The cost of variety: when we evaluate the impact of that same part throughout the range and the platform it belongs to, consider the volumes and the total number of parts linked to each other.

Often, when working on projects, the focus remains exclusively on the single piece cost, with the attempt to optimize a part, for a given project. Asking right from the outset how we can put all the costs on the scales of the decision-making process, from those of the whole production chain to those of the individual model, from those of the entire range to those incurred for the management of those models, brings us closer and closer to the objective of the minimum Total Life Cycle Cost of the family of products and not just to the optimization of part for a given project, which rarely guarantees the total minimum.

2.2.11 How Can We Establish Goals at the Beginning of the Project?

When we establish the goals to achieve in the project for a new product or new service, little attention is given to the "dynamic" aspects of the context in which we are operating. It is important to break the objective down into its component parts:

1. Cost goals
2. Performance goals
3. Product/Service Features desired

It is equally important to compare the goals regarding our future product with those of our current product, and with the objective data of competitors' products. In this section of the Concept Paper, we strive to understand the conflicting goals and reconcile them as best we can. The company may already have some feeling about these trade-offs but it is best if they can be quantified. Some companies, such as Toyota, have made **trade-off curves**, that is to say, correlation curves between the different functions of the product itself. For example, weight versus fuel consumption, number of components and cost, quantities sold and costs, etc. Why is this done?

Because in real life it is unlikely that all the specific conditions under which we have established the assigned goals will not be challenged during the project either due to technology or cost considerations. Something will change. This is the reason why it is always a good idea to establish project targets in terms of a range rather than as single point values. This makes it possible to look for solutions with greater flexibility, finding the most suitable project areas within the given range. For example, if we are developing a new training course, various things that will influence our costs and revenues may change, from the number of participants to the cost of the instructors, from the cost of the marketing required to promote the course to the costs of the sales structure needed to sell it, from the costs of rooms, hotels, and catering to the cost of handouts to provide the participants. If we are developing a new iron casting, there may be changes in the unitary costs of the cast iron, the weight, the performance of the product in relation to the type of iron used. Giving due consideration at the beginning of the project to possible variations in the main factors governing costs and revenues of the new product, and above all to how these factors influence each other, provides a much more complete vision of the risks and opportunities that can move us toward or away from our goals. Another benefit of this approach is we gain knowledge on how the sensitivity of the value of the product changes with regards to varying certain parameters. This will help us in the project to make better decisions based on a series of data and facts. In addition, this knowledge is sometimes called the *knowledge curve*, in that it often reveals the existence of genuine gaps in our knowledge that need to be filled with further data analysis during the project in order to gain the full picture.

If, for example, we consider the development of a new car, it is not hard to understand that if its target speed increases, the amount of noise it makes is very likely to increase, and the aerodynamics and, ultimately, the cost, will definitely vary. Without precise knowledge of how these parameters and what the areas of shared acceptance of the various parameters are, it will be difficult to make a sound decision based on facts. Rather, there are likely to be hold-ups, time-consuming discussions, misunderstandings, and wasted time during the project trying to re-align goals (or expectations) or worse a risky decision will be made based on "gut feel."

Making an effort to quantify the trade-off curves early in the project together with the objectives will help us to understand and avoid areas of risk, just as it will highlight what opportunities there may be. At the same time, we can create a map of the main *cost drivers* and of the characteristic functions of the product, that is to say, the factors whose variability can affect costs and sales. This more in-depth analysis upfront will make it possible to move forward more quickly during the development phases of the product, with a greater awareness of the key factors affecting the competitiveness of the product on the market. And the trade-off curves can become part of the knowledge database for other development programs.

2.2.12 Why Choose One Goal Value and Not Another?

Besides an analysis of the trade-off curves, there is another even more critical question that needs to be dealt with while defining the goals: why one numerical value and not another one? Generally, the numbers are defined on the basis of a utilitarian logic of profitability or statistics.

The decision to improve the performance or to reduce a cost by 5%, 10%, or 15%, for example, compared to a previous model or to the competition, *does not always follow the logic of the future client's perception of value, but that of internal improvement or optimization.*

Let's look at the chart listing the established goals for the successful launch of the Lexus LS400 in the United States (Figure 2.3).

We can notice something quite singular here. The maximum speed target was fixed at 250 km/h, compared to 222 km/h and 220 km/h of the BMW and Mercedes models, the main competitors in that bracket, while the other characteristics were not set so aggressively in percentage terms. Why? They could have decided on 223, 230, or 235, but the maximum speed value was fixed very high so customers could appreciate the marked difference of the characteristic to which they attribute value in that particular sales bracket.

	Celsior (LS400)	Mercedes 420 SE/ 560 SE (WG B)	BMW 735i (WG A)
Max. speed	250 km/h (Europe)	222 km/h (Europe)	220 km/h (Europe)
Consumption (Urban / Highway)	23.5 mpg or more (USA) 7.0 km/l or more (Japan)	19 mpg (USA) 5.4 km/l (Japan)	18.8 mpg (USA)
Noisiness	Quietness at high speed (58 db @ 100 km/h) (73 db @ 200 km/h)	Quiteness at high speed 61 db (100 km/h) 76db (200 km/h)	Quiteness at high speed 63 dB (100 km/h) 78 db (200 km/h)
Aerodynamic friction coefficient	.28~.29	.32	.37
Weight	1,710 Kg (USA)	1760 kg (USA)	1760 kg (USA)

Figure 2.3   Synthesized table of the Lexus LS400 target compared to the two target vehicles based on 4.2L engines. (Source: Liker J.K., *The Toyota Way: Fourteen Management Secrets from the World's Greatest Manufacturer*, McGraw-Hill, 2004.)

Only in this way could the car stand out clearly from the others. It was part of a series of winning decisions. Lexus blew away the competition, not so much on price, but on the much higher perceived value for the price compared to the competition in the United States. Fixing the goal at 250 km/h represented a level that was spot-on in relation to one of the most important needs of the target customer, unlike other characteristics, like the degree of silence at high speed—which, as you can see, is much closer to the Mercedes and the BMW—or fuel consumption. The shrewd choice of a goal to achieve, made through the eyes of the end customer, also helps in the delicate stage of the internal *buy-in*, namely, the phase in which the objectives have to be "accepted" within the company, not on the basis of orders from high or bureaucratic instructions, but on more negotiated and shared grounds, especially when very aggressive targets are involved. During this phase, we not only want to cascade objectives but we need to communicate to the project team *why* the targets were set at those levels so they can be better motivated to strive to achieve them.

When a project is being conceived, this phase is sometimes done too quickly, with a tendency both to lose sight of the point of view of the end customer, which translates into the loss of many opportunities, and to lose credibility within the company itself in the event of failures or difficulties in achieving goals that are incoherent or ill-defined.

When we talk about this example during seminars or in the course of Concept Paper workshops in companies, a number of questions recur frequently. We will examine these in the following sections.

2.2.13 Are These Objectives Really Achievable?

One question that springs to mind is why Mercedes and BMW did not set their target at 250 km/h.

The answer relates once again to the process through which the Concept Paper is elaborated, and not to the piece of paper as such. Toyota's Chief Engineer, in this case, took the approach of "no compromise." He firmly believed that he could achieve whatever aggressive targets he set and break through constraints. like high fuel economy means low power output. He knew he had to be the leader to convince people to stretch beyond their comfort zone and was willing to take that responsibility. Often. a goal is considered aggressive simply because it upsets an ingrained habit, a common-held belief or a conviction regarding the technological or scientific state-of-the-art, which then ultimately proves to be surmountable.

The more a company manages to sweep away these common-held beliefs, making itself unique in the eyes of the customer, the more it will be perceived by the market as innovative and providing a much higher value to customers. If there are competitors in the market, comparing the value attributes is relatively easy, providing there is a willingness to challenge the status quo and to really place oneself in the customer's shoes, as was the case with the Lexus, which at the time was a real breakthrough. It was an example not only of technological innovation that blew past the company's competitors at the time, but also of an intelligent and pragmatic definition of goals really able to meet customers' deep expectations.

Figure 2.4 contains a succinct scheme of the objectives for the Lexus LS400 project set by the Chief Engineer, Mr. Suzuki.

Sometimes, the goals of a complex project may appear to be in conflict, giving rise to various dysfunctions and waste within the working team. Placing all the objectives on the same plane could be counterproductive and sometimes even paralyzing. In the LS400 example above, they used "yet" instead of "or" and, through the passion of the chief engineer and the passion of the various engineers and teams, broke through paradigms.

1 – Great high-speed handling/stability	*YET*	A pleasant ride
2 – Fast and smooth ride	*YET*	Low fuel consumption
3 – Super-quiet	*YET*	Light Weight
4 – Elegant styling	*YET*	Great aerodynamics
5 – Warm	*YET*	Functional interior
6 – Great stability at high speed	*YET*	Great C_D value (low friction)

Figure 2.4 Summary table of conflicting objectives Lexus LS400. (Source: Takashi Tanaka, Lean Transformation Summit, London 2008.)

2.2.14 What If We Are Already the Market Leader?

When we are already at the top, as the market leader, the only way to protect that position is to challenge ourselves, both by activating internal processes so as to continually innovate to surpass our limits, and by drawing inspiration from other markets and technologies. Take the example of companies that introduce strong technological innovation borrowed from other sectors. Hybrid cars are a good example of this concept. But, once again, we need to be sure that the client remains the focus of our attention, even when we are engaged in a bold project of technological innovation. Can you remember the first hybrid car that came onto the market? We are almost all tempted to say it was the Toyota Prius, forgetting that it was Honda, with the Insight, that brought out the first hybrid car in 1999. Why didn't it have the success it deserved? In fact the small, two passenger Insight was a flop at the time, if compared with the success Toyota had a few years later with the Prius. Honda had shifted its focus heavily onto the technological aspect, supplying a car that functioned very well, had many exceptional features, and state-of-the-art technological performance. However, very little attention was given to what we have been talking about so far. There was little consideration of how the customer would use the product, how much space he or she would need in the trunk or passenger cabin, for example. The robust process of defining customer value carried out by Toyota, on the other hand, protected the company from this error. Asking the right questions meant that the Prius, for example, had four doors from the outset, a good sized trunk and many other characteristics that led to it being accepted immediately by the market. It was an unrivalled commercial success that once again left competitors trailing behind.

The term used nowadays in the United States is a *Package of Customer Value*, which brings together all the characteristics of our product, as opposed to exclusively technological considerations, which often lead companies to lose sight of the overall vision. Consider the success of products like Apple's iPhone. Though it is not technologically superior to many other products on the market, it has managed to interpret customers' needs, giving them emotions and value perceptions that, *overall,* are far superior to its competitors, thanks to the concept of the Package of Customer Value.

All too often we have seen the traditional equivalent documents of the Concept Paper, such as the specifications and a business plans, done and then left largely by the wayside during the phase of development. This means that in reality every time the team has some doubt about the initial targets or assumptions, the whole project goals have to be re-discussed and useless meetings held. By contrast, when the Concept Paper is done well, quite irrespective of its format in fifteen to twenty-pages, the initial degree of alignment of the team is so high as to provide an incredible momentum to the project. In the daily life of the project, the synthesis of the Concept Paper will then take shape in the *project room,* also called the *Obeya* (big room), where the objectives are stated in documents on the wall "in the face" of the project team. In the following chapters, we will see how the *project room* is developed and what advantages it offers.

Besides the content associated with the product/service that the team intends to develop, the Concept Paper should also clearly include the project plan, project organization, how trade-offs will be arbitrated, and any other internal rules that the team will subscribe to before the project becomes operational.

2.3 Concentrating Efforts at the Beginning of a Project

> The human mind is like a parachute. It functions better when it is open.
>
> **Albert Einstein**

Oppressed by the pressing sense of emergency prevailing in almost all the activities we do within and outside a company, it becomes very difficult to adopt the principle that has enabled hundreds of famous people and teams to achieve project goals on time and within allocated budgets. It is a rule that should be applied in the launch of a physical project, as in the development of a new website or a new software package, a new training course, or an insurance service. The principle requires discipline, creativity, and leadership: concentrate efforts at the beginning of the development of a new project in order to thoroughly explore alternative solutions when there is still the maximum scope for creativity. This principle provides the team with the time to use their intellectual energy to find those groundbreaking innovations that will please our future customers.

Seth Godin, a world-famous marketing guru, the author of scores of bestsellers translated in over twenty languages, and founder and CEO of Squidoo.com, approaches his projects as follows.[3] He uses the term *thrashing* to describe the activities of this phase of the project. Tearing to shreds, firming up, attacking, and bludgeoning are all activities that, metaphorically speaking, should take place early in the development phase. The Japanese often use the term *Kentou*, the "study" of concepts. We always ask teams to go looking for conflict when there are trade-offs to deal with and when it not only costs the company very little but can also yield solutions with lots of added value precisely because we are at the beginning of a project. Unfortunately, it is much more common to see conflicts, debate, debugging—thrashing—when a product has already been created. For example, when the software is close to being delivered, when any modification of the physical product will entail considerable extra time and expense.

To do what Godin suggests, and what is done in practice by firms that apply Lean Development, we need to accept a number of changes in our approach:

1. The greatest effort must be made during the first phases of the development of a new product. Historically, it is not unusual to use 15%–20% more resources in the industrialization phase than planned to rework designs and get the product to launch. Instead, we should front-load our efforts to design in the right solutions and thus these resources will be "saved" the effort and frustrations frequently found at the end of the project.
2. Parallel development of more than one solution rather than developing and iterating on a single concept from beginning to end. This can yield innovative solutions especially in the conceptual and preliminary planning stage, but can also be beneficial in the latter phases when the projects are high risk.

2.3.1 When Does a Project Really End?

If you look at the graph in Figure 2.5, you can see the different way of using resources in the two different approaches. The traditional approach is indicated with the pale shading, the Lean one with the darker color. With the Lean development approach, you can see that more resources are used at the beginning, but the work is completed on-time and, above all, there is an almost total absence of reworking after the end of the project. With the traditional approach, on the other hand, there are few resources at the beginning, but a whole heap of them at the end, and frequent re-workings, hold-ups in the work, and various instances of debugging that keep the whole team occupied much longer than predicted.

Besides Toyota, companies like Harley-Davidson, Ford, and Schumberger are now making increasing use of what is known as *frontloading* in the development of new products. This means committing more resources at the beginning so as to tackle from the outset all the potential risks and opportunities, as the end goal is to obtain a reduction in time and in the overall resources spent on the project. In our experience with projects, however, we have almost always had to deal with something rather particular. The perception of project duration is almost invariably very distant from the reality of what project team members experience.

Often, the project is erroneously considered to be finished when it is delivered the first time. Unfortunately, frequently resources are then committed to modifications and yet more modifications, but these are no longer thought to be part of the project. Finally, you see "swat" teams being set up to deal with constant problems regarding quality, costs, or product performance. At this point, these are no longer regarded as part of the development, but as normal, on-going product "improvement" which is frequently hidden in the overhead costs of the product.

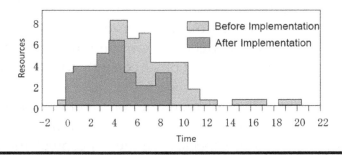

Figure 2.5 Comparison of the use of resources over time in a traditional project compared to one after Lean has been implemented.

We have been engaged for months in task forces where millions of dollars are spent on tinkering with products that have already been launched. But if perhaps we had spent several extra tens of thousands of dollars more, a few more weeks, and a few more resources in the early phases of the project, we would have avoided the task force, or at least drastically reduced the devastating effects. Often, these events are disassociated from the fact that a project has not been well managed at the beginning. In the best of cases, nothing is done to remove the causes of this waste, but instead, head down, all-hands efforts are done to quickly remove the negative issue of the moment. So why does this often happen?

2.3.2 Starting Out Already Late

Sometimes when we start a project, we are already considered to be late, because we usually start from the final deadline decided by the product plan. We then proceed to work backward, defining the activities involved: production, launch of production systems, prototyping and industrialization, planning, exploration of concepts, definition of the project specifications, and team formation. Here lies the paradox: if the initial phases—the Concept Paper and Kentou—have not been tackled thoroughly, it will be hard to define exactly what to do further downstream to satisfy the needs of the client on the one hand and the company's budget on the other. We find ourselves beginning a project already with very little time available and without having a precise idea of what to do.

Figure 2.6 illustrates the difference between the two approaches in terms of relative time. The short time allocated for initial, in-depth consideration in the traditional approach, as represented by the Concept Paper and Kentou phases, will has a snowballing effect in terms of more protracted development and industrialization phases. In contrast, the aim of the Lean approach is to make the latter two phases be more quick and efficient, by committing resources and creativity in the initial phases to design in the right solutions rather than deferring the solving of problems to the latter phases.

2.3.3 The Problem of a Sprint Start

Once started, something happens that silently undermines the controllability of the duration of all projects: a series of small, interminable iterations. We choose one of the possible solutions that we think can satisfy both the customer and the budget. We design it, develop it, and submit it to any one of

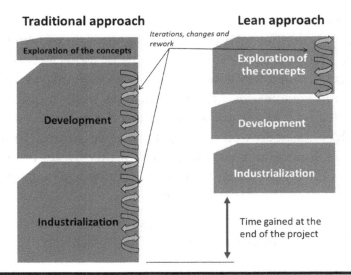

Figure 2.6   Difference in the approach to product development between a Lean project and a conventional one.

our co-developers within or outside the company: marketing, styling, quality, production, etc. Virtually every time some issue arises, a loop of iterations, modifications, improvements, and redesigns then begins. In these occasions invariably arise, from inside our company structure or from outside, observations that force us to rethink our design in some way. Either a comment to the effect that the pieces cannot be assembled well, that the form we had conceived is not good for the marketing people, and so on. And so we go back to the drawing board, experiencing a Stop and Go waste that amounts to a "circling around the solutions" (Figure 2.7).

If this phenomenon is multiplied according to the degree of complexity of the product and of the company you are part of, it will be clear why the majority of projects can quickly spiral out of control. In these conditions, it is almost impossible to define the standard duration of the events of the project itself due to this repeated circling. Projects are managed almost with the expectation that some surprise is lurking around the corner and that we will "find a way" to get back on track.

On the surface, we have a sense that we have a bias for action and we can get started straight away without stopping getting caught in organizational paralysis, but in reality it is not possible to predict either the duration of iterations, nor how many there will be, given that the phenomenon can recur frequently with a variety of subjects along the development path. The conclusion of all this is that the only thing we can be sure of is that we will not be able to say in advance when and how we will finish our projects.

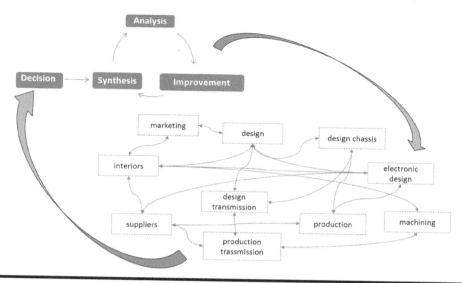

Figure 2.7 The sprint start requires a complex series of successive iterations and optimizations.

2.3.4 Iterative Models and Convergent Models of Development

If it is true that Lean transformation starts from our way of thinking, the model for creating and developing new products and services may paradoxically seem more confused and complex than the traditional one, because it forces us to open our minds and to consider, in the face of a single challenge, a wide range of possible solutions that have to be dealt with at the same time and from the outset.

What is presented in university courses as one of the most potent "heuristic" scientific models for the development of a solution, the iterative model (Figure 2.8), turns out to be quite ineffective and a great source of waste in a real and complex context like that of many companies, in which the need to satisfy multiple needs are spread inside and outside the company. By contrast, the convergent model, the same one applied by Seth Godin, forces us, especially when we are tackling an innovative project, to pull lots of alternative solutions out of the hat, immediately involving all the possible contributors to the innovation as soon as possible. Let's consider what happens when we have already built the equipment for the assembly line, when the product is almost on the market and we realize that something is wrong. Well, we begin to do cycles of modification, accepting whatever costs are incurred because we can no longer avoid them. In other words, we have to make

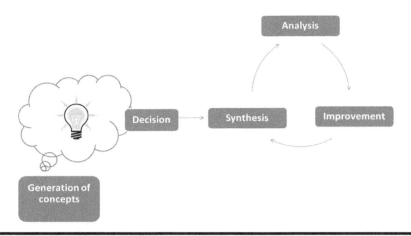

Figure 2.8 The iterative model of product development.

the solution work given all the constraints that are now imposed in the system. So much for fluidity and creativity and welcome to the world of firefighting!

This holds true not only when a physical product is being developed, but also for the planning of any kind of event, even in our everyday lives, when our choice is just one of various possible alternatives.

If, instead of accepting the best idea that comes to mind at a given time and doing it (and assuming, apart from anything else, that it is not possible to do any better), we were to stop and exchange ideas with others, asking them for further alternatives and additions, talking about different possible alternatives, and understanding the pros and cons of individual alternatives, we would understand that what appears superficially to be a waste of time is in fact an advantage, a clearing away the possible consequences of mistaken or imperfect choices and converging (Figure 2.9) to the best solution for our customer and our company.

2.3.5 Kentou and Set-Based Concurrent Engineering in Practice

The best way to get a good idea is to get a lot of ideas…

Linus Pauling

If we wanted to fix an appointment with an extremely busy person as quickly as possible, what would we do?

Undoubtedly, if we were dealing with someone who really is very busy and we were trying to get an appointment, succeeding at the first attempt would just be good luck. It is much more likely that we will have to try

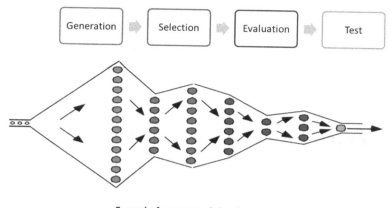

Funnel of conceptual development

Figure 2.9   **The converged model of product development.**

several times before succeeding in finding a free time slot. What can we do to cut our wait to a minimum?

We could propose a list of possible alternatives that are already okay for us, because the more alternatives we offer, the more likely it is that at least one of them will suit our busy colleague as well.

In fact, this is the guiding concept behind the principle of *Set-Based Concurrent Engineering*,[4] a proven method for every kind of product to be developed or for when we need to innovate to resolve a problem.

With Set-Based Concurrent Engineering there is a gradual progression from a large number of solutions to a single one for production. Through successive restrictions of conceptual parameters of design, we converge to the optimum solution that simultaneously satisfies in the best possible way the different spheres of feasibility of the various functions, and more importantly, meets the needs of the customer.

As we have already said, having the goal of creating different alternatives makes us invest more time initially, but it enables us to move a number of solutions forward, some of which will be gradually discarded during future integration events. These act as filters, the purpose of which is to permit methodological verification and also to develop an awareness of going with an optimum solution for everyone and not just for some, before moving on to the next stage. During this filtering process, some solutions are always excluded in favor of others, but the ones that are dropped remain in the project database as these learnings could be possibly reused in future projects.

In the course of the project, the set of different alternatives will open and close, radically changing the classical way of organizing in the exploration phase of projects. This will also help to create a mechanism for learning and for shared knowledge that will tend toward the maximum degree of satisfaction and added value both for the project that is under way and for those in the future, making the accumulated knowledge available in a structured manner.

2.3.6 Development Teams Based on Modules

In Lean companies, we can collapse the complexity of product development into two phases: a phase called *Kentou* or study phase, and a phase of *simultaneous realization*, which includes detailed design and industrialization. In the Kentou phase, the work is divided between various Module Development Teams (MDT), whose goal is to develop a subsystem of the final product. Each team is asked to come up with the highest number of possible solutions. MDTs are small cross-functional groups responsible for part of the system. In a car, an interior, for instance, there may be two designers, an assembler, a process engineer, and sometimes a supplier.

This study phase is where concepts are explored, and then narrowed down to a manageable number or one. It is fun and creative, and highly inclusive of groups in the company that traditionally are hardly ever included so early on in the development of a new product. It gives rise to descriptions, sketches, and drawings that are sometimes not even dimensioned. These concepts that are generated by each of these subgroups are done with the aim of seeing what possibilities can be put on the table to achieve the same project targets in accordance with the Concept Paper. This activity is carried out before establishing the definitive product concept that will then be developed and produced. The presence and the coordination of the Project Leader or Chief Engineer are strategic in this phase, because this person must see to it that the finished product targets (System Targets) are transformed into the sub-targets of the different modules (Module Targets), making sure the subgroups are sufficiently independent, but without ever losing sight of the interfaces between one module and another. For example, in designing a vehicle, the subgroups are tied to some parts of the car and sometimes have goals that appear unrelated. The goal is to give maximum freedom to generate different possible solutions, precisely so as not to limit people's creativity in a phase that is left deliberately fluid. The Chief Engineer's role then becomes one of system integrator to work with their module teams to find the best system-level solution for the customer.

2.3.7 *Reuse of Existing Solutions and Knowledge of Previous Critical Areas*

Many companies are discovering that one of the greatest opportunities for cost savings in design and manufacturing is reuse of standard parts, as well as developing multiple products from common platforms and architectures. In the case of Ford's renaissance, since near bankruptcy, the head of body engineering, Jim Morgan, displayed multiple vehicle hoods with the top sheet metal torn off. Half were Toyota-Lexus models and half were Fords. Each Ford hood had a different architecture for the supporting steel structure under the skin and for Toyota they were all identical. Developing standard architectures and parts saved Ford billions of dollars.[5]

Before beginning to invent new components or services, questions should be asked as how much can be recovered from solutions currently being used from previous solutions explored by other projects, but applicable in the current project. In this phase, it is important to ensure the MDTs have sufficient freedom of movement, and not to rush things too much, leaping hurriedly into the design and producing a sub-optimum solution, overcome by the anxiety to "get cracking." It is important in this phase to *go and see* firsthand what we have on the shelf, how the modules we are working on are used and produced in the plants, to get to know in practice the real problems that each component has in the real world, to see how their internal customer uses and produces these components. For example, go and talk to the assembly team on the line to understand what problems they had in earlier experiences of assembling the components we are designing. This type of activity is not left up to the good will of the individuals, but is done in a unhurried and systematic fashion. The same applies when the interaction concerns outside suppliers. If we are designing a piece that will be produced by the supplier, we need to go to that supplier to see what is really going on, not leave it up to others or at any rate not allow ourselves to be guided by convictions or hearsay. On the contrary, we need to go and see what is really happening on the spot. This is the *gemba walk*.[6] Exactly as the Chief Engineer does during the development of the Concept Paper, when he or she goes to see how the end client uses a given product.

In this phase of the project, this is the best way for filtering or optimizing the concepts that are generated. In addition to direct contact with colleagues, suppliers, and clients, it is clear that we should rely on common standards, guidelines, and checklists that are used in a disciplined way by all engineers. These documents represent everything that other working groups before us have learned and have made available in a structured and utilizable form, thereby supporting the process of convergence toward optimum solutions during the study phase. This helps the teams to use data and objective facts to make better decisions rather than being guided by arbitrary opinions.

2.3.8 Simultaneous Convergence of Different Modules

Everything we have said thus far is applicable to the different subsystems of any new product/service, including the production system, with its different alternatives in terms of equipment, machines, lines, and controls. The subsystems will converge in a series of steps toward the choice of solutions that represent the global optimum and not the optimum of just one of them as shown in Figure 2.10.

When we begin to embrace this way of thinking, it is fascinating to see how quickly people get used to developing, in a quite natural way, more than one solution to the same problem. The chosen solutions will have to be feasible from the point of view of the group to help guarantee the best advantage of the system. And if such a solution cannot be found during the initial search, efforts will then have to be made to either spend more time/effort to find more innovative solutions, or we may need to modify by loosening the restraints of one or more parts of the system. If, for example, we are trying to minimize the product cost, the work in this phase will consist of finding the overall minimum, because it can by no means be taken for granted that the sum of minimums of the individual parts corresponds to

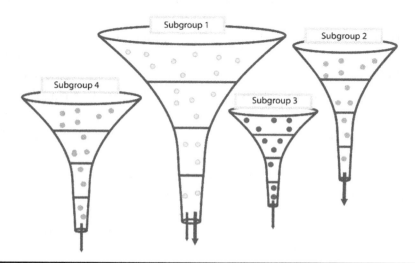

Figure 2.10 The converged model of product development for complex products.

this result. Sometimes, the minimum piece cost of a given component does not correspond to the minimum cost for the system if it drives higher performance (and cost) in another part of the system. And so it becomes fundamental to adopt both a different way of thinking and a concrete and effective way to quantify such effects. In all our years of experience, the minimum total cost product is rarely achieved, precisely as a result of cultural barriers, distortions in measurement methods, and poorly developed mechanisms for the financial incentivization of the various groups within a company.

In the example of Figure 2.11, you can see how each MDT has explored different feasible solutions from their own point of view, occupying their "set" of alternatives in the subsets of the Venn diagram. When the different sets of solutions are compared, it turns out that among the many feasible solutions, the optimum ones occupy a limited part of the overlap between the subsets. It is reasonable, then, to eliminate solutions lying outside this area and to focus time on the analysis and in-depth study of those that remain in the overlapping design space.

In one example of a systems supplier to automotive, they did in fact benchmark each individual subsystem on cost against the best in the world. They found the lowest cost solutions for each part and created a "Frankenstein" model of the best solution for each part and based their target cost on that— a 40% cost reduction. They realized they could not use those parts as they would not work together as a system. But they set a 30% cost reduction target and through systematic investigation of alternative solutions converging to one they achieved the 30% reduction (Liker and Franz, 2012, chapter).[7]

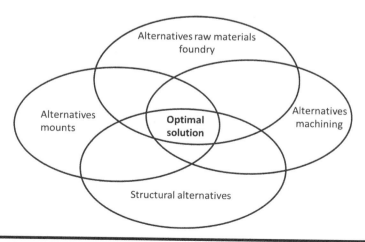

Figure 2.11   Example of evaluation of different alternatives: the best solution is one that meets at the same time different feasible areas.

2.3.9 *The Case of the Prius*

The original Prius hybrid, the first mass industrial case of hybrid car technology, was, for Toyota, one of the projects with the greatest time pressure, because the goal was to enter the market within fourteen months in order to successfully compete with Honda, which, despite showing signs of weakness, was already on the market with the Insight. So did they forego thinking before acting? Did they skip the Concept Paper and the rigorous application of SBCE? On the contrary. They demonstrated that the more time pressure there is, and the more risk there is of making mistakes, as in this case with an innovative technology, the more the approach bears fruit, making it one of the fastest cases of the introduction onto the automotive market of a completely new technology.[8] And for them, it must have been particularly difficult to do without all the learnings typically derived from previous experiences, such as trade-off curves, guidelines, and checklists, in that they had never produced hybrid batteries or engines. The approach in the case of the design of the hybrid engine was the following:

- Consideration of eighty different types of hybrid engines in the first exploration of concepts
- Reduction to ten in the second phase of selection
- Further study of the ten solutions in order to choose the best four
- Computerized simulations and in-depth tests to choose the best of the four solutions

One of our clients, hearing me talking about this case, said one day that it would be culturally impossible for us to get people to think about and discuss eighty alternative solutions with so much time pressure. Indeed, if anyone were to carelessly propose such an absurdity they would be considered out of their mind.

Are we really in a hurry? Let's slow down then. Are we afraid of releasing a poor product onto the market? *Let's find as many solutions as come to mind and compare them.* Let's stop to think, rather than to redo and improve something umpteen times along the way.

Eighty different types of hybrid engine are considered, reduced to ten through a system of evaluation made as objective as possible in order to narrow down the solutions to a more manageable, but still high number. There is incredible pressure, but no justification for dangerous shortcuts and no reason to opt for the traditional approach. The higher the pressure, the more Toyota took pains to consider various solutions, precisely because they wanted to get to the end on time with the winning solution. Then they moved forward to the computerized simulation phase with four different solutions. It was only after this that they chose the final solution, bringing it out onto the market within the given timeframe.

2.3.10 Group Brainstorming? No Thanks

How should we begin to develop concepts using this approach? How many solutions should be generated? How many times should they be narrowed down?

There is no general rule applicable to all cases and circumstances because each time it is necessary to take into account the available time, the possible, feasible technologies to choose from, the degree of innovation needed, the size of the teams, and so on. But one thing can be said for certain: the first step in the Set-Based methodology is to get the various groups to develop as many solutions as possible quite independently, which is in contrast to what happens in traditional group brainstorming sessions. The idea is to give people the greatest breadth of individual creativity at the most appropriate time. When people or subgroups meet after having developed possible solutions independently, the comparison and evaluation of ideas always produce more new ideas thereby enlarging the creative sphere. "We learn from all the set," the SBCE experts say about these types of creative work sessions.

Each subgroup is free to develop the concepts of different solutions within the parameters of action of their own area of competence, represented by assigned quantitative targets and by the set of restraints and interfaces with other subgroups. For a car headlight, for instance, there will be objectives such as luminosity, cost, light characteristics, size, and interface with the fender, hood, and bumper. Within these parameters, the team will be free to give full rein to their creativity and then compare notes with their colleagues on the module team.

2.3.11 What Happens if the Solutions Are Incompatible with Each Other?

After exploring the concepts of each subgroup, the next step is to compare the various sets of alternatives and to define those solutions that work well for everyone. So, if subgroup A has found five solutions and subgroup B has found four, it is necessary to understand which of the respective solutions respect the constraints of both while meeting the system-level goals. Lucky scenario: among the solutions found there are already some that work well for both. Consider two possibilities. Less fortunate scenario: the two sets of solutions are far apart and there are no optimum solutions between both subgroups. What do we do now? Crisis! It might be big or small, but this is the right moment for it to happen. Better now rather than shortly before the finished product is due to be delivered to manufacturing or just before it is to be launched into the market. In this situation, one of the two subgroups may have to reconsider their constraints, loosening them and/or one of the groups will have to extend their set of solutions by doing more innovative research to find a point of overlap.

One example might be the attempt to find a point of contact between the solutions proposed by the styling center and those developed by manufacturing (Figure 2.12). Manufacturing have come up with a list of possible solutions they can live with and that can achieve the objectives of the Concept Paper. Likewise, the styling center has produced various bodywork designs.

Again, lucky scenario: there are at least two bodywork designs that overlap with the producibility criteria of manufacturing, and which can be made with equipment judged to be possible by the manufacturing team.

Less fortunate scenario: none of the bodywork designs created by the styling center can be produced with any of the solutions proposed by manufacturing, and so we have two sets of solutions that are completely detached and which do not overlap anywhere. In cases like this, the risks of the project emerge immediately, and the corrective measures are managed during the project in the early phase while the design is most fluid, when

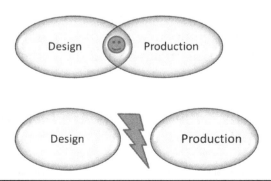

Figure 2.12   Example of searching for an optimal solution under exploration of concepts.

other solutions or compromises can be found without great upheavals to the entire product.

2.3.12 *Excessive Harmony Does Not Yield Good Products*

It is not true that better products are obtained with harmony and agreement. We need to know how to arrive at constructive conflict in order to have state-of-the-art products. *The truth of the matter is that there are moments in which we must spark a crisis* if we want to integrate the different points of view, *but some moments are more opportune than others.* For example: if we have to choose between a moment when manufacturing has already defined and built almost all its equipment two months prior to the start of production, and a moment when the designs of the product and of the equipment needed to build it are still on paper or in people's heads, which would you choose? In other words, it is a question of managing to focus the attention of the subgroups on solutions that, all things considered, do not seem to be all that urgent, because the potential crisis we are accustomed to is still a long way away. But it is precisely in the early phases and thanks to this different spirit of Set-Based design that it is possible to avoid the classic sub-optimum iterations that are all too familiar to us later in a project.

In Lean Innovation, we actually "love" sparking crises in this phase, because we want people to face up to the risks of the project as soon as we discover them and then using the right analytical tools and techniques that are available for resolving the situation at a reasonably low cost. What will happen in this situation? Coming back to our prior example, the styling center will take the opportunity to modify one of its bodywork designs to permit easier assembly, or manufacturing will make some alterations to one or more pieces of equipment to adapt one of the styling's design. The designs thus gradually converge toward the global optimum rather than favoring specific optimums that do not yield the best solution.

2.3.13 *From a Good Product to an Excellent One*

When selecting the concepts that have been explored, the tendency is to choose what is regarded as the best solution, but it is worth giving some consideration to the word "best": compared to what? What works well for a specific need might conflict with a different one. Without this broad vision of the whole field of the system's functions, we might end up making some really huge blunders. To avoid this, it is worth reflecting on how the key characteristics and the performance of the various solutions behave relative to one another. Technically, the curves representing the variation of a performance with respect to a variable are called *trade-off curves*. If we have the data, it is worth drawing them to help make an objective analysis, as in the example of Figure 2.13.

In this case, we can discern how it is possible to conduct a technical and/or financial evaluation with a quantification of the optimum solution in the whole field of functioning, as opposed to the identification of a "merely good and acceptable" solution.

2.3.14 Two Small Secrets

2.3.14.1 First Secret

In many projects, we see a quest to achieve 100% performance in all the subsystems. But there are times when the attempt to obtain 100% in everything does not lead to success. When we have an overly innovative solution, it is a good idea to protect ourselves with a "backup" solution that may only be 80% okay, which, in the event of difficulties, can protect us from the failure of the entire system. This is the reason why,

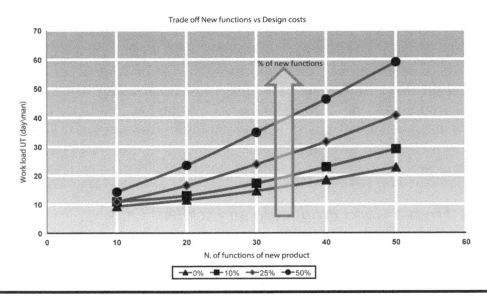

Figure 2.13 Example of a *trade-off curve*.

when developing new products, Lean companies have the good habit of coming up with at least one backup solution for those parts of the system where they can see risks. Would you prefer to have a product consisting of parts theoretically delivering 100% performance but where there is the risk of a product recall due to a quality problem, or which does not even get through the testing and validation phases, or a product that contains a few parts with 80% performance but which are reliable and guarantee a problem-free market launch?

This is the small secret that enables many Lean companies to be sure of obtaining, within the established time frame, the solution with the greatest final quality, by carrying forward backup solutions right through to the end of the development phase, ready to enter the field of play when things get too risky. In fact, this is often the secret to ensuring the successful on-time completion of the project with minimal risk.

2.3.14.2 Second Secret

When we advance the development of various parts at the same time, it is likely that some will converge sooner, managing to define the best conceptual solution to carry forward into the next phase of the project. What can happen in this case is that the slower subgroup comes up with solutions that "do not fit" well with the already advanced ones, forcing the entire system to embark on fresh iterations and stops and starts during the project. Another thing that can happen is that one group prematurely accepts a solution that offers it lower costs but do not offer the real minimum total product cost. How many times does it happen that we carry forward solutions, moving ahead more rapidly than other colleagues, only then to be brought to an abrupt halt or required to revise what has been done? To avoid this, the Chief Engineer or Project Manager must be capable of slowing down one or more groups to ensure both synchronization of tasks and the best system integration in the least amount of overall time. This will help to have the smallest possible number of modifications downstream for the team.

In other cases, when we can decide early on a part of the product, it allows us to release that part early for tooling. This is called "staggered release." For example, Toyota will release some steel body parts early for the development of molds rather than send a huge batch to body development all at one time. This smooths out the workflow for the downstream operations reducing overall lead time and often improving quality.

2.3.15 When the Supplier Teaches Something to the Client: The Denso Case

Overly precise specifications at the beginning of a project delivered to a supplier or a designer may signal that concepts have been explored only roughly or that a Concept Paper has been poorly conceived. Why? Because at the beginning of a project, it is unlikely that all the details of a design solution will be known. Certain things might be known—the price and cost targets, the general characteristics of the product, or service to be developed—but it is practically impossible to ask a supplier for an object or service with specifications and requests that have been firmed up too far in advance. This, on the other hand, is what many purchasing departments ask or hope for, in order to wrap up negotiations purely on the financial and business level. But it is hardly ever considered that design solutions evolve along the way and that contractual dealings cannot be set up prematurely. On the contrary, it is not yet known how the detailed product will turn out. This approach then gives rise to the never-ending churn of modifications, renegotiations, unexpected price hikes, and a colossal waste of company time and resources. Such situations arise so often that it is quite legitimate to ask: How can all this happen?

Let's look at a case with a company called Denso. Denso is a supplier of car parts, including radiators. One of its customers, a well-known car manufacturer, had asked them to develop a new radiator, giving them product specifications and requesting the definitive quote. However, certain aspects of the performance specifications in the Request for Quotation seemed contradictory even after trying to clarify them with the customer. What's more, the specs came with a mass of detailed information and requirements that seemed to be at odds with the real state of advancement of the project. For example, there was little correlation between the functional characteristics requested and the cost goal imposed. In the face of these doubts, the technicians at Denso, already accustomed to working with the Set-Based Concurrent Engineering approach, decided quite independently to develop some mock-up prototypes with different possible solutions and variants to submit to the client, even though these had not been requested. One of the variants coincided closely with the requested specifications. But as they considered other solutions, some of which would actually be less costly for the client, the decision to explore different concepts seemed the most sensible path to take in order to understand what the client really wanted and to make the client clearly see the trade-offs that needed to be made. Three sets of solutions were proposed: the most expensive one, high performing; a solution geared more toward middle performance; and one set mostly focused on cost. Each set of solutions also had three to four variants. Obviously, the prototypes were rather rudimentary means with a view to the speed of execution, but were sufficient to help the client to achieve a rapid understanding. By "seeing" the set of possibilities, the client was better able to articulate their true needs and collaboratively work through the trade-off decisions to be made. Thus, Denso was carrying out at the same time an SBCE-style process, involving the client in the phase of convergence to try to avoid iterations, delays, and modifications that would have been normal with a traditional approach.

The SBCE approach can, therefore, be a tool in the hands of the client, to guarantee optimum solutions in a limited period of time, or an excellent tool in the hands of a highly evolved supplier to get the client to modify vaguely defined specifications on the basis of objective facts and parameters. This holds true above all when the specifications and other documents from the client are characterized by excessive paper-pushing and bureaucratic zeal that aims for a single solution that frequently squashes innovative opportunities. This is an example where facts, numbers, and concrete things were placed on the table, providing the elements for a more effective choice. Not a battle of words and negotiating gamesmanship, but a reasoned and mature presentation of different technical alternatives made available in a structured (and creative) way to find the best overall solution that was a win-win for both the client and the supplier.

2.3.16 Problem-Solving Resolves Everything... But How Much Does It Cost?

Eliminating problems before they arise is one of the guiding principles for the development of a new product or service in a Lean company. For this reason, a hunt starts during the Concept Paper and Kentou phases, for all the weak signs that might arrive from various areas of a company in a structured way. That is why efforts are made to uproot the causes of possible future problems by going to see what is going on where a problem is first detected—in the factory, at a supplier, retail outlet or the client's site. In every case, there is always a clear mission, namely, to resolve the problem but just as importantly is to capture all the learnings to make them available to colleagues and partners.

Many companies fall in love with (retrospective) problem-solving methods and tools, for instance, the whole *six sigma* framework,[9] forgetting, however, the enormous potential that resides in the healthy capacity for *predictive rather than retrospective problem-solving*. Sometimes we attend task-force working group sessions and observe people with great experience working in firefighting mode only once the problem has already exploded. Paradoxically, we do not always see this same experience and energy working to prevent the problems. Wastes such as product costs are too high, transport problems, fluctuating performance, customer complaints, unexpected losses in market share, and so on. In the majority of cases, these problems were predictable. During our Lean workshops, we sometimes devote whole days to understanding, together with the project team, how we could have prevented one or more recent headaches encountered on current projects. Almost always there would have been a way, and we can assure you that calculating how much time and money this lack of prior attention costs the company provides considerable food for thought on the virtues of firefighting. It is more convincing than a whole lot of philosophical talk debating the subject.

There are three basic rules for predictive problem-solving in the development phases:

1. Immediately: every time any kind of risk is feared, tackle it straight away.
2. Go to the source of the problem: the potential problem must be dealt with by removing the possible causes at the roots, and not just treating the symptoms. This can only be done by truly grasping the situation firsthand.
3. Focus on learning: having dealt with the root of the problem, capture and pass on what you have learned, taking pains to inform others so that the same problem will not recur in the future. Formal documentation in checklists or know-how databases is even more powerful.

If the focus is more on making sure that problems do not arise rather than solving problems that already have happened, this attitude will become a new way of thinking that supports a proactive problem-solving culture. In fact, in this type of culture, every time there is the whiff of a possible problem that might crop up, it is obvious to everyone that it is pointless to put it off and that getting a grip on it before it explodes in our faces is the most effective path for the whole company. Such an approach inevitably requires a "go and see, and get your hands dirty" attitude, especially in the product development phases. This is the very first concept Luciano learned in the field with his Japanese *sensei,* Masaaki Yutani. Being a good former Toyota manager, and perhaps because he did not fully understand our Italianized English, he always tended to go to the production line to find evidence of what he was being told. We might be talking, for instance, about standards of cleanliness in the department, with everyone swearing that it was impossible to do better, and we would see him get face down onto the ground, wriggle right in under the machines (getting up visibly dirty), demonstrating to us that he was totally unafraid of *going immediately to the heart of the problem*. The process he taught us, by example, is the fundamental importance of *focusing on learning*. When, as a recent graduate, Luciano compared him in his mind with many other managers he was getting to know, he noticed a big difference. In the space of a few minutes, and with a minimum of words, he taught Luciano much more than a master's course on advanced problem-solving techniques. He would state bluntly, "Never allow weak signals to crop up again as future problems," and he would try to make Luciano understand how important it was to have the same widespread will at all levels of the company.

Too often, we are accustomed to action, to solving problems and moving on. We are unconcerned about other colleagues who may face the same obstacle tomorrow, about how we can stop them encountering it, about how we can make available to them the solution we have found today. And more often than not, guess who ends up in the shoes of that colleague? We do.

2.3.17 *When Simple Steps Yield Solutions That Avoid Serious Consequences*

Sometimes it is hard to avoid certain technical problems, even serious ones, because "time is not lost" in the design phase on examining experiences prior to the project in question, or because not enough time is invested in evaluating the feasibility of a solution together with those people who have the practical knowledge to quickly pinpoint technical risks and opportunities. For example, we might see, in relation to pieces produced through casting and heat-deformation processes, the recurrence of problems already experienced in the past— such as deformations, cracks, ruptures due to over-rapid cooling, non-optimum molds, or logistics issues. This happens every time we skip simple, sometimes obvious steps, like going to see what is really going on in the prototype department, or seeking the opinion of those directly involved in the production of those pieces. We do not necessarily need to have a structured Knowledge Management system, we just need to be guided by a healthy focus on continual learning. In a Lean

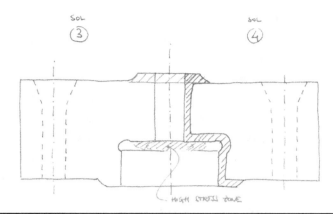

Figure 2.14 Example of technical problem solved in the bud.

approach, efforts are made by the project team to ensure these simple steps are taken frequently, as in the example of Figure 2.14.

Above all, you will note how the initial solutions have been presented in this case: in the form of an old-fashioned pencil sketch, and not on a finished CAD model. In Figure 2.14 you can see a comparison of two solutions, number 3 on the left and number 4 on the right. The sketch of solution 3 had been immediately "blocked" by the person with responsibility for production, due to producibility problems regarding a part and its transportation that would lead to waste in his facility. On the basis of experience and standards, the production engineer identified various possible problems in this design condition, including mold stability and the movement of materials. The designers therefore made modifications leading to the next solution, number 4, maintaining the functionality of the item but eliminating the producibility risk at the outset, while it was still on paper, without waiting for it to explode once production was under way. Early identification of the problem gave engineers more freedom for coming up with possible solutions, because the design was still flexible. Redesigning the solution in this phase of development was not expensive, the only cost being the time to use one's head, a little discipline, and commitment in tackling a problem so far in advance and not being in a state of emergency.

The importance of introducing the phase known as Kentou, the preliminary study of alternative concepts, proves not only to be strategic to the pursuit of innovative solutions with higher end-customer value, but also indispensable for channeling our creativity to avoiding heaps of internal costs arising as a result of having designed solutions that initially worked well for someone, but were not optimum from the company's point of view.

2.3.18 It Is Advisable to Make Modifications Early On

Lean companies must live with modifications. Indeed, there may be, on some projects, more modifications in the design process than with traditional companies. However, the advantage is that they make them earlier. As has been already mentioned, they actively go looking for them in concept and development where the disruptions are few and the costs of modifications are typically lower. Look at Figure 2.15.

A good way of gauging the "leanness" of a company is to monitor the period in which modifications are made during projects and during the life of their products. The more modifications are made at the upstream end, the "leaner" the company is in the development phases and the less it will clearly spend on modifications just prior to production. Among other things, modifications made upstream can be more radical and less of a "patch" solution, as happens when modifications are made close to or after production has commenced. The more effort is made at prevention at the beginning, the less rework has to be done just before production, when the cost of the *quick fix* is typically more expensive to implement. As an American colleague said: "You pay much more for a late change and you usually get a less robust solution!"

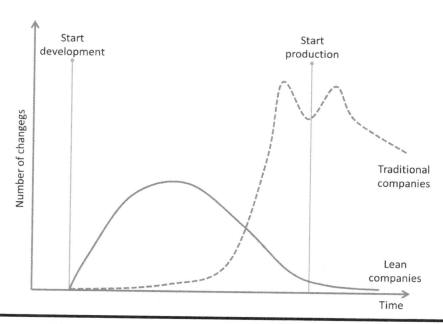

Figure 2.15   Different models of approach to change. (Source: Drogosz John, *Lean Product & Process Development Handbook,* **University of Michigan, 2007.)**

2.3.19 When a Limited Budget Makes No Provision for Additional Expenses

We have often had direct experience of conflicts arising from not being able to spend a few tens of thousands of dollars in the development phase, due to budgetary problems, and then having to spend hundreds of thousands of dollars two or three years down the line to resolve the problem once it exploded when production was under way and the product had reached the end customer. In retrospect, the budget argument simply does not hold up. The money has to be spent at the right time, otherwise the consequences can be significant in terms of lost profit margins or even worse loss of customers.

The paradox is that, with the emergency, the focus now shifts principally onto the customer. A couple of years earlier, the focus was short sightedly on the budget, rather than on the risk to the customer. Often, it is the mental attitude of managers and technicians that makes the difference. Policies and procedures have little to do with it in these cases even though they are frequently the scapegoats for the aforementioned behavior.

Usually, the fundamental cause of this rather narrow-minded attitude lies, once again, in considering the short-term financial constraints, rather than attending to the long-term value of the company. Very frequently those same managers who favored short-time choices will, after two or three years, have changed job role or company, leaving the old problem unsolved in the hands of someone else.

The development of a product is strategic, not tactical. Companies that are leaders in innovation are fully aware of this, and really do consider customer value from the very earliest phases of development. They do not waste time eaking their way through each quarter counting money, but work energetically to "make money" in the long term, demonstrating that the value of a company is a consequence of the sum of all the decisions that are taken to bring value to the customer.

2.4 Value Stream Mapping to Understand the Real Current State and Creatively Envision a Desired Future State

Discovery consists of seeing what everybody has seen and thinking what nobody has thought.

Albert Szent Gyorgyi

In companies, whether big or small, we often act without being aware of the patterns we repeat every day—actions performed repetitively either as individuals or as a group, both when these bring good results and when they bring bad results. In managerial jargon, such patterns are called processes. And here arises one of the most common errors, which I see repeated in companies of all sizes. What is a process?

Almost all companies, when they decide to represent themselves in terms of processes, choose the short and easy route, with purely formal procedures and heaps of standard operating procedures describing the various company processes: production, administration, design, logistics, and so on. Above all, the objective is not to use the charts and descriptions of company processes as tools for continuous improvement, but to arm themselves with reassuring procedures to give a semblance that they have the process under control.

To what extent do you think these thousands of written procedures are a faithful representation of real company processes? Of what really goes on? Of the real habits that people have acquired over the years? Often, they are only so in theory, and are only produced with a view to getting through a quality certification every few years. Who has written these processes and procedures? Were they written by the people who perform them or by someone else on their behalf? And above all, why were they written? Many times, they are summarized descriptions of process flows, as you can see in Figure 2.16, where, in the first line, there is an example of activities that describe a possible process. Linear, neat, and tidy, offering a good representation of what we think, or hope, is the reality. Unfortunately, though, in the majority of cases the representation is far from accurate.

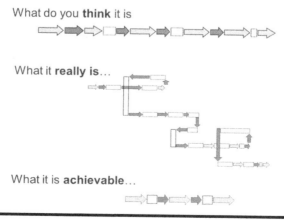

Figure 2.16   Comparison between different interpretations of a process.

What happens in practice is much more difficult to represent than what is shown in company procedures, which is why it is much simpler to produce a thick file, bind it all together nicely, and get ready to pass the certification test. Representing the "what it really is" in all its complexity is a much more difficult task. Above all, it requires a willingness to see the deep-down reality and the waste associated with the current processes. Various examples spring to mind, some of which we have already discussed in previous sections, where "everyone knew, but nobody said anything," thereby burying problems and real habits until the arrival of the next crisis requiring urgent resolution, at all costs and in any way possible.

How can we learn to represent reality faithfully, with the aim of using this representation as the basis for making improvements? In order to move from a genuinely complicated situation, but faithfully represented, to an improved and potentially achievable situation, as in the second of Figure 2.16, we need, with great humility and honesty, to sit down and represent the real process. It is hard work, but necessary. By doing it, we can turn this process mapping into an activity. This almost always involves a cross-functional team with a skilled facilitator to encourage everyone to take ownership of their processes and attack the everyday wastes that stand in their way of delivering innovative products to the marketplace faster, cheaper, and with higher quality. This must be followed up in regular meetings, at least weekly, to discuss the actual state of the project and deviations from the plan. They can then convince themselves of what is truly achievable for their process once waste is removed as is shown in line three of Figure 2.16. Above all, we must realize that in every company big or small, information, material, and communication flows are complex, and may pass from one person to another and one department to another several times, as in Figure 2.17.

It is necessary to accept the fact that process mapping involves several people, who are often performing activities in different places and at different times. At Lenovys, we begin almost all our projects in companies with a representation of their reality, which starts from the simplest element, a basic block of activities, and the cross-functional team went over this in detail developing an increasingly complex representation of everything that is performed in the activity flow under examination. In the early 1990s, Daniel Jones and Jim Womack gave this technique a name, Value Stream Mapping, adapting the original Toyota technique called "material and information flow diagrams." Originally, this technique was used to analyze production processes in order to identify all those activities that added value,

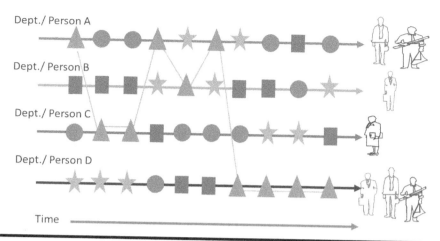

Figure 2.17 Example of real flows to be mapped during product development. (Source: Drogosz John, *Lean Product & Process Development Handbook*, University of Michigan, 2007.)

separating them from those that did not so that the identified wastes could be eliminated.

Through a highly hands-on activity carried out in the workplace, "gemba" style, all the various phases of processing, handling, transport, control, packing, shipping, construction, assembly, and so on, are mapped. The ultimate aim is to reduce the time all this takes, to increase productivity with the same resources, and to limit gaps through a systematic hunt for waste. Consider the example in Figure 2.18.

When attempts are made to apply this technique in the office and above all to the design, creative and intellectual activities workflow, a considerable number of problems arise. Compared to what has been done in manufacturing, these techniques are relatively little used to represent real process flows in the world of product and service development. Why?

In manufacturing, most of the flows are linear, and mapping what happens on a production line is much easier for various reasons. First of all, due to a question of time. The time it takes an item to go down a production line might vary from a few minutes or a few hours through to a maximum of a few days, a few weeks for more complex cases, if we consider partially offshored manufacturing and transportation by ship. It is never like what happens in the development of a new product, where we may be talking of up to a few years. In such cases, it is difficult, even mentally, to map and trace the path that is taken. Reconstructing various months or years of activity is hard work, but necessary, if we want to gain a picture of the real

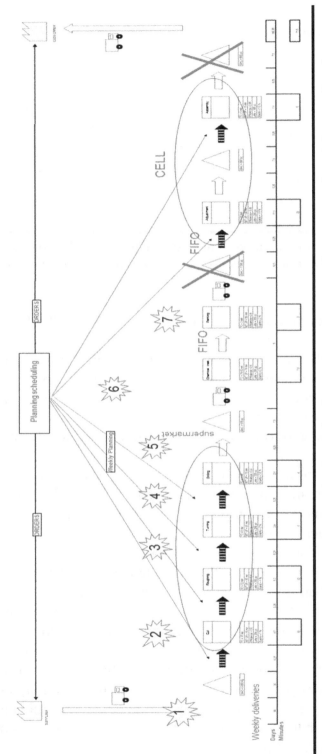

Figure 2.18 Example of Value Stream Mapping in production. (Source: Drogosz John, *Lean Product & Process Development Handbook*, University of Michigan, 2007.)

situation, however complex that may be. This is the best way to get a profound understanding of why often unseen or underestimated problems are occurring, because cause and effects relationships cannot be seen immediately but only after months or even years. Another typical problem associated with the development of a new product or service is that the flows are never linear, and there may be many locations involved depending on the process being analyzed. Also, while in manufacturing you can go and see, in the true spirit of Japanese "Genchi Gembutsu," and gauge and measure scrap, inventory, and the cycle times of the various activities, in intellectual activities like those of design, it is hard to find objective data. For example, when I ask designers what they do exactly, how long their typical activities take, and when a specific activity can be considered complete and no longer in their hands, the initial response is invariably very ambiguous. It is hard for them to say what they do exactly, both because they are not accustomed to "mapping," describing, and measuring, and also because intellectual activities tend to be entangled with others, in vast oceans of multitasking and hard-to-articulate interactions that can vary from one project to another. The initial struggle is to have the team try to "see" the activities they do, through the experience of a "reality mirror," represented by representation, on a big wall, of their process, or Value Stream Map. This early frustration, this looking in the mirror through frequent leaps into the past and into real everyday experience, gives way to enthusiasm when people see themselves represented not just directly, but also together with the various interactions with their working groups and their colleagues in other departments. All this takes place in a clear, simple, and direct way, so as to encourage a full awareness of what goes on. The problems become more visible and the team sees that it's not *my* problem or *your* problem but rather *our* problem and we need to work together to fix it.

2.4.1 *Value Stream Mapping in Practice*

Here, we look a bit more closely at Value Stream Mapping, which will hopefully be useful for anyone who wants to try out this technique for mapping any kind of administrative activity. Every activity that an individual or group performs can be represented by a block of basic activities. Simply arm yourself with bits of card or sticky notes and start jotting down the activities performed by everyone. Although software packages are available to support us in this task, we advise to use simple means such as sticky notes, marker pens, and free walls. There are various reasons for this.

1. Speed and simplicity of execution, modification, and representation.
2. Facilitation of socialization and interaction.
3. With a computer, the focus tends to be on the single person working with the computer, who is controlling the activity.
4. With computer tools, there is a tendency to think more about the tool and the form rather than the content and the real aim of the exercise.
5. With a computer, even if images are projected on a large wall, there is no possibility to interact quickly and physically, with simple, concrete activities like moving a sticky, adding another one, or making a change. With a computer, you cannot stand around talking and reflecting in front of the wall on which we have built up our Value Stream Map, which becomes a true mirror of reality, constructed together with all the participants.
6. With the computer, there is always the risk of Stop and Go waste while everyone is waiting for the person to type in all the information and the team loses momentum in effectively following the process. In fact, some people may get frustrated and mentally detach from the activity.

Only when the group concludes that the crude hand-written map is a reasonable model of the processes the team can, after having completed the work, transfer everything to a computer for easy distribution to a more broad group. Note, we said reasonable model, as there is enough variation across projects that a perfect representation is not possible, nor necessary. What we prefer to do, then, is to begin with the human contact and by filling out sticky notes: name of activity, description, who does it, and the task time. Each activity is then labeled as to whether it is value-added, necessary waste, or pure waste. Sometimes, it is not immediately clear how to distinguish between waste and added value, because the tendency is always to justify what one does a priori. Modifications, repetitions, redundancy, and waiting for things are some examples. To categorize it correctly, we must adopt the end customer's point of view. As we have already seen in other parts of the book, if the customer sees it as value added that they are willing to pay for, that activity is value-added. Other activities may be necessary, but non-value added. For instance, a verification of compliance with existing government requirements are activities that do not actually bring any added value to our end customer, but they are necessary for legal purposes. Still other activities are pure waste: for example, when we repeat an action that has already been done, or repeat a drawing, a document, specification, or modification. I use a nice bright red marker to distinguish these from the green (added value) and yellow (necessary waste).

Another strand of information that needs to be traced is the net duration of the individual activities under examination, what John Drogosz calls "task time," which is then compared with gross time or "time in system": in other words, the real duration of the activity in the system I am mapping. For example, I may have done a drawing in two to three hours, but in reality that drawing may have spent two days on my desk. Seeing the reality of the situation and the real figures, accepting the fact that you have a "time in system" of two days compared with a "task time" of three hours, begins to stimulate people to ask "why." Deeply involved in the mapping activity, they begin to identify an endless series of wastes, causes, and ideas for improvement. The most important part of the mapping consists precisely of this, of measuring activities with impartial eyes to create a common awareness. As this spreads, barriers between people begin to crumble. When approached with humility and pragmatism, the mapping activity naturally leads people to open up and to try to understand the reasons underlying what is happening in their processes. For example, the commercial people become more aware of the challenges faced by designers, who become more receptive toward production's concerns, and so forth. Understanding that we are all in the same boat paves the way for collaborative efforts to identify the possible causes of problems and make sustainable improvements.

To standardize the activity and to ensure it is a tool that can be used by everyone, below are some standardized icons (Figure 2.19) that are similar to traditional Value Stream Mapping in production but adapted for product development processes.

Some frequently used icons are the triangles to represent the myriad delays that occur in office processes. Another important set of symbols are the arrows that makes it possible to distinguish whether an activity has been "pushed" or "pulled." What happens in the vast majority of cases seen thus far is that all projects are "pushed" by someone and not "pulled." Typically, when initially mapping processes, they tend to be full of "push" arrows: Project Managers who push their various requests, designers who have done some drawings and then push them on after they have finished, and so on. Over time, you will see the evolution of the Value Stream Map, with the introduction of elements where activities effectively pulled by the needs of those further on in the value chain. Another common symbol, perhaps the one we see most often in the mapping of processes, represents the iterations of individual activities. Two, three, and sometimes even a generic "n,"

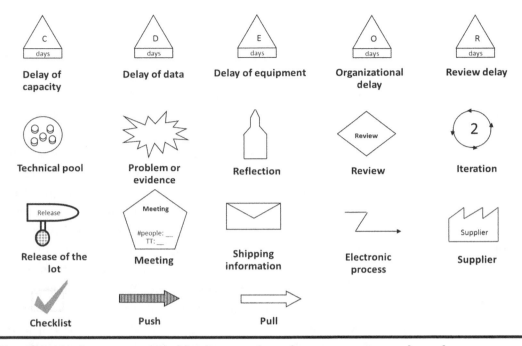

Figure 2.19   Icons more used in the mapping of processes, research, and development.

simply because people are unable to calculate the number of times an activity has been repeated. And this, we can assure you, is one of the findings that is most eye-opening and gets participants thinking about how they can improve their process. In one case of a company making gas-electric turbines, the iterations were due to an inability to model combustion accurately so testing was a necessary waste. Reducing lead time required reducing the time of testing cycles, which also allowed more cycles if necessary to optimize the design. This led to a multiyear project, first to dedicate a test cell to design (previously it was shared with manufacturing) and then increasingly eliminate waste in the test sell. Visual management of the process allowed the team to understand incoming work, lead times, and how the product was moving through various steps in the prototype build and test process. It also because a hangout for combustion engineers who were able to see and learn in real time the results of their design concepts.

2.4.2 The Steps of a Value Stream Mapping Event

Applying Value Stream Mapping to the form of a workshop has been proven to be the most effective way to drive improvements. As a start, it is important to properly scope the process(es) that will be improved. This includes defining the boundaries of the processes to be mapped, choosing the product we will follow through the processes, setting initial improvement goals, and identifying the people who need to be involved in the Value Stream transformation.

Figure 2.20 shows a standardized process to conduct a Value Stream workshop. During the workshop, the first thing to grasp is who the customer really is. This is less obvious than it might seem, because frequently the entire team lacks knowledge of who uses the product and what they value from the selected process. This happens both in relation to internal and to external customers. Often, there are different clients, and it is vital not just to be aware of this, but also to know what each group actually needs. Take the case of Harley-Davidson, which has quite a complicated structure. They need to satisfy the needs of various kinds of clients: the end customer who buys the motorcycle, the sales dealer client who sells it to the end customer, the bike enthusiast who buys spare parts to enhance his or her bike in latter years of ownership, and the mechanic who services the product. For each of them, it is important to know the different needs that they deem as value-added. Remember what was said about the Concept Paper, when we talked about the different customer needs. If we are unable

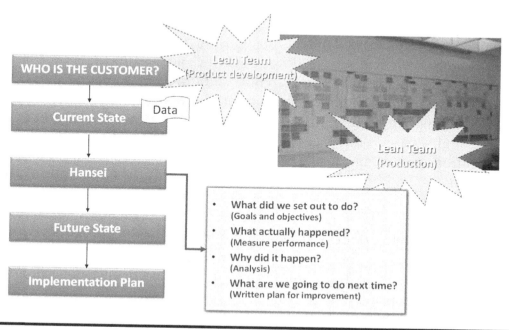

Figure 2.20   Scheme of the improvement process. (Source: Morgan J. and Liker J.K., *The Toyota Product Development System: Integrating People, Process, and Technology,* **Productivity Press, 2006.)**

to clearly distinguish between added value and non-added value, from the point of view of the customer, we will never be able to "see" waste in our processes. It is important to be ruthless while doing this, if we really want to understand whether what we are doing adds value for clients or not.

The question that needs to be asked every time is this: would the customer pay for this? If the answer is 'yes,' it is then important to consider that the customer will only be willing to pay once for the same product or service, or part thereof. Stepping into the shoes of the specific customer provides a picture of everything that is waste and not added value. And what amazes all of our clients is the ratio between the sum of added value activities and the total of the activities performed to obtain that value. The proportion of added value is so tiny that it almost always represents a powerful stimulus toward action and improvement, in order to move in the direction of obtaining more value with less waste.

After defining the specific customer(s) and those customer's needs, the next step of the process mapping is to create a representation of the "current state." Here we will always try to add in as much detail as possible regarding reconstructed activities, durations, iterations, dead time, flows between groups, and other relevant facts for the given product we are mapping. The goal is to have an understanding and facts about the process, so as to be able to identify problems and wastes. We use horizontal swim lanes to represent the activities of different functions. Across the columns at the top there is time so we can see the flow of activities across functions over time.[10]

Between the mapping of the current state of processes and the future state, we use a tool as simple as it is powerful. The Japanese call it *hansei*, which simply means "reflection." *Hansei* is a key concept in Japanese culture, and is based on the simple idea that there is always something to learn from past events: from one's successes, in order to obtain further improvements, and from one's errors, so as to avoid them in the future. This approach is also used as a means of regular verification during the course of a project, to capture learnings. We will discuss this in detail in Chapter 4.

When the habit of doing *hansei* is cultivated with the team during the Value Stream Mapping, many issues are surfaced, wastes specifically identified, root causes are analyzed using concrete facts and finally suggestions for improvement are made to improve the process. This naturally leads to the next step: the creation of the future state of the processes.

In the definition of the future state, the team is prompted to draw up a new and improved process that removes the wastes and includes the suggested improvements that came from the *hansei*. Exploiting the lessons learned from past experience, an attempt is made to establish not only the new process but also the tools, and habits needed to make the process work.

Once the map of future processes has been charted, we clearly have a whole set of opportunities that have been included in the future state. Then comes the final step: definition of the implementation plan, with the choice of priorities, the timing of improvement actions, and the assigning of responsibilities.

For the process to work well, it is important to have a skilled facilitator. Our role in these workshops is to facilitate the process and more importantly stimulate the team to come up with their own solutions to address the problems that are inhibiting them from doing their work effectively so they can have more free time to innovate. At the same time, as outsiders, our most important job is to develop internal facilitators so we are no longer needed.

2.4.3 *Why Not Start Immediately with Tried and Tested Solutions?*

When applying Lean in the innovation and product development space, there is not a single validated recipe for everyone. Each time is a new discovery for the teams and for us. Once, we did the same type of work with three different business units from the same company. It was essentially the same process but three different products, ultimately leading to three different versions of future maps and three different implementation plans. The workshops are focused, intense and relatively brief, lasting at the most three to five days, but nonetheless are incisive and readily accepted by whoever is involved. This way of working puts you in much closer contact with people, and with their real world. There are no general or abstract solutions. Instead, it is necessary to "get your hands dirty," in an effort to understand what is really going on, guiding a process of increasing awareness and enhancing the maturity of the people involved. The role of the effective *sensei* is to be a humble coach who leads the team in shaping a leaner operational future. Once this step has been done together, points of view change, and the "project game" moves to a different level of performance, because no one is imposing anything, because people believe in what they are doing, and because this is what provides the extra impetus for the subsequent implementation of what has been defined by future state. This is in contrast to what happens in the traditional consulting approach, where the tendency is to impose universal, or benchmarking, models and schemes, without showing any great respect for the human and technical context in which one is working.

Not infrequently, clients ask us to come to them with ready-prepared solutions to apply, in order to avoid the effort of the initial mapping. For traditional consultants, the pre-ordained solution is perhaps the ideal modus operandi. Traditional consulting activities include preliminary interviews, almost always individual, elaboration of the initial state, comparison with reference models, and a virtually unilateral proposed solution for the revision of processes. Take it or leave it. And often, attracted by the apparent financial benefits that are promised, the proposed solution is accepted, after which begins the difficult task of trying to put it into practice. The social aspect of the problem is ignored altogether. In a genuine Lean spirit adapted to the context, using a proven methodology, the processes, solutions, and project plans are devised by the people who then have to implement it. It is no longer something that just concerns the Project Manager or the consultant, but the whole team, who are instead lead by the Project Manager and coached by *sensei*.

As John Shook says, "it's not about the map." The real added value of this activity is not the map, but the very fact of having activated a process of awareness-raising and self-improvement among the people in the company. In cross-functional workshops, agreement begins to emerge about what really happens and as the future state is developed commitments are made by each function that will be necessary to make the new process work. For example, in the same gas-turbine engine case, the purchasing department agreed to violate normal policies and order parts as their design was complete instead of waiting for a complete design of all parts in a final engineering database. The casting supplier who was in the room agreed to prioritize these small batches as long as engineering did all they could do to commit to these designs and not change their mind multiple times. These representatives then met in weekly meetings to implement and remind each other of their agreements. The result was the fastest lead time for a similar product in the customer's history—on-time, with quality, and at budget.

2.5 How to Get the Intellectual Juices Flowing without Obstacles or Interruption

> Those who make the worst use of their time are the first to complain of its brevity.
>
> **Jean De La Bruyère**

After having defined customer value and given maximum importance to the initial phases of the project set-up, it is important to see how we can stimulate the creativity and innovation of our people while speeding up the phases of project execution.

Often, one of the obstacles we come across in improvement activities and in the running of Lean Innovation projects in companies is voiced by many people as: "I like it, and I agree with it, but I haven't got time." At first, everyone appears too busy running around trying to deal with urgent matters, which sometimes turn into emergencies, and they do not have time to deal with "less urgent" activities that potentially could reduce the burden of urgent ones in the future. Two key elements need to be considered here.

1. *Effectiveness*: habits acquired in the choice of the "things to do."
2. *Efficiency*: habits acquired in the choice of "how to do things."

As we deeply explain in the Lean Lifestyle® framework, it has been amply demonstrated that the majority of us are no longer accustomed to really choosing what we do. Instead, we live in a continual "reactive state." This state makes us respond constantly to events, stimuli, and input from outside—television, newspapers, family, colleagues, bosses, friends, and so on—rather than setting out to make conscious choices regarding what is really important for us and for our company in the precise moment in which we are acting. From a neurological point of view, the habit of behaving in a reactive way is plausibly explained by the slow release of dopamine every time we react to urgent input. Dopamine, in fact, is one of the principal neurotransmitters involved in the mechanism of pleasure and reward in our brain. It plays an important role in all those experiences that offer gratification to a subject, both physiological and pathological, in particular in addictions to substances or behaviors. We are effectively "addicted" to our habits of living in a reactive state.

2.5.1 The Myth of Multitasking

Scientific research demonstrates that incoming email, phone calls, and other information can modify the way we think and behave. It alerts us to the fact that our attention capacity is undermined by the abundance of information. The reference here is to the primitive impulse to respond to immediate opportunities and to threats. The stimulus provokes excitement—a dopamine rush. In the absence of stimulation, people get bored. While lots of people think that multitasking makes people more effective and productive, scientific research shows that the opposite is true.[11] People who do lots of activities in parallel, male or female, experience difficulties in concentration, and are unable to ignore irrelevant information, ultimately suffering from a greater degree of stress. In addition, research is also discovering that, once the parallel activities are finished, a "fragmented" mode of thought and difficulties in concentration continue to persist. More generally, cell phones and computers have transformed our lives. They enable people to work anywhere, away from the office. They shorten distances and manage innumerable small everyday tasks, freeing up time for more interesting things. In one way or another, media consumption has literally exploded. In 2008, people were absorbing three times more information every day than in 1960. Clearly, some multitasking is needed in the office but when too many tasks are being juggled at one time and they begin affecting the quality and output of the tasks, we know we have crossed the line from efficiency to ineffectiveness. This is particularly true when dealing with intellectual activities, when innovating new products and clarity of thought is must.

In the specific context being dealt with here, what we do with ourselves and our customers is to try to identify and develop new habits that replace previous ones. The aim being to literally recover lost energy: for example, learning to carve out invaluable time to "reconnect," on a weekly and daily basis, to focus on chosen prioritized activities, in a genuine process of conscious self-regulation. The key word to developing a new routine is "repetition." We must over and over practice the new behavior until it overwrites in our brain the neurological patterns of behavior we are trying to modify. It is, in fact, practically impossible to remain connected with oneself if this process is lacking in the world we live in, so full of input, information, and stimuli. The process must be entirely personal, but it cannot bear fruit unless it becomes a structured habit.

2.5.2 Queuing Theory and Intellectual Efficiency

Few people devote attention to the concepts of *leveling* and *sequencing* with respect to their activities or those of their project group, because of the widespread conviction that the important thing is to "get things done." In actuality, what we achieve—our output—depends a great deal on how we set up those activities. We would like to draw on *queuing theory* to illustrate a very simple, but fundamental, concept in determining the time it takes to respond and close activities. The duration of an activity, its *cycle time* within any given system is not directly proportionate to the saturation of the system itself, but is correlated exponentially to the degree of use of the system's resources. What does this mean in practice? If we have a group of people utilized at 90%, the cycle time to perform any given activity will be greater than a case in which the same group of people are only 50% saturated (Figure 2.21). Every extra activity that comes in from a certain point onward, in the vicinity of 80%, not only slows down the group's performance, but makes it hard to predict when it will be done as well.[12] For example, an activity with an average duration of two days, when the group is utilized at 80% or less, may take from four to eight days if that group is excessively loaded.

Therefore, not only will it take much longer, but we will not know exactly how much more. The same thing applies to any system. Every variability within an already saturated group of people leads almost to paralysis, in addition to the indeterminateness of the real completion time of the activities. It is important, then, that a group of designers called upon to solve a problem has a sufficient level of flexibility to accommodate the variables that kick in during the various phases of design. This will enable us to avoid the risk of response times stretching beyond estimated times, which are almost always calculated without considering the impact of the rigor and following of the planning itself. What emerges from this is the importance of understanding what can help to balance individuals and working groups so their level of saturation does not go beyond a certain limit.

Think of what happens on a highway with heavy traffic when there is an accident. The traffic slows down more and more, coming to a complete standstill until the damaged vehicles are removed. The same accident on a

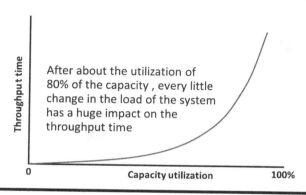

Figure 2.21 Effect of overload on the development time. (Source: Morgan J. and Liker J.K., *The Toyota Product Development System: Integrating People, Process, and Technology,* **Productivity Press, 2006.)**

fast highway with light traffic will not lead to the same queues. The traffic will continue to flow at practically the same speed (Figure 2.22).

The lesson here for our teams trying to innovate the next product or service is that they need the time to think if they are to truly innovate. If they are overloaded, then their ability to come up with great ideas will also be slowed down (or even stifled) as they try to navigate through the excessive loads of work.

2.5.3 The Eight Principles of Flow in Intellectual Activities

There will always be "accidents" or unexpected surprises in our working days. We can work to minimize them, but we cannot eliminate them all. It is essential to try to understand how to make ourselves and our product groups more flexible to deal with these surprises without having them upset the entire system.

Techniques exist that, if adopted, can bring benefits to your daily work and your project teams. We have summarized them in the following eight principles, with the aim of making them "usable" by anyone in any given project.

2.5.3.1 Level the Arrival of Work

Fluctuations in the arrival of work to be done inevitably causes queues in any system. For example, if four arrive today, one tomorrow, and ten the

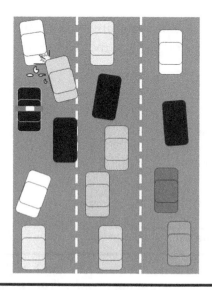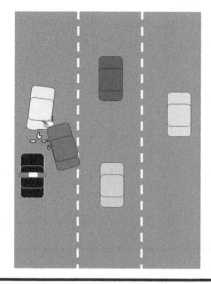

Figure 2.22   Queuing theory and comparison with highway traffic.

next day, this will lead to interruptions and to material lingering on our desks, in our PC, in our heads. The time it takes to clear the work will tend to be variable and will inevitably be longer. It makes sense to try to "level" the arrival of work in coming to us and our team members. In the work teams we deal with, we always try to put into practice anything that favors as consistent a workload as possible—for example, doing things so that information comes in and goes out in "digestible portions," rather than "fasting" one day and "getting indigestion" the next. We need to be constantly receiving work, but not overloaded. Our minds always need something to think about, otherwise, it will do it by itself. This is one of our biological characteristics.

Greater attention toward a pragmatic leveling of incoming work for ourselves and others will help to increase fluidity and intellectual performance. The same principle holds true when we organize our days. If, for example, we arrange packed programs without inserting breaks or buffers between certain activities, it is very likely, if there is the slightest interruption, that the project timing will fall apart, landing us quickly in the situation of paralysis we just talked about. It is therefore worth incorporating buffers of unfilled time into our days and weeks, so as to provide a cushion against variables that we cannot predict to ensure that downstream customers have a consistent and predictable arrival of work.

2.5.3.2 Minimize the Number of Activities in Process

The previous discussion regarding multitasking brings me immediately to another effective technique for ensuring a constant flow of activities. If we reduce the number of activities on which we are concentrating, in any given time, we will undoubtedly favor not better flow, but above all higher quality in the completion of the activities themselves.

We often tend to overestimate our short-term capacity and reciprocally underestimate our medium- and long-term capacity. This leads us to overload ourselves by starting lots of activities that end up sitting on our desks. If we learn to dose activities, tending to limit them to a few at a time, our performance over time will certainly increase, as long as we condition ourselves to live with the apparent state of frustration of having to put off some things rather than others. We say *apparent* because one thing is to begin lots of things, another is to complete them on-time. In fact, we often delay the closure of activities when we try to simultaneously manage more of them than is humanly possible.

Working according to this principle of small batches means making an effort to subdivide everything into small pieces, moving work forward in small steps. Focusing on small steps, in all the projects we have experienced, has always created a favorable climate for success, positively reinforcing that the project is truly moving forward. Success breeds success, failure breeds failure. Our minds do not distinguish the small success from the large success. Emotionally speaking, every success counts, large or small. Planning a small thing and succeeding in finishing it on time is a powerful mental weapon that gives us the strength to keep moving forward, much more than planning a big thing and waiting for its successful conclusion over a longer period of time. We might say, and plan, that we want to lose twelve pounds in a year, but it is much harder to accept rather than a goal of a quarter of a pound every week. Our minds will tend to put up much more resistance to a big, daunting objective, even if more time is allowed for it. We will never tire of repeating that in managing projects, the key elements are the people. Therefore, we must never lose sight of what encourages change in people and what, instead, blocks it. In this case, not only does working in small batches improve flow but it also improves morale. Some Lean development organizations have used the concept of "WIP caps" to limit the number of different projects active in a work group at a given time. When one is complete a new one can enter the system and begin to be worked on.

2.5.3.3 *Reduce the Size of Activities*

This principle is a close relative of the previous one, and consists of reducing the size, in addition to the quantity, of activities under way. If we want to become masters of flow and timely execution, we must remember: "Simple is actionable, complicated is interesting."

Simplicity is something we can act upon, complexity is interesting. Interesting for whom? It is interesting for our mind, which must "keep busy," but is it really value added? Often we confuse the things we actually complete with the things we have the illusion of doing just because they have entered our vortex of thoughts.

The American scholar Tony Schwartz has spent many years studying the factors that favor the performance of people engaged in office and intellectual activities in general. What supplies energy and what drains it. Schwartz affirms that the average length of time any person can give with maximum intellectual productivity is no more than seventy-five minutes. And so, Schwartz claims, it is not clever to fill our days with activities that exceed this time span, if we want to simultaneously pursue results and a profound state of well-being.[13] About 72% of people have serious difficulties in focusing on one thing at a time, causing slow-downs and dips in energy that impact both on our psychological and physical state and on company performance. What can be done? Well, divide up, for instance, our activities into blocks of no more than one hour, excluding for that hour everything else. Immediately afterward, plan to insert mental breaks, in order to regenerate and prepare ourselves for another high-concentration session. Training ourselves to finish activities, and not just to get them started, is fundamental. We have never seen forms of stress appearing in really productive people who are continually able to manage their energy. Keeping the size of the individual tasks small is not just indispensable, but crucial, because it sets in motion virtuous, emotional circles that project us into more creative thought over time. We become masters of flow, effective creativity and consistent action.

2.5.3.4 Establish a Regular Cadence

To explain this technique, we want to relate an example from one of our projects. The whole group was accumulating delays in the project plan. Thanks to weekly alignment meetings, as an analysis of the causes of various anomalies were undertaken, it had become clear that one of the designers was in the unhappy position that he had become a bottleneck for that working group for about three weeks in a row, slowing down the work of his colleagues, who were waiting for his designs and for information from him in order to move on with their own activities. When we tried to see why these delays were occurring, the "truth" soon emerged. The designer had a second task besides that of working on the project for the new product: he was also responsible for solving technical problems associated with existing products already in production. That is to say, technical modifications, revision of designs, and assistance in solving problems for already-launched products posed various kinds of problems in the assembly or testing phase prior to shipping to customers. Colleagues from the production department called him up frequently to sort out problems, demanding his attention, pushed by the "rush" to meet imminent delivery deadlines. He was forced to frequently interrupt his design activities, and in the end spent whatever remaining time he had on the project. To make matters worse, he could not even provide a reasonable estimate of when he would finish his design activities. He was frustrated because the interruptions made him lose concentration, time, and effectiveness, and because the number and duration of his interventions in the production department were variable and unpredictable. The solution was to move toward standardizing and planning these interruptions. This was done by assigning a predetermined duration for the interventions: regular cadences. We began by setting aside a daily slot, which was initially in the early afternoon from 2pm to 3pm. His colleagues in production were asked to prepare for that session, drawing up a list of problems requiring solution, to clarify the scope of the problem, and to focus on the fact that the discussion needed to be completed in the allotted time slot. This apparently simple change in direction led to some initial difficulties due to the resistance to changing habits of the production personnel and the designer himself.

The instinctive and immediate phone call had to give way to a laying out of the problem in a notebook or, even better, on a board, for a subsequent focused action to resolve it. In the face of the fear that it would take longer to solve the problems, statistics came to our aid: the average wait for real, post-call intervention and for definitive resolution of the problem were almost the same as the time scheme we were proposing, the difference being that the enormous amount of wasted time generated by the calls themselves, frequent interruptions, lack of concentration, and variability in the duration of activities was eliminated. It was great to see the phone ringing less frequently, hearing much less shouting, and at the same time to see more problems being solved at a regular cadence while also seeing the project work move forward in a more leveled manner. After a few weeks, the designer was no longer a "bottleneck," and the meetings in the production department went from being daily to being every other day, because with this type of intervention, the group became not only more efficient in using its time, but also more effective in solving problems.

During a seminar, after we had described this case, one of the participants exclaimed:

> One thing I've understood... by doing this, people, besides waiting, also learn to think... I kept the phone off all day today, following your instructions. I understand why, when I turn it on at the end of the day, I will find, as on other occasions, about ten unanswered calls... but the great thing is that I'll find that eight of the problems, the reason for the calls in the first place, will already have been solved!

As we can see, it is critical to set up a kind of "heartbeat" within the working group, in order to make as many things as possible happen in a routine cadenced fashion. The first thing to do is to avoid the typical chaos of input and output, that is, in statistical terms, to avoid excessive variability in input and output for the typical work centers of a project: individuals.

2.5.3.5 *Plan Results and Not Activities*

What does this mean in practice? We have already seen the importance of a regular cadence in project activities. Let's now look at another aspect.

Often, there is a tendency to plan activities and to focus attention on doing, rather than being guided by a plan based on the final, and intermediate, results to be achieved throughout a project. It is not enough just to set up routine meetings with the team. It is also important to organize them not only to talk about or to do activities, but to evaluate the intermediate results of single activities.

This is a basic concept, yet it involves a completely different mental attitude. Each individual and each subgroup in the team always works on something concrete, which at a certain point will be presented to the rest of the team. For example, if the team has decided to meet once a week, it is not sufficient to have a status report; it is equally important to predefine the outputs to be evaluated during each of those meetings. The idea here is to plan, over time, not activities, but real output, which must be rendered visible in a clear and unequivocal way at each meeting so a decision can be made.

The focus shifts from the planning of activities to the results of those activities, at a predetermined pace. If, for example, we are talking about design activities, the activity of "designing" is divided up into small packages of drawings so that each design is literally "pulled" through time at the pre-defined cadence. During the periodic sessions with the other team members, the focus will remain on the results achieved in the form of small packages of concrete, drawings, which will be physically evaluated with the rest of the team. Whenever we succeed in introducing "rhythm" in individuals or groups, we benefit in terms of creating focus, a sense of urgency, and ultimately project efficiency. This same concept is valid both in our private lives and in the running of professional projects, big or small.

2.5.3.6 *Pull Planning*

Another high-impact technique, to be used whenever embarking on a project involving a lot of people, is *Pull Planning*. This approach can make a noticeable difference in meeting the schedule. Imagine you have to get objects from one end of a tube to another, but that the order, sequence, and type of objects required are known only to the person at the other end of the tube. Would you dream of beginning to push your objects through the tube? Or would you prefer to get them pulled by the person at the other end? In a restaurant, unless we are talking about an establishment offering a fixed menu, no one would start bringing out food to the tables without having consulted the diners first. Too often on actual projects, we "push" forward the fruits of our activities—drawings, elaborations, sums, assessments, decisions, and so forth—based on what we do ourselves, and the pre-established project plan, without really considering that in group activities we not only need to deliver what is required, but when it is required, and in the right amounts and at the right place. This applies to all types of information, physical objects, designs, decisions, assessments, elaborations, approvals, etc.

Think about how often we have to go back to something because we did not take the trouble to find out exactly what was needed from us, when it was and who needed it. During Lean training and workshops, we run various trial simulations to ascertain the difference between "push" planning and "pull" planning, measuring variations in performance in the two cases. There is always a surprise for participants when looking at the marked difference in progress the simulated project makes at every stage and the associated benefits become apparent. It is a fun way of stimulating reflection and learning at the same time.

Every resource involved in a project responds to the needs of one's internal and external clients, and should only produce what is requested and when it is requested. This facilitates communication, effectiveness, and team members' morale as they feel they are better supported by getting what they need at the right time to do their job.

Even if this seems so obvious to the reader, why is this so difficult, and indeed almost never happens, in real life?

Because both suppliers and clients have to communicate their needs at the beginning and constantly throughout the project. In the gas-electric turbine company, they have established pull through boards at each step of the process. It is like Kanban in manufacturing. Each step of the board has cards showing what work has come in that is waiting to be worked on, what is being worked on, and what is completed for their customer—the next step of the process. When work in the next process is complete then the next work product they require is passed along and the boards are updated. A task is complete and goes out and another task in queue is started. There is a cap on work-in-process to limit the individual tasks worked on at a given time which helps timely completion of each task.

2.5.3.7 Avoid Overloading

In addition to the queuing issues mentioned in the prior section, what do we risk when we find ourselves at the limits of capacity? Instinctively, perhaps, one of the first thing we might say is that "there is no time to think." Another response might be "loss of flexibility," or "no room to deal with certain problems in depth." All this is true. To these answers we might add a consideration. Our performance, in terms of duration, quality, and punctuality, together with that of our groups, will, in the long run, be heavily influenced by this sense of "activity suffocation." We will tend not to clearly see the quality of our work, we will have no room for improvement activities, and for the inevitable surprises that crop up in any context. In a word, we will no longer be able to see beyond our noses. This is why excellent companies give great emphasis to the concept of resource leveling, especially in the development of new products. If we want to maintain a high performance level of innovation, it is important to keep checking that we and our colleagues are not becoming overloaded. In the following pages, we will try to understand how it is possible to tackle the question of resource leveling and of the standardization of capacity and processes in order not to end up being "suffocated" by the activities themselves.

2.5.3.8 Minimize Interruptions

The principles discussed thus far help not only to establish agreed frequencies and duration for personal and group activities, but inevitably encourage the creation of new rituals and new mental attitudes. People become aware that many areas of inefficiency can be eliminated with appropriate preventative activities. As we said when talking about multitasking, one of the most insidious forms of inefficiency in group activities relates to continual reciprocal interruptions.

Since notable improvements can be gained just by applying the seven previous principles, with the ten recommendations grouped below, it is possible to achieve a *state of genuine hyper-productive calm*, channeling activities fluidly while encouraging individual creativity without sacrificing the maximum amount of collaboration within the group. Let's look at them one by one.

1. Create and use checklists. Companies such as Toyota, use Engineering Checklists (now computerized) during their projects. These enable the rapid resolution of a problem proactively based on past experience.
2. Define in advance the answers to recurrent questions, just like the FAQs often used online and share them with the entire team.
3. Supply as much background information as possible when assigning a task, calling a meeting, or communicating knowledge to someone, so as to minimize the interruptions from people asking questions afterward.
4. Take the trouble to train people before they commence a task.
5. Do not just delegate activities, but also responsibilities. Assign complete tasks that encourage others to be responsible for a given end result that needs to be achieved.
6. Group together similar activities (batching), especially when these consist of a large number of small but potentially "distracting" activities, because they are liable to arrive when you least expect them (email, administrative matters).
7. Fix "windows of availability" in advance with your colleagues and assistants for them to be able to collaborate with you.
8. Carefully organize the archived so it is easy for everyone to find materials, drawings, and information relevant to the project in hand. This saves a lot of time searching or having people disturb others re-requesting information.
9. Learn to carve out "sacred" time slots—moments of isolation lasting sixty to ninety minutes, during which you cannot be disturbed for any reason. Mark these in your calendar.
10. Work empty timeslots into your schedule for rejuvenation, on a daily, weekly, and monthly basis, alternating them with periods of high concentration—like an athlete, who always rests between one training session and the next. If we do not arrange them in advance, our bodies and minds will do so of their own accord, because it is impossible to remain continually under tension without burning out. Individual activities such as exercise or meditation and team activities such as team building exercises or outings are a few good ways to rejuvenate the creative energy of yourself and your team. Good sense and intuition will help you to learn how often and how long to do these.

The table below summarizes the eight principles of flow for office activities. Practice them and you will see your team's effectiveness, and your own, will improve and your daily stress will be reduced.

The eight principles of flow in intellectual activities
1. Level the arrival of work
2. Minimize the number of current activities
3. Reduce the size of activities
4. Establish regular rhythms
5. Plan results and not activities
6. Pull planning
7. Avoid overloading
8. Minimize interruptions

2.6 Resource Leveling in a Complex Project

There is the risk you cannot afford to take, there is the risk you cannot afford not to take.

Peter F. Druker

However much planning we do, there will always be some moment in a project when you find yourself having to deal with the unexpected, areas of criticality liable to throw your schedules, and project results off course. In these moments it will be necessary to increase capacity, the number of resources required, to get back on track. A "bit more time," a little more effort, a few extra people, a few more hours, days, or months to "do things well" and finish on time. Whether we are part of a large company or a small one, whether we are part of a big group or even just on our own, we are all likely to face such problems at some point in the course of a project. How do we make this happen?

2.6.1 A Model for Leveling Workloads between People

To deal with variations in required capacity, Lean companies use methods that are truly unique in certain respects, and which yield unexpected positive results when applied in any kind of business. Figure 2.23 illustrates a possible model for the use of human resources in the course of a project, drawing upon real cases. In the case illustrated, note that resources need to be increased from the second month on, the phase in which the project moves toward the "freezing" of the designs. This is the period in which the exploration of concepts, what is called Kentou (study) in the Lean Product Development terminology, is completed. In the graph, you will see various bands relating to the different people engaged in the project. We observe that the product engineers are assigned permanently to the project and are supported by technicians and designers, who belong to a central group and who go to lend a hand when there are workload peaks in various projects. In the example, you can see that in the first two months after Kentou, there are up to ten people working on the project. This figure then rises to thirteen, thanks to the assistance of the support technicians over the following three months along with the help of designers and their co-development supplier, before dropping back to seven through to the end of the project. This resource flexibility in the course of the project is made possible by a strong standardization of methods and tools, without which it would

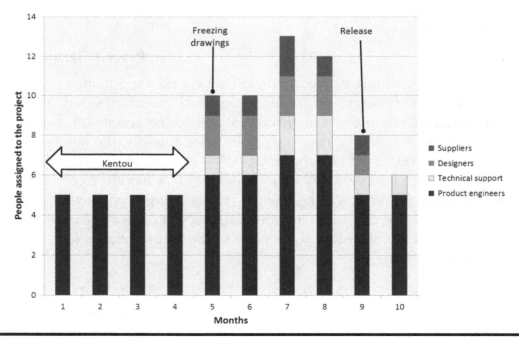

Figure 2.23   Example of leveling resources in a complex project.

be impossible to quickly flex in fresh resources as has happened here. Without good standards, an enormous amount of time would be wasted while the new arrivals tuned in to different working groups' ways. It is very important to have these safety valves, whereby technicians can go where there is greatest need. The central services group, in agreement with the various Project Managers, decides whether intervention is required or not. These technicians are never transferred permanently to individual departments, because this would make it impossible to continually distribute resources between different projects. This group of technicians should not be confused with designers and suppliers from outside the company, who may be called upon to perform certain tasks, for instance the preparation of drawings of components designed by the product engineers or the suppliers themselves.

Obviously, what we have seen here is just one example. In different areas, the percentages and periods may vary quite considerably, but the most important thing, the key message we want to convey with this example, is to have you reflect on the importance of analyzing workloads upfront and plan as best you can for the invariable peaks that will occur. We can either assign our own project resources, so as to ensure a leveling of workloads and/or resort to external or other internal resources, creating a kind of buffer to avoid problems when needs arise in the course of a project. Not doing so, and hoping that everything will work itself out somehow, or worse, waiting for the problem to explode in our faces, places us in a position where delays will be almost inevitable and the degree of stress higher. One final tip, if you decide to employ this technique: using human resources from outside the company could potentially lead to a loss of know-how. Decide in advance what is core business/knowledge and what is not, i.e. what is valuable for your competitive edge, and then decide what to assign to internal company resources and what can be done by people outside the company.

2.6.2 What Happens if There Are Just a Few of Us or I Am on My Own?

In this case, paradoxically, the problem of balancing and leveling workloads is even more critical, because every obstacle will reflect directly on the final outcome of your project, in terms of time and quality. The available tools are the same as the ones used for large projects, but here it is particularly important to personally address the following issues:

1. *Delegate*: you must learn to delegate in advance anything that does not have to be done by you. The more you train yourself to apply the concept of delegation in managing a project, the better you will learn to really grasp what it is important for you to do on that project to add value to the customer and where others are able to help. Here, a bit of humility helps. Frequently, we delude ourselves that we are the only ones who can do it right. If that is really so, then we need train others so they can do it in the future.
2. *Flexibility buffer*: plan in empty space for unplanned/unknown activities. Your days are short, and your capacity finite. Bearing this in mind from the outset will help you find the time needed to take the difficulties you encounter in stride.
3. *The eight principles of fluid activities*: application of the eight principles described in the prior section can help you to eliminate many difficulties in the management of your projects, at the same time enhancing effectiveness and individual well-being.

2.7 Lean Project Management: The Art of Surfing Applied to Projects

> You can't always get what you want. / No, you can't always get what you want. / But if you try sometimes, you just might find / You get what you need.
>
> **Rolling Stones**

2.7.1 Taking Project Times and Deadlines into Account

In a long-term product strategy, missing a deadline is often more serious than miscalculating a cost or not quite meeting a performance target. Imagine subdividing an entire project into ten subgroups. Imagine making each subgroup then responsible for 10% of the cost and 10% of the time of the entire project. Now if the head of one of the groups makes a 10% error in his costs, this will cause a 1% cost problem for the entire project. If instead the same person fails by letting 10% of their target time slide forward on the critical path, this will cause, in most cases, a 10% delay in the entire project. A delay like this will also have an impact on other projects, creating what the British call exhaustive "scattering," as well as leading to the loss of market opportunities for the entire organization, i.e. unforeseen impacts on other factors, future projects, changes, unforeseen work, costs of efforts that are taken away from the new products, and customer satisfaction. This is a well-known concept at Apple, where they have always given priority to the timing of the project at the expense of other factors. Remember the first iPhones and iPads on the market? They were sometimes imperfect, but available, to the great satisfaction of old and new customers. Late projects and uncompleted cycles, at the individual level, are the main obstacle to the development and release of new energies and opportunities.

2.7.2 Is the Right Information in the Right Place at the Right Time?

There is another common question that arises during management reviews: will the project be completed before the deadline and with good results? Unfortunately, there is no guaranteed answer to these questions. During a project, the information is there, true, but the project is a dynamic entity. Plenty of information will arrive eventually, but almost always late and piecemeal to answer the questions.

And the managers?

Often more concerned about the results in the short term rather than the processes that lead to the results, they may find that they have no real confidence in the progress of a project in terms of cost, quality, content, performance, times, and deadlines. They will try to trust the information provided by their people, but basically the elements that they traditionally had access to for an objective comparison are almost always anecdotal words, status summaries, or plans that are drafted, re-drafted, and revised many times during a project.

One of the most common beliefs in conventional systems regards the cause of project delays it is believed that every delay is due to a departure from procedures and standards, together with the fact that their people are unable to meet the targets. Following this logic, the most common cause of delays would be the widespread lack of discipline. If so, all it would take to eliminate the problem would be greater discipline…and in fact many companies invest time and money in large bureaucratic efforts, the construction of planning sheets and highly detailed processes, at least detailed on paper, that in the end turn out to be slow and costly. The conventional Project Managers attempt to respond to the doubts and questions that I have given you so far by creating highly detailed plans and desperately try to stick to them giving them the illusion they have everything under control.

Instead of learning to "surf" the waves, conventional organizations try to control them.

But this almost never works.

It almost never works to tell everyone what to do in the greatest detail possible. It almost never works to do such detailed planning and scheduling in order to make things happen in the right sequence. It almost never works to try to make the knowledge flow through channels in an extremely rigid, predefined way.

Lean companies have learned over the last century how to "surf" the waves during projects, without vainly wasting time in order to control the waves themselves, to proceed without major disasters or glitches, and with great flexibility from start to finish. In addition to the eight principles of fluid activities illustrated in Section 2.5, other differences emerge between traditional systems and Lean Project Management systems.

2.7.3 Value Creating Management

This definition comes from Dr. Allen Ward, one of the first people to have studied the Lean Development model in both Japanese and American companies. According to Ward, project supervisors, managers, Project Leaders, and entrepreneurs should create value by designing product development systems and spreading knowledge of them. In this way, the activities of team members are not tightly controlled, but the plan is used for overseeing and guiding them.

What does "thinking more about the process" mean? First of all, it means understanding that whenever an expected result is not achieved it is because there is a problem at the root of the process and not because one or more people have simply "failed." People are, in the vast majority of cases, working in good faith.

We have rarely witnessed people who had deliberately decided not to achieve the pre-established results, but *if something goes wrong there, is almost always a systematic cause that needs to be identified and removed.* This should be the main job of the manager in a project team.

The manager must strive to see his or her own system in this light and therefore always seeking ways to help teams achieve better results. This also means being there for the team, to remove barriers and obstacles that hinder the achievement of results. The more managers learn to observe their processes and teams, the more they will learn to understand the real causes of inefficiency and ineffectiveness.

Why do we embrace this approach versus the traditional command and control approach? The better the system results are, the more successful managers will be, and vice versa. But if managers only continue to be "part of the system," they will not be able to continuously improve their team's performance. So they have to take a step back to see the system in its entirety, attempting to understand what actions must be taken to increase the effectiveness of the system itself. As coaches for their teams, commanders of ships and their crew, they must try to take the type of actions that create value for the customer.

The manager's only goal, in the spirit of Lean thinking, is to increase the percentage of added value with respect to waste, because every time this is achieved, the team and the system acquire a little extra speed, do more things in less time, and with less waste. Therefore, the manager becomes *a system designer*, and not an authoritarian manager who gives orders. He or she adds and spreads knowledge.

2.7.4 Who Promotes the Principles of Flow on a Project?

For complex projects, the Chief Engineer is the person who manages the pace of a project, and the one who shapes the true rhythm of the project. The flow and control of the workload are supervised by the Project Managers, who must guide teams in such a way as to ensure that there are always adequate resources and that there is always a cadence to the project. In many projects that the author has guided in Italy, he always introduced the concept of Lean Project Management. In this new perspective, a team leader is identified and given the responsibility of being the "father" of the project, and increasingly becomes the figure that gives the rhythm to the whole team, having first made sure that everyone knows the rules of the game, i.e., they all understand the Value Stream of the project.

The principle of Pull Planning mentioned earlier in the chapter comes into play here. In 2004, when Luciano visited Toyota in Japan, he began to learn to recognize the characteristics of winning teams and individuals. Here is an example. No manager in a meeting would accept someone stating after the fact that they were late with an activity, perhaps because they did not have the information from a certain supplier or a certain colleague. The concept, which they took for granted, is that *those who are responsible for an activity must always obtain what they need to achieve the result.*

Therefore it is the "customer," internal or external, who must shed light on what is needed, and after having done it, they must make a personal commitment to effectively communicate and gain consensus with their "supplier," and even go physically get what they need, if necessary. This is a full dynamic pull. The management of the project is much lighter, leaner, because first and foremost, care is taken to effectively spread and communicate the overall vision of the project. An effort is made to have a series of events that are very well defined and clear from the start, and within these, the project now relies on micro-planning what is done by the individual players in the project. In this way, the various departments and different people clarify the information that they all need, because their real goal is to reach the next *target event* in time.

The Project Manager focuses his or her energies on the critical factors that lead to results, rather than on reporting and the continual updating of plans. This involves having a clear map of the project, controlling the pace and the planning of these target events, with a clear indication of what one wishes to achieve. At the same time, care must be taken to provide the knowledge that is shared by everyone, putting in place the conditions to encourage the spreading of physical, virtual, and computer information. In practice, the Project Manager is the one who must create the right conditions for events to flow at predefined intervals. It is important that there be a "rhythm" for individuals and for groups to keep a sense of urgency throughout the project and give the team confidence that the project is truly progressing.

So we can then say that when the conditions of "flow" and "pull" are embedded in a project, it will always be the customer of a downstream process who will "rhythmically" ask for what he or she wants from their own upstream supplier. Here is a summary of the criteria used to give rhythm and pace to a project.

- *Target events*: (Design Review and Project Review) to "pull" the development of the team forward and ensure the success of the project.
- Supermarket of *shared information* from which people can "pull" what they need.
- *Predefined rules* of the project, so that people know how to get information from each other to minimize interruptions.

- *Rhythmic cycles* for all development activities so that everything will proceed in a regular way and the knowledge will be channeled in a smooth flow.
- *The value-creation oriented attitude of managers*: rather than just give orders and ask for demanding and complex reports, they must effectively support those in the front line of the project development by removing barriers to flow.

2.7.5 How Pull Planning Is Put into Practice—A Real Case

In the example in Figure 2.24, we can see a real case of the development and validation of the new products of a well-known company. Note the presence of five different working groups: product developers (group 5), designers (group 4), logistics for ordering the pieces (group 3), assembly line for the construction (group 2), and validation and final testing of the finished components (group 1). In this case, the previous local improvements of the various departments had resulted in a lengthening of overall lead times, as well as an increase in the stock of semi-finished components that had been developed or were in the process of being developed. Despite the fact that the various working groups had done some internal Value Stream Mapping, with a view to reducing waste, the total time was

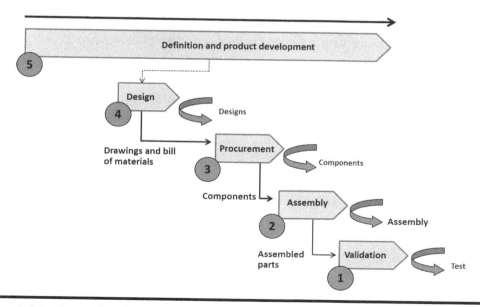

Figure 2.24 Example of Pull Planning. (Based on case implemented by J. Drogosz at a large industrial company.)

still not materially shortened and a lot of overtime in assembly and validation was done to crash the schedule on certain projects. When the whole team stepped back and looked at the entire system, the true wastes inhibiting flow came to light. For example, the planning time of validation (group 1 in the figure) was one month in the project plan, but in reality, this month was made up of many small activities often lasting far less than a month. In fact, the validation team ran on a weekly schedule while the projects used monthly views of the schedule. By lining up the tests, as they really happened in validation, they were able to discover the real weekly material and information needs required to achieve each individual test. In the true "pull" logic, the assembly department (group 2 in the figure), was "pulled" by the customer (validation), focusing its work on assembly, exactly as requested by its customers downstream.

This meant no more requests for a large batch of components and information for a period of one month for the validation, but requests for what was required in the same department week by week, piece by piece, until one group was in "full pull" with another. This meant forcing group 2 to assemble the parts needed exactly in the required sequence, drastically reducing both the number of parts constructed and not used, as well as the dead time between one department and another. What happened as a result? Group 3, the logistics group that ordered the parts from suppliers, was involved not in ordering the whole quantity of necessary components all at one time, but the parts that would be used in the correct sequence, synchronizing and aligning itself with its own customer, group 2.

This part of the work was the most difficult for several reasons which we will explain in detail, because it exposes a very common problem. After putting group 2 into "pull" with group 3, it was natural to do the same thing with group 4, or with those who do the designs, and therefore doing things in such a way as to no longer have designers who complete their designs independently of the rest, but designers who execute their designs exactly in the sequence identified by group 3. In doing so, a new bottleneck actually emerged after there was flow between the departments: the logistics group.

Why?

Because, in reality, they were used to doing things once a month and had also reduced the number of people in the department, inasmuch as they were not needed every day. Therefore, they did not create the conditions to work fluidly and in a synchronized way with their own internal customers and suppliers. *The local optimum, at times, does not match the global optimum.* This case study illustrates why it becomes important to establish what is best for the entire system before one decides on the right number of people to be added at the various points of the system. The ultimate goal for the interests of the company is always a goal for the entire system, not the individual department.

Once the new method of synchronization and "pull" of the various departments was defined and shared, it was then made visual. This technique, similar to *fundoshi scheduling* at Toyota, allowed for the visualization of all the deadlines within a project: all the materials, designs, and information that are linked to one another. All this was done with large, clearly legible billboards so everyone clearly saw what was expected in each group, each week. This is an example of Lean at its finest: simplicity and attention to effective communication. People no longer have to go in search of the data, no longer have to make an effort to discover problems, and no longer have to even ask for information.

Giving high and shared visibility to the planning of needs and the extent to which those needs are met leads to management benefits that are absolutely underestimated by those who continue to trust in nothing or in highly complicated models and control schemes that are only visible on individuals' PCs. When the data and the information were readily visible, to the engineers, operators, and the Program Managers, the focus shifted from going over all the details to the management of the exceptions and the real critical points. It would be enough, for example, to go twice a week past the billboards and information to verify "live" how things are actually going, to immediately identify the priorities that deserve action, and to easily see that small problem before it becomes a large critical problem. No manager would (or could) open a table or matrix on their own PC, because it is complex and difficult to "navigate." Instead, when the information is communicated in an easily visible way, we realize that the more easily we learn to access critical information, the more easily the problems come to the surface and again the more easily we can resolve them as a team.

2.7.6 Detailed Planning of the Flow of Materials and Information: Fundoshi Scheduling

Let us take a more detailed look at the tool of *fundoshi scheduling*. This consists of a large billboard on which all the steps needed to move materials and information within a project are scheduled with precision, guided by the final goal. The final delivery date is connected to the target dates of the submission of each design, passing through all the intermediate operating phases.

The great value is in creating detailed links between the individual elements of the entire chain: from the date of submission of each design to the forecast dates of delivery of that component, and from these to the expected dates of manufacture or assembly or testing, up to the delivery of the finished product. Effectively, a chain of dates is being created, going backward to link each individual project event in such a way that it provides the exact target sequence for all players involved in the project, internal and external.

How is this useful?

Let us imagine, for example, a product composed of a number of components equal to approximately two-thousand units.

Is it possible to turn out all the designs in a single day? No.

Is it possible to turn out all the designs in a week? No.

In fact, the work that is done by designers, logistics people, assemblers, and suppliers can require anything from a few weeks to several months, depending on the type of product. In order to safeguard the needs of those who will be using the designs down the chain from the designers, it is advisable to make a detailed plan of the correct sequence of designs, taking into account the functional, technical, and design characteristics of the product, but also the presence of any technological and logistic constraints that make it impossible to design one particular piece before another. All of this has the goal of making the entire flow as fast as possible without unnecessary glitches or delays.

What is the starting point?

The starting point is that date in which we wish to complete the final product. Starting from this date, we begin to go backward, inserting the dates that are part of the natural evolution of the product, which, in the case of the example mentioned previously, could be as follows:

1. Final testing.
2. Component testing.
3. Instrumentation.
4. Final assembly build.
5. Sub-assembly builds.
6. Deliveries from suppliers.
7. Internal manufacturing.
8. External manufacturing.
9. Orders to suppliers.

10. Issue of bill materials.
11. Issue of the final drawings.
12. Development of component drawings.
13. Development of the system.

When the sequence of target dates for all events is clear, the list of target dates required for the issue of the individual components becomes equally clear. At each step, there is a discussion between customer and supplier to define needs, identify constraints, and agree upon final delivery dates. Next to the entries for individual target dates/quantities, the actual dates and any roadblocks will be posted on the billboards. As soon as there is a deviation from the target dates on the billboard, it is easy to see the "danger" points in the project, and the entire team can take appropriate countermeasures.

2.7.7 *The Management System and Review of the Whole Project*

In Figure 2.25, you can see how the entire pace of a project can be planned from start to finish. It is a fundamental process for all projects that we call the *Project Review System*. It starts with a subdivision of the entire project into different macro-phases. A key date is established for each of them, by which the "salient events" of the project in relation to that particular stage must be completed, the so-called *key deliverables*, documented and objectified.

The activities required for realizing the *key deliverables* are included in the detailed planning sheets, which are managed directly by the individual responsible for each *key deliverable*. The progress of each element and the person responsible for it are clearly charted, allowing for a visual control of the entire project with a single A3 sheet.

In the example in Figure 2.25, the initial stages of development of the project were entered: this included the Concept Paper, the exploration phase of the various conceptual alternatives, the Kentou (study) phase of the product, the system design phase where the whole architecture of the complete system chosen was designed, then moving on to the stage of detailed design and prototyping. The testing and validation phase always precedes the mass production phase. In this case, since we are talking about mass production, it is essential that the final phase of analysis of market feedback is included.

The choice of the macro-phases can change from one project to another, but it is essential that the entire project is divided into phases that are easily understood by everyone, within which the information, materials, assessments, and decisions flow easily. At the end of each stage, the so-called

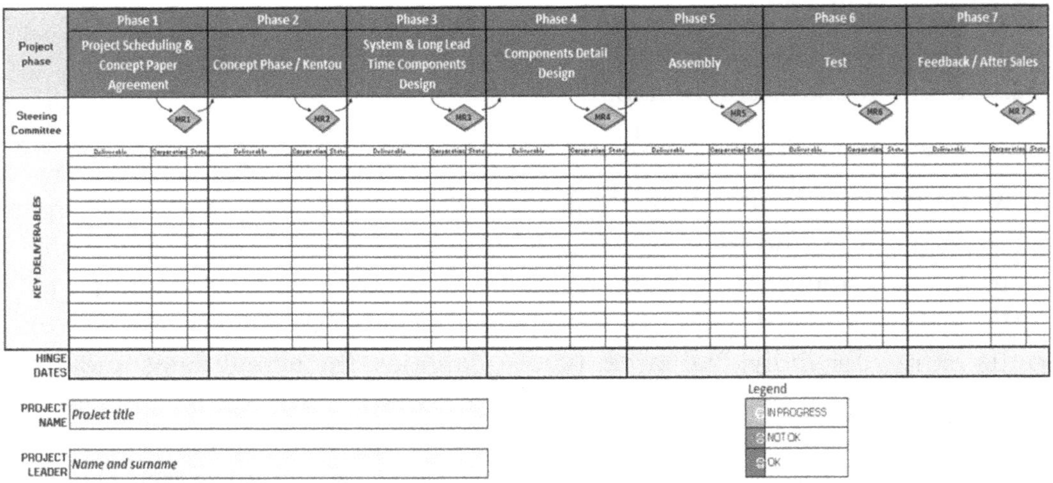

Figure 2.25 Lenovys Model of Project Review System.

Project Review must be completed. These are similar to the Milestones in the Stage-Gate product development processes used by many major companies, including Procter and Gamble and Siemens. These are times when the entire team critically reviews the project's progress by reviewing the output list that should have been delivered by the end of each phase. However, in this case, we are talking about actual commitments that are made within the entire team and not arbitrary times based on traditional phase gate templates. This will then establish the formal rhythm for the project. Having key deliverables met and checked during these reviews brings a tight focus to the activities of individual team members between one review and the next.

As we were saying, we have seen similar methods in different companies, and once again we want to emphasize *that it is not the document that makes the difference, but the social process that brings it to life.* The difference between a successful project and a mediocre one lies in building the above with the project team and obtaining their buy-in. With this approach, the team can them make it visible in an Obeya space, and manage through exceptions to address or prevent problems as they arise. The ability to involve and empower people in the acquisition of all the data needed to successfully meet and surpass all the requirements of the upcoming review is a powerful technique. The Project Review System outline can help synthesize all these factors and simplify management with respect to traditional project management, organizing the project according to the desired pace to achieve success. Some of the advanced companies we have worked with hold their milestone reviews in the gemba and have dispensed with powerpoint entirely. They view creating the powerpoint and presenting it in a conference room as pure waste. After all, they have been reviewing process through mini-PDCA cycles, every week in their Obeya meetings, so there should be no surprises in the milestone review. *The success here always lies with the real processes and people, not the tool employed.*

2.8 Standardization and Creativity: The True Strength of a New Product

> There are only 3 colors, 10 digits, and 7 notes; it's what we do with them that's important.
>
> **Ruth Ross**

When it comes to innovation and new product development, we often fall into the trap of a limiting belief: the standardization of methods and processes is an enemy of creativity. Unfortunately, due to this conviction we have been witnessing, within our companies, various "dysfunctions":

- Great variability in the duration of the processes related to the development of products and services.
- Difficulty in predicting the actual output of creative staff members.
- Levels of quality that vary from person to person, from product to product.

Before understanding not only how creativity and discipline can coexist, but also how one helps the other, we think it is important to clarify what it means to standardize, and, above all, at what levels it can be introduced.

1. *At product level*: to introduce features into our products that avoid reinventing something that has already been invented, in order to have a common architecture and reusable components, and to introduce concepts such as modularity and platforms to design a range of different models. Therefore, this means anything that can be standardized in the design of our products or services without undermining the value and uniqueness of the end customer.
2. *At processes level*: the second aspect of standardization is related to the development and design process. Seen from this angle, standardization means having activities that are repeatable, and first and foremost, activities that can be replicated by others, and that are measurable. This

concept is important because by having repeatable and measurable activities these can be replicated, transferred, and improved. Often, you do things that you cannot transfer objectively and therefore they can no longer be repeated or delegated and even improved. They do not have to be transferred exactly, as in copied, as each situation is somewhat unique, and we want to encourage kaizen. But the basic concept can be learned from.

3. *At people level*: an additional level of standardization is related to the ability of the people involved, their level of training, and ability to work in teams. When two colleagues differ substantially in these things, whenever they are called upon to perform similar tasks, there will inevitably be differences in performance. The output and duration of their activities will be clearly different. Therefore, managers need to align and standardize the technical and social competencies (skills) of their employees, if they want to systematically increase the performance of their system. To achieve this level of standardization, it is necessary to make "knowledge management" a vital part of the organization, with good planning in both the collection and stratification of corporate know-how, as well as its usability. This also needs to be coupled with intensive mentoring to develop the tacit knowledge of our people.

Everything that refers to a company's know-how, in relation to the product development phases, can and must be stored in such a way as to ensure the capture, sharing, understanding, and most importantly, the applying of knowledge.

In some companies, this tool is called the "know-how database," and is a veritable repository of corporate knowledge. Some typical elements include design guidelines, *trade-off* curves, reusable and scalable design packages, standard parts, production process information, supplier information, checklists, the *lessons learned* from the previous projects, test results, and directions for avoiding the same mistakes *(error proofing lists)*. It is not a case of adding more "procedures," but of capitalizing on real experience, the things that went well and those that went wrong. Some of these will be general knowledge such as how to use a 3D solid modeling system and others will be peculiar to a subsystem, such as plastic-injected molded parts, and needs to be owned by the deep functional specialists in that group. Thus, not everybody needs to look at everything. This is a precious treasure to be protected more than anything else in the company because, if it is well done, it will contain years and years of practical and usable knowledge that can be used by all to make the best possible future products and services for our customers.

2.8.1 The Basis of Standardization: Knowing How to Use the Data and Knowledge in Our Possession

We already mentioned in the chapter on the Concept Paper the importance of the knowledge, or the *trade-off curves*. These curves represent the relationships between parameters considered important to the customer. There is a strong link between these curves and standardization. Imagine, for example, the case of an automotive exhaust system. The main drivers can include the mass of the exhaust, the engine's power, or the exhaust backpressure. With well-constructed *trade-off curves*, we will have many diagrams that describe the variation of one parameter with respect to another.

Each time a new need is identified by a customer, or when a problem has to be dealt with, the first thing we try to do is understand where we find ourselves on the curve. It is important to be able to understand the impact of a new request or a change in one variable with respect to the others, because by studying these characteristics, it is possible to take quick decisive action exactly where necessary in order to meet the new demands, without adversely affecting others from a technical or economical point of view.

The construction and use of these curves fit perfectly in the spirit of Lean management applied to the development of new products, because it aims to thoroughly understand the reasons behind everything that happens in the entire operating range of a product, before inventing and testing new solutions.

2.8.2 How Do We Collect Data for a Trade-Off Curve? We Make Better Use of the Way We Already Do Things and the Data Already Available to Us

To better understand this concept, I want you to think about the basic difference between testing and experimentation, between the traditional way and the Lean way. It is common practice in any company to submit products for testing and validation prior to release. These activities verify the product's ability to meet operating conditions for the entire life of the product itself: endurance tests, vibrations, breakage tests, functional tests, etc. In traditional companies, most of the times that a product is tested, it is compared with a set target for passing the test. It is important to know whether you have passed or failed that test, with the assigned target for the given project. Therefore, there is often a final validation report that is a list of tests that have been carried out with the outcomes that say whether or not the test was passed or failed. If, for example, our target is to verify that a device functions for at least two million cycles, traditionally it is enough to stop at two million cycles plus one.

In a Lean company, during these phases of testing and validation, components and systems are tested to their limits whenever possible because we want to "map" what happens in all potential ranges of operation. This is done in order to learn as much as possible from a test and may help us to reuse this knowledge in future products. At Toyota, Honda, Tenneco, and many other companies, although they have clear test target specifications, it is preferable to program the test to the point of complete failure, for several reasons. If we are dedicating our time, energy, and resources in the validation of a product, it is smart to map everything that happens up to the point of failure, in order to be able to reuse data and trials for different products. Furthermore, as good as we are with statistics, in reality, the validation only measures a part of the real population and a small number of components. This is why it is preferable to have as much information as possible on the basic characteristics of this product, for its entire operating range.

Paradoxically, companies that follow this approach have, in the long term, less need to continuously test and validate components and products. Take, for example, Honda, which is a company with one of the highest rates of technological innovation and new product development in the world, but also has a relatively low rate of prototype production. They have fewer prototypes but extensively test them to the point of failure for critical parameters they do not fully understand. Despite taking up more time with validation devices to test their prototypes, they gain capacity rather than losing it in the long term, due to the fact of very effectively being able to "capture" knowledge of their components and devices. Practically speaking, they have less need to test everything thanks to extensive use of trade-off curves, obtained through a judicious use of testing in the past. This way, the conditions are created for not having to test some parts of the new products, because, for example, they already have the test results from previous designs.

2.8.3 Standardization of Components, Reuse of Know-How, and Corporate Profit

Imagine what happens to a company's profits when you can reuse most of the components, including a new product and the previous one of the same family. Or if you can use the same components extensively on various product platforms. Toyota has historically re-used up to 70% of its components on different platforms, ranging from the compact car to the latest luxury flagship vehicle. And no one is upset (or even notice) when they find the same door handle on both the Toyota Corolla and the Lexus. This shows that some details only have added value in the heads of the designers or accountants, rather than the final customer.

In order to have access to the extensive use of components between different families of products, to benefit from past trials of similar products, it is important to make the accumulated knowledge accessible. As discussed above, the so-called Books of Knowledge or know-how database play a key role. The fact that we are not used to managing corporate knowledge well can become devastating in the long term. Think, for a moment, that *approximately half the people who work in the company for you now, ten years from now will be gone: retired or elsewhere, taking with them what they have learned.* And the company will be forced to start all over, again bearing the costs of learning and slowing down the real innovation of products and processes. This happens more often than you might think, but we are less aware of it because it is a phenomenon that is distributed over time, ultimately slowing down innovation in the company.

The reuse of components provides significant advantages associated with industrial purchasing strategies, with the reduction of warehouse space associated with the lower number of part numbers to manage, in the number of different tools required in the factory and the ability to do mixed model production on the same line, in administrative, managerial, and technical-productive terms. One fewer component is one fewer component that has to be designed, ordered, purchased, manufactured, controlled, managed, packed, etc. Saving on total cost goes far beyond the mere cost of the material, and often has an even greater hidden cost that can magically appear and disappear. Let's see why.

2.8.4 Releasing Energies to Make a Real Difference

A strategy that can lead to unimaginable results in increased value to the customer, and at the same time free up internal resources, requires a whole new *mind set*: learning to focus our energies on the critical 30% of the design activities that ensure a 90% increase in perceived value from the point of view of the customer. In this *mind set*, we encounter one of the most sensitive aspects of the development of new products: the ability to combine standardization, discipline, and creativity. It requires profound technical and mental discipline to be able to approximately reuse 70% of designs that are needed for the product but not necessarily coveted by the customer. If we manage not to concentrate too heavily on issues that are of little importance to the customer, then we will be able to put our best efforts into true innovations that really matter in "making a difference" to the customer. However, if we focus our creative energy on that 30% that the customer sees and values, applying structured innovation processes such as Set-Based Concurrent Engineering, we drastically increase the probability of success delivering the right product at the right time to the customer. In so doing, we essentially release enormous pockets of energy otherwise dispersed. The distribution of energies we are talking about is the road that has so far been followed by companies such as Toyota, Apple, Honda, Procter and Gamble, and Diesel, with impressive results. Think of a next-generation iPhone and compare it with one of the previous generations. You will notice that at least 70% of the components remain the same. Then think about the iPhone, iPod, and iPad. Look at their operating systems, their software, and their components: you will be impressed by the percentage of shared (or scaled) parts. Now also think of how many models Apple has on the market, compared to those of their competitors. Finally, ask yourself which company in that sector makes the most profit and who has the largest market capitalization. The answer is obvious.

You can understand, then, what it means to run a business and really care about the product and the customer, and what really makes the difference, while reusing knowledge and standards for everything else. This approach has been taken by countless successful entrepreneurs who have been able to focus their energies on the few value-added innovations that stimulate the customer, rather than trying to do everything in an average way.

2.9 Summary of Key Points in Chapter 2

1. *Processes as a response to problems.* Before providing solutions or defining any new rule or process, let's ask ourselves what the real problem is that we need to solve. When this is clear, we can analyze the given process for gaps to the ideal process and identify the root cause of the gaps, remembering that all activities in product development are bound to each other like links in a chain.

2. *Before starting a project, define customer needs and the business constraints by applying a thorough, structured process.* The Concept Paper is the document that sums up and formalizes this vital process. This process should be done before embarking on any project activity, to align people toward the final customer value while accounting for corporate constraints.

3. *Concentrate efforts at the beginning of the project in order to explore alternatives while there is maximum ability to innovate.* A key strategy for achieving the optimum solution in the shortest possible time, with the fewest number of modifications and iterations later in the project. Set-Based Concurrent Engineering is a structured methodology to help spur creativity in the early phase of the project.

4. *Map processes to distinguish between waste and value-added activities.* There is no universal recipe for improvement. It is fundamental to train yourself to recognize the principal sources of waste in your own specific working context—in product development and other intellectual activities. Value Stream Mapping of processes leads to a greater awareness of the people who will actually have to guide and effect change in the company.

5. *Get intellectual activities to flow by minimizing variation.* Apply the eight principles of flow, applicable to individuals and groups: level incoming work, minimize the number of current activities, reduce the size of activities, establish regular rhythms, plan for results and not activities, Pull Planning, avoid becoming overloaded, and minimize interruptions.

6. *Learn not to get overloaded.* The ability to predict and control the level of work in the system ensures the quality of work, respect for deadlines, and individual well-being over time.

7. *Lean Project Management.* Create the right conditions to make projects flow, rather than concentrating on control of all the details. Become experts in understanding the process and guiding teams to tackle problems as they arise on a project.

8. *Standardization of products, processes, and competencies.* Vital for effectively utilizing scarce and valuable resources. The best-in-class companies manage to reuse approximately 70% of existing components when moving from an old product to a new one.

9. *Maximum value with minimum effort.* This strategy is complementary to the previous one and concerns the ability to see what delivers maximum added value for the customer and channeling creative energies to innovating products and processes that customers really want.

Resource

https://www.lenovys.com/en/case-history/frigoglass/

Notes

1. Devised by W. Edwards Deming in Japan in the 1950s. In those years, production quality was guaranteed merely by testing stages. All post-process inspections could achieve was to discard defective items; according to this logic, the increase of quality would mean an increase in inspections and therefore of costs. Waste and costs were not in tune with the concept of quality that the Japanese wanted. So they turned to American experts, including W. Edwards Deming, to introduce tools to ensure a gradual improvement in quality.
2. For more on this specific issue, see the Appendix.
3. Godin S., 2010.
4. Walton M., 1999; Ward A.C., 2007; Morgan J., Liker J.K., 2006.
5. Liker J.K., Morgan J., 2011 ("Lean product development as a system: A case study of body and stamping development at Ford." *Engineering Management Journal*, Vol. 23, No. 1, 2011, pp. 16–28.
6. Jim Womack describes the "gemba walk" as all the "strolls" in the field that are normally done in a Lean company when we want to gain an in-depth understanding of a given issue.
7. Liker J.K., Franz J., *The Toyota Way to Continuous Improvement,* N.Y.: McGraw Hill, 2012, chapter 11.
8. Morgan J., Liker J.K., 2006.
9. *Six sigma* is a methodology born in the United States at the end of the 1980s, and was used in the 1990s by companies like Motorola, Allied Signal, and General Electric. The stated aim is to offer products to end consumers with the highest possible quality and lowest possible cost, by applying statistical tools and methods that help people to measure, analyze, improve, and control every type of process.
10. Morgan J., Liker J., 2006.
11. Richtel M., 2010.
12. Hopp W., Spearman M., 2007.
13. Loehr J., Schwartz T., 2005.

Chapter 3

People: The Engine for Creativity at the Heart of Long-Term Success

In business, we often think that results are achieved thanks to having chosen the right strategy, the right product, and the right actions. But these traditional elements of corporate governance are rarely insufficient for ensuring prosperity over the long term. A winning organization on paper with a good plan of action and performance monitoring systems can lull managers into believing that the success of their companies is assured. But as Freddy Ballé says: "It is not a question of machines, or of organization, or even money. It's the people … Leadership. It's all a matter of leadership." The ability to deeply engage people, motivate them, really put them at the center of the corporate transformation process is the key factor that ensures the full sustainability of any change in a company. In this section, we will explore some strategies to better unleash the enormous potential of our people too often hidden in companies today.

3.1 There Can Be No Innovation without People

> Go to the people. Live with them. Learn from them. Love them. Start with what they know. Build with what they have. But with the best leaders, when the work is done, the task accomplished, the people will say: "We have done this ourselves."
>
> **Lao-Tsu**

What stimulates innovation in a work group most of all? A fine article in the *Harvard Business Review* in May 2011[1] reported the results of observing hundreds of individuals including professional research groups from industrial engineers to famous inventors. The most powerful leading to a high rate of innovation in the groups was a "sense of progress." Based on their conclusions, the more we become accustomed to experimenting with small units of progress, the more the emotional side of individuals and groups are fuelled, making them more "creatively productive" over the long run.

This article made us think long and hard about the usual behaviors observed inside and outside a company. What motivates people to improve themselves, to change, to innovate?

Imagine researchers struggling with their long and tiring laboratory work, often lacking any dramatic results. They are often working at a base salary. What drives these researchers to move forward in their work? Or imagine an athlete who is training hard for a competitive event, day after day, week after week, month after month. What drives this athlete to continue?

In both cases, certainly not the things that are tangible from the outside.

Motivation often comes from a series of seemingly intangible elements, in particular the search for and attainment of signs of progress, which at times are really quite minor, but are enough to keep our "internal engines" running. For an athlete, this might mean an improvement in trial times by a few tenths of a second, coupled with a winning vision of him or herself in a race, even if it is months away. In the case of researchers, it might be a small sign such as passing the alpha test in the laboratory. In both cases, the researcher or the athlete will "feel good" when they experience this sense of progress. And the better they feel, the more confidence they will exude and hence will continue to be productive in their endeavors.

3.1.1 Are Corporate Productivity and People's Well-Being Compatible?

All tools for improving productivity are useless unless they are tied to a change for the better in the emotional state of the people within the company.

We have personally been involved in company improvement projects for many years, as employees, managers, consultants, and entrepreneurs. From what we have seen, when the link between productivity and individual well-being is lacking, you cannot effectively create, let alone sustain, innovation and continuous improvement in a company. We have seen many projects fail and many initiatives lose their drive for this reason. As long as our companies are made up of people, it will be up to the people to ensure the success or failure of any activity or initiative.

As a prerequisite for initiating and making projects succeed, the skillful involvement of people is vital. This is done by bringing people on board from the beginning of any change effort, not only to share the business reasons with them, but also to listen to their individual motivations, ultimately leading to a common view of the "urgency for change." Concentrating on the welfare of the people, together with the need to increase productivity and innovation in the business, is the only way to guarantee sustainable structural change over the long run.

If we want our businesses to grow, we need to grow people; and growth is not possible without well-being.

In a company, the state of well-being of its people comes from a blend of emotions, skills, motivations, and perceptions of their everyday working experiences. The previously mentioned results of the research conducted by Teresa Amabile and Steven Kramer bear this out. Some behaviors on the part of management might favor a truly virtuous cycle of improvement and innovation, others may hinder or even discourage it.

Setting clear short-term micro-objectives, as well as a long-term vision with broad goals focused on positively influencing customers, allows ideas to flow within a work group and can be real "catalysts" of progress. Recognizing and valuing the contributions of each member of the team while encouraging and supporting those in difficulty, can be emotional tools that fuel the sense of progress and belonging. However, other behaviors, have the potential to hinder progress. These include: creating unclear or contradictory goals, taking responsibility away from the employees (micromanaging), punishing or "demeaning" in the case of honest errors, suppressing new ideas, favoring one person's ideas over another's, showing a lack of respect to team members, and rewarding individual achievement above team achievement. All of these aspects can create a sense of antagonism within the team that will clearly reduce its effectiveness.

The examples given above show the link between the external dimension of the company, comprised of facts and objective results, with the internal dimension of people, that are comprised of motivations, emotions, and perceptions. When we neglect to tie the two dimensions together, we distance ourselves from that virtuous combination of productivity and well-being.

Too often, the focus of top managers is to "organize" better companies and individuals, usually through structural changes on paper. If their focus was more oriented toward creating the conditions which encourage progress and ongoing improvement in the company, many more people would feel a sense of success in their jobs. And, as a logical extension, there would be greater guarantees of the company succeeding over time.

How can managers encourage a sense of progress with their team members? Let's find out...

3.1.2 What Does It Mean to Become Lean? The Principles of Lean Leadership

What does it mean, in fact, to become "Lean"? It does not mean introducing some process or instrument copied from elsewhere and pasted into some areas of your business.

> *Becoming Lean means creating a system that ensures the capacity for continuous autonomous improvement on the part of the people in the company, in order to raise performance in that company's business, forever.*

An environment supporting continuous improvement makes it possible to achieve and maintain excellence, but it also presupposes a willingness to accept new challenges constantly. The real key to individual and corporate success is based on the proper balance between "technical" and "social" excellence.

Successful companies have been able to build a system of leadership that can support and guide people's behavior, making it possible for the processes to function.

Jeffrey Liker and Gary Convis have summarized the model of such successful companies in four stages of development, calling it Lean Leadership.[2]

1. *Self-Development*: People must be able to continuously learn, improve, and constantly question themselves and thus lead others by example and with passion.
2. *Develop the full potential of the team*: knowing how to enhance and stimulate the real potential of one's own team, guiding them not as

"bosses," but as "coaches." This means taking to heart their continuous learning and their autonomy. Motivating and getting people involved are key to sustainable improvements.

3. *Support daily improvement to achieve results*: setting up systems and habits that can facilitate the achievement of concrete results on a daily basis *(daily management),* in keeping with the spirit of continuous improvement *(kaizen).*

4. *Create aligned vision and objectives*: to promote the solidarity of the entire company in regard to a common vision, sharing the reasons for the distribution of aligned and complementary objectives that are never at odds with each other.

Promoting values and beliefs that favor a "viral" diffusion of the same philosophy within all personnel in the company is key to Lean Leadership. These values incorporated as the foundation of The Toyota Way 2001 are the spirit of challenge, the *kaizen* mentality, "go and see," teamwork, and respect for people.[3] What Liker and Convis emphasize is there is something of a sequence to these four steps, though not in lock step order and they can be viewed more as a constantly spinning wheel. Leaders cannot be teachers developing others until they learn themselves. What do they need to learn? Obviously, they need to learn some technical skills and knowledge, but, in addition, they need to become expert at process improvement to drive the organization forward. As they learn to do the work and lead to the improvement of how the work is done, they need to learn how to teach these skills to others, in a way that is empowering and motivating. Rother calls these first two steps the "improvement kata," a set of routines for improving things, and the "coaching kata," a set of routines for teaching others the improvement kata.[4] As senior leaders and middle managers learn the skills of improving and developing others, they can drive this down to the work group level to support daily management. Only then, the organization is ready to achieve breakthrough objectives with all aligned toward common objectives.

This happens at the company level in Toyota through their annual process of strategy deployment, called in Japanese *Hoshin Kanri*. It also must happen in a micro-version within any development project to cascade the product and process vision and targets to every working level so the whole team is aligned. In advanced organizations, this includes outside organizations like parts suppliers, equipment vendors, and dealers. Obviously, we cannot wait to set stretch objectives for everyone to mature to a perfect state, so we need an iterative process of developing people, setting challenging goals, coaching people as they work toward those goals, reflecting on what happened, and continually improving the organization, people, and products.

3.2 Coordinating and Integrating Development through the Chief Engineer System

> Leaders are people who do the right thing; managers are people who do things right.
>
> **Warren Bennis**

The loss of global responsibility is one of the less visible wastes or dysfunctions often present in many companies, due to the fragmentation of decisions, tasks, and roles between different people and different departments. Much of the waste typical in the development of new products and processes is exacerbated by the lack of a unified view of the entire project, as well as by the lack of a clear and unambiguous responsibility for the final product and results.

In companies that have a strong focus on the effective development of new products, and in those which apply Lean Thinking in their development processes, the role of the Project Manager often entails far more pronounced responsibilities than elsewhere. At Toyota, this figure is called the "Chief Engineer," and is a shrewd mix between the figures of the Project Manager, the authoritative social leader, and the technical "system integrator." The Chief Engineer, or the equivalent figures at Apple, Procter and Gamble, and other companies becomes the real "parent" of the new product and is responsible for the complete product from setting the vision and requirements to the technical and financial results. They have a clear knowledge of the progress of their project at any stage in the product's life. The Chief Engineer is responsible for guiding teams to find solutions to technical and financial challenges and making multidisciplinary decisions. This requires deep technical knowledge combined with superb social skills.

In the development of a new product, the function of the Chief Engineer is to "keep it all together" from the beginning to the end of development. With authority and leadership, this figure is able to interact with all necessary stakeholders, asking everyone involved what is needed, at any time. From the CEO to the team members, everyone recognizes the Chief

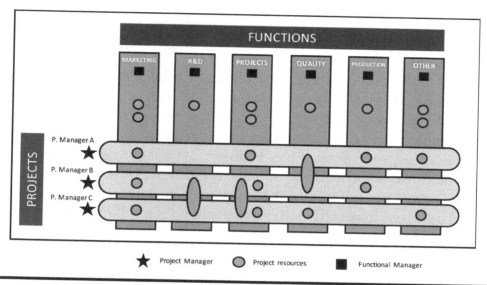

Figure 3.1   Organizational model for Project Leader/Chief Engineer.

Engineer to be the voice of the customer in the company, as well as the one and only person in charge of the product.

As shown in Figure 3.1, the structure of a Lean company, usually matrixed, is designed to ensure support for the Chief Engineer to develop exceptional products. In addition, technical excellence is promoted in the individual functions that have the task of developing and managing specialized knowledge within the company. The Chief Engineer, one for each product in the company, ensures the release onto the market of the products themselves, working right across the entire organization to "pull" the right resources and expertise from the functional groups to ensure the success of their project.

Despite not having a direct hierarchical responsibility, the Chief Engineer is the real "glue" for the entire project, always ensuring that the focus is on the product and the end customer without the risk of getting lost in the details of managing the technical departments.

3.2.1 Matrix Structure?

The model shown in Figure 3.1 is a version of a matrix organizational structure, in which specialized organizational groups coexist with transversal project leads, as in the case of the Program Manager and various department heads. But there are some subtle, but significant differences compared to what we more typically see in matrix organizations.

1. There is no ambiguity in role and authority between the project lead
   and the functional manager, as in many matrix organizations. The
   functional manager is the supervisor of the employees in that function—there is no dual authority role in a formal sense. As such, the
   functional specialist's boss leads the career path of professional growth
   and development, performance evaluation, and the allocation of tasks
   and projects to be worked on for each person in their department. The
   project lead, such as the Chief Engineer, is treated more like a customer
   of the functional specialist's service, not another boss as is typical in
   most matrix organizations. The functional specialists must be properly
   prepared and managed by the functional boss to understand the program requirements, become a productive member of the team, and
   satisfy the customer—the chief engineer. The fact that the customer
   is right cannot be applied better than to the relationship between the
   technical specialist and the chief engineer. Chief engineers are not the
   boss of the person, but have ultimate authority over project decisions.
2. A profound respect for the role of the Chief Engineer, quite irrespective of that person's formal position in the organization. This allows the
   Chief Engineer to lead without invoking formal authority, and to lead
   both vertically, project team members, and horizontally, executives of
   other functions like sales and supply chain. To develop the track record
   to earn this respect, bordering in worship, takes many years of success
   starting in the trenches. Thus, inexperienced managers with great educational credentials and expertise in project management software do
   not have a chance of successfully filling this role. The Chief Engineer
   has the experience and credibility to be the arbiter who can facilitate
   the right decisions in cases of conflict between functional groups,
   bringing consensus ideally, but deciding if necessary.
3. Clarity of Direction and Roles. The Chief Engineer is clearly and
   unequivocally focused on the success of the overall project, achieving
   the maximum value of the final product for the customer with the minimum waste for the company. On the other side, the focus of the other
   functional managers is clearly oriented toward providing the specialized
   technical resources and solutions to the project team to achieve their
   goals. There is a very careful and deliberate process of breaking down
   the goals from the overall product vision, to specific requirements, technical, business, and timing, to the specific targets for each group supporting the project. Through regular meetings, at least weekly, it is clear
   who is on or off target.

As mentioned in Chapter 2, the skillful integration of the parts is mainly achieved through an informal organization process that the Japanese call "nemawashi," in other words, careful management of all the micro-negotiations between departments. Nemawashi literally translated uses the nature metaphor of *transplanting a tree from one place to another*: it would be impossible to transfer it from one terrain to another without taking extreme care of the roots, and the breakage of certain parts of the tree, the characteristics of the terrain etc. Similarly, there is a complex process of gaining a degree of consensus among group members in a complex process and each member must be carefully prepared, and their input seriously solicited, so that ideally any formal decision in a meeting has already been agreed to by all participants.

In *The Toyota Way*, Liker provides a detailed account of one of the most famous Chief Engineers in Toyota's history, considered by Toyota associates in the United States to be the "Michael Jordan of Chief Engineers." Ichiro Suzuki was directly appointed in 1983, by then Toyota Chairman Eiji Toyoda, to direct the launch of the Lexus brand. This brand was very soon to become the absolute benchmark in the field of luxury cars. Suzuki occupies an important place in the history of Toyota for having demonstrated how to guide without commanding, but spending a great deal of time in understanding how to remove technical, social, and motivational barriers along his path. He was entrusted with the task of launching a car whose performance was out of the ordinary for Toyota to compete for the first time with the top-ranked Audi, BMW, and Mercedes models, which had control of the market at that time. To realize how exceptional this feat was, considering that by the early 1990s, a single Lexus model had sold nearly three times the amount of the three models in the same range sold by the competitor Mercedes,[5] upwardly repositioning the technological paradigms used to build that type of car.

There is an emblematic anecdote about the conflict Ichiro Suzuki had with the company's vice president of Powertrain, a person high up in the organization, hierarchically with more authority than him. His goal was to break a trade-off that he noticed among Toyota competitors—the trade-off between noise in the passenger compartment and power of the engine. His philosophy was this yet that, so great power with a quiet ride. To do this, he determined he needed to eliminate noise, vibration, and harshness at the source, which required building pistons, cylinders, and other critical machined components with tolerances that were far more precise than those that had ever been achieved. The first time he presented his request to the VP of Powertrain, he was literally laughed out of the office.

"Are you crazy? We can't do that! You are asking us to reduce variation in the machined parts to lower levels than the variation in the machine tools themselves."

The Chief Engineer, at first feeling dejected, went back to the VP and convinced him to build a single prototype in order to accurately assess the technical feasibility, despite the evident difficulties. The engineers who designed the engine personally assembled the first prototype, to assess the positive aspects and defects for themselves, and subsequently mounted it in their largest car at the time. As they came out of test driving this car at the test track one by one, they said they had to figure out how to make a mass produced version of this engine. The driving experience was simply so exciting that it unleashed a passion to meet what seemed to be an impossible challenge. The Chief Engineer had to creatively lead the team past their paradigm of "it cannot be done" to "how can we get this mass produced." There was no one brilliant idea, but rather through thousands of small improvements, even assembling the engine in a clean room to avoid dust, the mass production version was achieved.

Ichiro Suzuki is a testimony to the fact that the real work of a leader to create an innovative, great product is not so much about managing budget and timing, but about removing the obstacles that prevent the product from coming into being. The fact of living slightly outside bureaucratic constraints allows the Chief Engineers to stay focused on the things that add value to their product, with relative flexibility and freedom, rather than being forced to micro-manage operational constraints and organizational details.

3.2.2 What Skills Should a Chief Engineer Have?

Generally, there are two levels of responsibility. The first level is technical, the second one is management-related. The key competencies necessary to be a successful Chief Engineer are listed below:

1. *Technical integration of the system.* The Chief Engineer's task is to first clearly understand the needs of their customer and effectively communicate them through a formal document called the Concept Paper. This document contains the program's objectives, product architecture, performance, and desired technical specifications. Then, the skills of a technical "integrator" are required, in order to manage the technical trade-offs and arbitrate technical issues among the entire development

team. The role of the technical arbiter is important, dealing with different solutions and requests from different parts of the company, each of which is a specific part of the product. The objective at this level is to find the optimal solution for the customer and company.

2. *Project management.* The next level of responsibility is tied to monitoring and achievement of the objectives of the project, including functional performance, cost targets, and project deadlines. This is done formally through project reports, Design Reviews, and Project Reviews. Nowadays, Toyota religiously uses a "big room," called the *Obeya,* in which key data on the progress of each functional group is visually posted. This was pioneered by Uchiyamada, chief engineer of the first Prius (see Liker, *The Toyota Way*). Beyond this, the Chief Engineer is constantly traveling to the gemba in Japan, the local countries that are customers of the vehicle, sales offices, manufacturing plants, and through informally building relationships and checking the process doing a lot of the coordination behind the scenes.

Becoming a Chief Engineer requires years of technical and management experience in order to establish capability and credibility to lead cross-functional project teams and to develop exceptional products.

3.3 Cross-Functional Cooperation to Effectively Develop New Products

Cooperation isn't the absence of conflict, but a means of managing conflict.

Deborah Tannen

While developing any product or service, harnessing the expertise of various technical disciplines to meet the customer and company needs requires strong integration skills and is always very demanding. But it is absolutely vital to make successful products for the marketplace. In a Lean development system, cross-functional integration is considered to be essential to reduce the wastes of synchronization, unclear responsibilities, excessive handoffs, and poor communication. Responsibility for the management of the new product is always given to a person with a strong orientation toward the product itself, the Chief Engineer, as we have mentioned above.

In addition, a strong project team is needed to get the product to market. The composition of this team reflects a highly "product-centric" vision. Of these, the staff leader is the figure that, in the traditional corporate culture, would be called "Program Manager," because he or she deals with the more administrative part of the project: timelines, product costs, budgets, etc. The more technical role of the System Integrator is always kept separate, to ensure that all the pieces of the system are "glued" together, and can be carried out by the Chief Engineer. The Chief Engineer's small core team members (assistants to the chief engineers, sometimes called executive program managers) are organized around the subsystems of the product and act as a subsystem integrator to manage that part of the product to completion. In addition, subsystems lead engineers responsible for daily development decisions. Furthermore, to core engineering team members, there are support specialists to assist their Chief Engineer in some of the project management functions such as tracking product cost, managing the prototype schedule, etc. The rest of the organization supports the product team. If, for example, we need to integrate key functions into the development of the new product, such as marketing, quality, and purchasing, we will not have those representatives participate directly in the product team through the entire project: the Chief Engineer, in the moment of need, directly "pulls" the information that is needed each time. Certain critical roles will participate in Obeya meetings.

While the Chief Engineer is responsible for resolving all conflicts between departments, the heads of the other functional departments have also clear responsibilities. What are the responsibilities of the department heads?

1. Developing the competencies of their engineers and technicians in their own specialties.
2. Periodic reviews of the growth and performance of their employees.
3. Development and maintenance of engineering checklists which represent the know-how accumulated in their own specialties.
4. Maintaining the state-of-the-art of individual specialties.
5. Technical coordination, such as ensuring the use of common parts across multiple products whenever possible.
6. Co-design with suppliers of components and continuously improve the suppliers' skills.
7. Assigning the right resources to projects to support the needs of the various Chief Engineers.

To summarize, the Chief Engineer and their team are responsible for integrating the various resources to ensure the success of the project, while the functional departments pursue developing technical excellence and making highly qualified people available to develop new products.

3.3.1 Who Makes the Decisions?

Most decisions are made at a "low" level between the engineer-designer, functional leads, and assistants to the Chief Engineer as they have the most knowledge and information. Few issues reach the Chief Engineer, because most conflicts are left to be resolved where the problems originated. This is a considerable cultural shift. How many times have we seen problems arise that could have been solved at the local level instead of making them rise up the chain of command? However, the Chief Engineer is the one responsible for leading what was written in the Concept Paper so major system and project-level trade-offs and decisions are managed by him/her. This clear decision-making process reduces the typical delays, slow-downs, discussions, yet more discussions, and appeals for the intervention of this or that manager. At the base of a Lean system, there is always a high degree of trust in the skilled people with an *empowerment* sufficient to ensure confidence and autonomy in the problems' resolution.

3.3.2 What About the Other Departments Not Strictly Related to the Product?

As for departments such as marketing, quality, and purchasing, as well as other staff departments, after their strong involvement in providing input to the Concept Paper in the initial phase, the Chief Engineer pulls in people whenever needed, as well as inviting participation in periodic alignment meetings in the Obeya.

For the development of manufactured goods, production plays a vital role. How should it interact with the rest of the organization during the development of new products?

In many Lean companies, there is a key liaison role between production and design. It is called the *Simultaneous Engineer*. From the world of production engineering, a group of experts working in the plant, are called upon to participate in the subsystem development groups during product development.

From the beginning to the end of the project, they are the people who must represent the voice of manufacturing while coordinating the introduction of the new product into the manufacturing facility.

The Simultaneous Engineers are very experienced people, the ones most familiar with the manufacturing issues, having already experienced and resolved many issues firsthand. They are entrusted with the duty of not repeating the same mistakes of the past, enriching and transmitting their own expertise to the project teams. They also contribute to the engineering checklists which are part of the know-how database for particular product subsystems.

3.4 The Value of Competence

Do the ordinary in an extraordinary way.

Saint Catherine of Siena

The secret to the success of many companies often lies in the specific "technical excellence" in their given industry that they are able to develop in people. Look at the cases of Toyota, Apple, Google, Ferrari, Luxottica, and Samsung where the heart of the success resides in the exceptional quality and uniqueness of their products and in the technical pride with which engineers and developers continue to perform research to unceasingly develop new solutions for their customers.

To develop excellent technical skills in the workforce, it might be inadvisable to excessively rotate personnel in different tasks. This is unusual if we think about employment today and how much more easily people change companies and careers than in the past. However, let's examine some key concepts regarding the development of *technical excellence* in the company. In general, there are two models that represent the paths of development for a company's employees. Both revolve around the position of the letter "T." In one case, the normal "T" model, the employee begins in a specialized area and after having vertically acquired a great deal of experience, is transferred, often as a promotion, to a different job in another part of the company, where they begin to move horizontally, rather than vertically in the organization. The depth and breadth along portions of their "T" are different from case to case. A reasonable "T" path can, for example, be ideal for many managerial roles. The other model, as you can see in Figure 3.2, can be represented by an inverted "T" shape, where an employee starts with

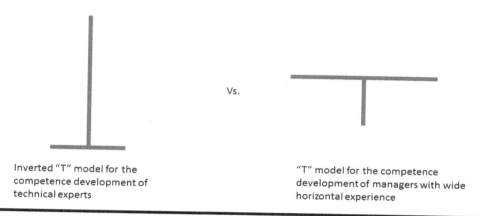

Figure 3.2   **Different T models for the competencies and career development.**

broad path and then proceeds with developing expertise in a certain area, as might happen for an engineer.

3.4.1 *Example: The Typical Development and Career Path of a Toyota Engineer*

As discussed in Liker and Morgan's *The Toyota Product Development System*, Toyota heavily invests upfront and throughout an associate's career in developing their skills. The path of an engineer who joins, for example, the body engineering department, begins with broad exposure and then the development of deep technical competency over several years.

In Japan, the associate begins with a month of general training, for the most part carried out by teachers and mentors within the company. They then spend about three months in a manufacturing plant, as an assembly-line operator and working with production engineers. Afterward, they spend another three months in the sales department, in close contact with end customers, to sell product and often to deal with their complaints. Therefore, the first goal is to become acquainted firsthand with the two essential customers of the fledgling engineer's future designs: the worker who will assemble the product and the customer who will buy it.

These are long-term goals that require a short-term investment. In this apparently uneconomic choice, the new employee is paid a salary of approximately eight months before his or her real potential is ever applied.

So, what is the advantage to this? In the long term, this person is not likely to engineer something that cannot be produced or assembled because four months of that person's life have been spent realizing design choices that do not take into account productive and logistic needs. He or she will think deeply about how to design for the customers, because that person has listened to their grievances and got to know them firsthand. In your opinion, would a designer or engineer simply hired and "thrown" into the job of designing, have the same sensitivity? The ability to understand the profound impact that each tiny point of a design will have in the real world? In your opinion, will the others have the same real knowledge of the company and the market?

But that's not all! After the first eight months, the new engineer will spend another four to eight months doing a "freshman" project with a mentor whose task is to monitor progress and pass on experience and know-how of the technical discipline. They then will spend some time in the Computer-Aided Design department learning the system, so they can engineer at the computer instead of passing on work to a pool of CAD experts. The next step is *"intensive on the job training"* by the mentor on their first project. In Japan, Toyota expects engineers to go through two complete design programs before they are considered a "full engineer," which means it takes from six to eight years to be respected as an autonomous contributor to engineering. Training continues throughout their career as they climb the technical or managerial ladder.

The Toyota approach to developing their people clearly demonstrates the effort and the benefits for companies that continually invest in their people over their entire career within the company.

3.4.2 What Is the Best Way to Develop Human Resources in Your Company?

When we talk about developing such deep technical excellence during our seminars, many people ask if it is anachronistic to invest so much in the initial training of a person. They ask whether it is even feasible, with the strong cost pressures we have, to "waste" time and money this way, especially in light of the great risk that the "highly priced" trained person might then leave the company. They ask if it might not be more profitable to risk less and hire good competent people from the market and place them directly and quickly where they are needed.

Before jumping to this solution yourself, you should consider a few factors. First, ask yourself how much it really costs to recruit highly skilled people brought in from other companies? Can you even find them? How long will it take to integrate them into your culture? Second, if you have people in your company who are not adequately trained, what wastes and costs are you incurring today? Lastly, who will bring you more value, the person who has followed the structured path to develop their skills or the person who has not followed it? Is it better to plan for the long-term success of your company or try to avoid spending time and money with a small number of people who might leave the company?

As one Japanese sensei put it:

> Frustrated Executive: "What if I invest in their training and they leave?"
> Sensei: "What if you don't and they stay?"

3.4.3 *Personnel that Leave and Enter into the Company*

The rate of staff turnover in companies that take the approach of developing expertise with their new recruits is typically much lower. Let us try to understand why, suggesting that it is not the Japanese culture that makes the difference, but the value system that is put in place in a company that truly makes the difference.

Companies achieve long-term results thanks to systems that integrate beliefs and values, principles, philosophy, and processes, which provide the basis for the results themselves. In our experience, this is the receipt used by companies that have achieved exceptional results in any geographical location and in any industry. Let us return to our new employees.

If a company invests up to three years in guided and structured training upfront and continued development afterward, trainees receive the message that the company believes in them, that they are so important to the company's success that a serious investment is being made in their personal development. Over time, we have seen people in these conditions pass up opportunities for higher paying jobs, as long as they continue to be valued and given challenging work. Historically, companies that have the lowest *turnover* rates are not the ones that pay more, but those that have created the social conditions that drive loyalty in the person. First and foremost among these conditions are the values that the company puts into practice. What are some of these values?

1. A belief in the value of developing and sharing knowledge.
2. A mentoring culture, the importance of having a reference point, an internal coach, an expert who is able to provide guidance when there are problems.

3. A culture of encouraging and rewarding personal growth.
4. A culture that continuously challenges its personnel to grow and learn.

These are just some examples that help forge the bond between the individual and the company and grow the human and professional capabilities within the company itself.

3.4.4 School, Apprentices, and Artists

When speaking about people development, some people ask us if it is right that industry has almost replaced traditional schools. It is true that in companies like Denso, Toyota, and Apple, in the "internal training classes" prefer internal teachers to those who come from outside.

This concept reminds us of the distant past, the Italian Renaissance, when in the artisan workshops the master blacksmith taught the apprentice, who went into the workshop to learn from his own master or teacher. This is something we almost never see today, even in places where it should still be a sound rule. In our world, we have lost the culture of handing down experience. However, Lean companies, in spite of modernization at any cost, go back and relearn the "basics" when it is necessary, proving that true innovation can also hide behind methods and systems which have long proved successful in ancient times. For a company, the "craft or occupation" that originated a long time ago is know-how accumulated over time, a mix of techniques and principles that cannot be delegated either to school or external lecturers. The school can provide basic knowledge and encourage the mental openness required to face the complex world of work, but it will never replace the "craft" of the company. Together with the techniques and principles, the values of a company cannot be taught by others, but rather it is the company itself that should teach them and live by them, especially their own managers.

You cannot hope to achieve certain results without first creating the right competence to obtain them, and without running the risk of falling into the wishful thinking typical of many people and many companies: achieving results without the right people and processes to achieve them.

3.4.5 Superstars or Normal, but Competent People?

At the system level, this attention to the corporate standardization of high levels of competence addresses the need for flexibility in selecting the resources to be allocated to a project. Often, we are used to selecting the resources to be allocated to a project by using personal judgments, sympathies, relationships, and competency demonstrated in the field. All valid reasons, but that can become an arbitrary process that values some people over others. There is also the waste of time in negotiating and vying for certain resources to be assigned to one project versus another.

At a company level, it can also cause a loss of flexibility because managers will gravitate to the same people while not giving others a chance to grow. Over time, this leads to overburden for the "high performers" and a stagnation of skills for all the others as they are not given the chance to expand their skills on more challenging projects. It leads to an imbalance of skills across development programs depending on the network and influence of the project leader.

On the contrary, with a standardized system for developing people, the company has more flexibility in effectively utilizing the skills of their people on projects. In addition, the choice of the person to be included in a project becomes more objective (and more peaceful) as people will have more standardized skills. The Chief Engineer does not need to waste time in vying to get the right person for each job, because they know that there is a system that provides a level of skill and that the risks of having less experienced people are mitigated with the mentorship being done by a senior specialist.

3.4.6 Specialists or Generalists?

Developing specialists today remains one of the few hopes for achieving true and sustainable technical excellence. Personally, we have little faith in those companies where one does a little of everything or where supposed technical experts are rotated frequently to ensure they can continue to "progress" in their careers. It's like telling a good heart surgeon to change their specialization after a few years, in order to keep their skills from stagnating. If you are looking for a good reliable heart surgeon, who would you trust more, a specialist who has worked in that field for years or a generalist who has broad exposure by changing jobs every few years?

3.5 Suppliers or Partners: Mirage or Reality?

The biggest mistake you can make is believing you can do everything yourself. After a more than thirty-year career, I still dedicate a lot of time to choose, firsthand, partners and employees, and I am still eager to learn the things I don't know from others.

Renzo Rosso—founder of Diesel

This subject is increasingly debated in many companies. Today, even more than in the past, a significant part of the value of a company's products is determined by outside suppliers. For an automobile, an industrial machine, an electronics, and many others, purchased components can be up to 75% of the final product's cost. Therefore, it should be unthinkable not to apply exactly the same principles we do with our employees to our main suppliers.

For companies with a strong innovation and frequent rapid renewal cycles of its products, it is vital to be surrounded by technically competent suppliers to develop and design new solutions, rather focusing solely on production capability. These key suppliers need to be appropriately involved in the early stages of product development through the use of appropriate management tools, such as pre-development agreements or the use of the supplier's resources located within the customer's company *(e.g. full-time resident engineers)*.

In a company that relies and focuses on innovation, strategic suppliers are managed and trained almost the same way as internal human resources. They are an integral part of the process of generating customer value, and therefore requires close collaboration to be sure the right value is delivered at the right time with the lowest total system cost. Suppliers are a natural extension of our company, and this is the reason we should think of the suppliers as part of our technical departments' extended network.

3.5.1 How Should We Choose Our Supplier-Partners?

For the definition of the relationships and the strategies with suppliers, the goal should always be to look at the total cost generated. The price of the component is not the only cost to be considered, but all the direct and indirect costs connected to that supplier should be taken into account. The costs of transport, internal handling, quality defects, poor technical or production performance, and delays in the delivery of a prototype are just a few examples of what can be avoided by careful selection and development of suppliers. Therefore, it is not simply a matter of assessing how much we pay for the component that we are buying from the supplier, but of *learning to truly assess all the influences that the component will have on the rest of our company and our customers, in the design, production, and sales and services phases of the product.* In production, for example, we could have components that we paid less for, but that lead to unforeseen costs in labor due to logistical or quality issues; in design, we may have difficulty with a "low cost" supplier, who fails to give us suitable solutions for reducing the cost of the product, or who is always late with the delivery of prototypes. Each of these simple examples is unfortunately considered normal waste in many companies and is often hidden in overhead costs.

3.5.2 Different Categories of Suppliers

The purchasing and integration strategies should be determined on the basis of the impact that a supplier carries in relation to the value and costs it generates in the final product. In this sense, we can divide the world of suppliers into three categories (Figure 3.3) depending on the actual effect they have on a business in the long run.

So-called marketplace oriented suppliers require a more basic business relationship as they provide commodity products with relatively low value-add in the product. In this case, we are talking about parts and components with a secondary impact on the final product and process, easily available everywhere, with a level of standardization that does not require special co-design activities. In this case, the more traditional supplier relationship based on production quality, delivery, and cost is important and the company can leverage price and volume to minimize costs.

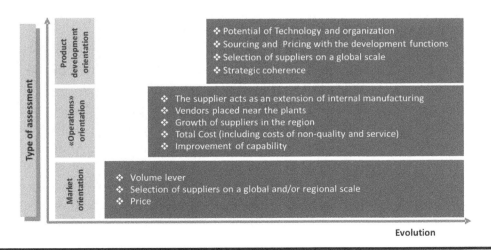

Figure 3.3   Categories of component suppliers.

In the middle range of suppliers are those who have a heavy impact on the production of the product, and then on the performance of the customer's production plant. Nowadays, it is important to properly evaluate the total cost of supply, including the costs of poor quality and level of service, the supplier's ability to continuously improve, and the distance from the customer's factory, because, in this case, the supplier can be considered an extension of the plant's production capacity. This time, the selection criteria should consider the most thorough evaluation factors, typically classifiable in tools and processes of *Vendor Ratings*, that assess the overall performance of the supplier over time, even going to the sites of the supplier to fully evaluate their processes, management, and tools to guarantee the objectives of the final production plant. An example of a Vendor Rating used in the past is shown in Figure 3.4.

Finally, the third category contains those suppliers that design and manufacture strategic parts that greatly impact the performance and/or cost of the final product. With these providers, we must expand the criteria for selection and evaluation from the prior categories. It is clearly absurd to adopt the same criteria for a supplier of screws and a supplier of strategic products such as circuit boards that control the major functions of a product. Unfortunately, this mistake has been made by many companies.

3.5.3 How Do I Know If It Is the Right Supplier for Me?

Choosing a supplier is always important, but when it falls into the third category, it is necessary to pay more attention, given the real impact the choice will have on the entire organization over the long term.

The process of selecting and "developing" a supplier-partner in a Lean organization is, in some ways, similar to the engineers' one within the company we discussed earlier in the chapter. It may take years to develop the skills of a supplier before it becomes an integral part of the organization. This is a process that cannot be driven solely by the final piece price for a given project. In addition, the company's product development capabilities and its willingness to collaborate and learn over time must fit the company's needs and values. In other words, we need to consider the technological, organizational, and management capabilities of the supplier, as well as the cost of their products. For components in this group, *it does not matter so much where in the world the supplier is located, but that the knowledge and the capabilities delivered can truly make the difference to my*

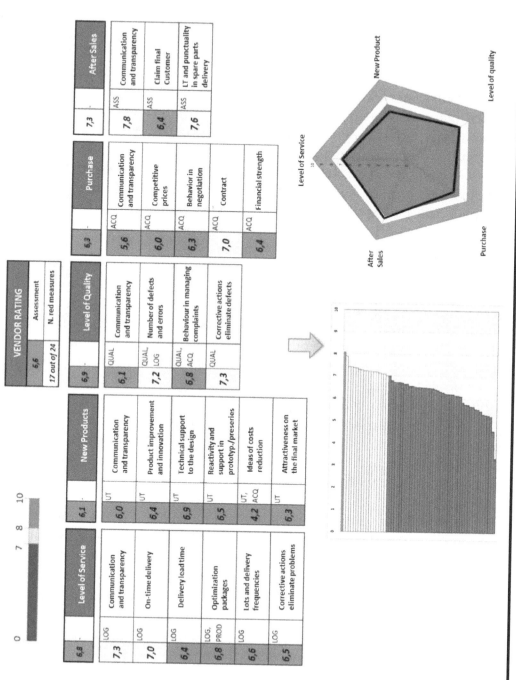

Figure 3.4   Example of Lenovys model for evaluation of key suppliers.

product and my process. There are specific factors that, in our experience, should be evaluated before the final choice. These are not the only factors, but they represent a useful base for understanding if you are choosing the right supplier-partner.

1. *Uniqueness*. The ability to deliver components, modules, and services with distinctive and unique features in terms of functionality, price, or other intangibles such as styling. Generally, it is decided to try this type of company, evaluating new concepts for a product or service not yet offered by other partner suppliers.

2. *Complementarity*. The ability to integrate the supplier into our Value Stream. This requires time to evaluate the actual performance of a new supplier as it relates to product development, production, and product support. It is best to start with a small, low-volume project to see if the potential partner and the company can fit.

3. *Speed*. In the early stages of product development, it is vital to be quick. The evaluation of this aspect of our suppliers is often underestimated. Think how important it is, for example, to quickly understand the new technical requirements, provide multiple concepts, build and deliver the required prototypes, carry out the required product testing, and send the results. For critical components, this can make or break your project timing.

4. *Aptitude for improvement*. During the development of any new product, it will be impossible to avoid changes and "adjustments" based on learnings from testing and field evaluations of the first prototypes. A supplier who is unable to adapt, improve, and propose fast new solutions will undoubtedly create problems and delays in the development process.

5. *Willingness to invest*. It is important that our budding partners have the desire and ability to invest with us to receive greater benefits for both, over time. This is not a purely speculative matter, but it involves an assessment of the supplier's predisposition and orientation over the long-term. In other words, do we see that our new supplier is more interested in working with us to find the right solutions or are they more focused on getting paid for every little change that happens during the development? Do they spend the time to "go and see" at their customer's technical center? Do they invest time and effort in developing their own suppliers?

In order to assess the above factors, it is best to start slowly and gradually build the relationship with a potential supplier-partner. For example, a small project could be used to start to test their product development capabilities in terms of generating innovative concepts, developing robust designs, delivering prototypes, and testing capabilities. In addition, it could be best to stipulate the initial contract for a small volume project so that you can become better acquainted with each other over the long term and mitigate risk to your company. Based on the first product cycle, the company can then decide whether the relationship is growing as planned and continue with more challenging and larger volume projects. As a caution, the faster a new partner is pushed into a business, the greater the risk is of spending extra time and money later on to remedy the situation that turned out not to be in line with the strategies and values. Take your time to properly assess and develop your key supplier-partners and you will come out with better products while reducing a lot of waste in your product development Value Stream.

3.6 Constant Learning and Continuous Improvement

> There can be no knowledge without humility and willingness to learn.
>
> **Mahatma Gandhi**

The ability to learn and improve is the greatest sustainable competitive advantage for individuals and companies. Those who know how to learn the quickest from the market, from their own mistakes, from their competitors, and from their suppliers will be more prepared to make major gains. Those who seek to continually improve their activities, without necessarily waiting for "big" changes, but by taking small steps every day, will be more inclined to achieve truly sustainable excellence in their industry.

Tactically speaking, this can only be done in one way: it must be practiced every day in everything we do and encouraged by our management. In Lean companies, there is an overarching belief that the full potential of the individual and company can only be realized by developing the ability to learn, and aim for continuous improvement, *kaizen,* as a personal and professional way of life. This approach is what makes continuous corporate growth sustainable and therefore must be felt as an important value at all levels, from the management to the workforce.

3.6.1 Big Initiatives

A company that embraces Lean values at a deep level is not obsessed with the big initiatives typical in many corporations. For example, *six sigma* or *world-class manufacturing* projects, or Lean Manufacturing itself, are all too often treated as mechanistic tools for corporate improvement and not as a set of values and principles that can be practically applied to continuously improve.

In some cases, these major initiatives are launched with great fanfare, formally structured, fully fledged, and chock-full of report outs on improvements that have been made and the money saved. A number of managers are giving more attention to the tool and the initial results than the actual process of cultural change and sustainable development of new beliefs in people. It often happens that these major initiatives then begin sinking, more or less gradually, and people do not understand why.

There might be great initiative from time to time, the so-called *kaikaku* or "radical improvement," but it is the everyday kaizen lead by individuals and small teams that leads to the steady sustainable improvements in world-class companies.

3.6.2 Learning and Continuous Improvement: Visible and Invisible Knowledge

While knowledge management is a well-discussed subject in industry and academia, many companies struggle with it. Part of the challenge is defining what is knowledge and recognizing that it comes in different forms. One category is *explicit knowledge* or more generally, "information." The other is *implicit* or *tacit knowledge*, or generally, "latent know-how." We can find explicit knowledge in many streams of information that flow into the company. Posters, cards, procedures, operational information, and emails are just a few examples that represent forms of knowledge and information provided at all levels in the company. It is easily codified into the form of facts, idiomatic phrases, and is transferable without much loss in the transmission. Sometimes it makes us smile to see the pictures framed and hung on the walls of the offices in which the company's Vision and Mission statements are prominently displayed. Often, it is a good example of explicit knowledge, but a bad example of tacit knowledge, when they do not line up with the real corporate culture and values experienced in the company. And in many cases, we see that many people do not even remember what is written in those framed pictures.

The more difficult knowledge to share is the tacit knowledge. It is knowledge that is not transferred in simple, linear ways. In fact, it is sometimes difficult to draw out. "We know it exists," but we cannot always see it. It often happens in the company that we know things about a number of topics, many details, and a great deal of information that is not however captured anywhere. We sometimes know who has that precious information and where to find it. If we don't, it can take time to find it or, worse, we move on without it and repeat the same mistakes. This confirms the fact that the layered knowledge built up over the years in people and in the company is not only complex and deeper than we might believe, but it is also difficult to transfer because it requires close ties between people and a lot of time to learn. When someone is able to decipher, organize, and share this type of knowledge, a true strategic competitive advantage can be clearly gained by the company.

3.6.3 Making the Intangible Tangible

Every time we create the right conditions for hidden know-how to emerge and make it available to colleagues, several positive things happen. Through this passage of conceptual transformation, both the person who possesses the information and the person receiving it are enriched. Consequently, this helps to enhance the business's learning culture, which, even if it is so difficult to measure, it is so strategic to determining success over the long run.

Several methods and tools can be used to capture, share, and further grow tacit knowledge both within and outside of the company. Some examples seen at companies such as Toyota include:

Supplier know-how exchanges. Through regular and structured sessions of technology "demonstrations" in areas of interest organised by suppliers, it is possible to share new concepts, technologies, and tools in a structured way. This provides access to new ideas, due to having a view of new solutions that are just outside the borders of the company. Companies can also broaden this approach by exchanges with other companies or institutions in other industries to gain new and innovative knowledge.

Benchmarking: internally and external competition. The benchmarking phase that in technical jargon is called the *teardown*, a competitor's product is taken apart piece by piece, in order to learn from it, quantify the costs, decode the production technology used and study everything that can be gleaned by dismantling the product.

When there are no physical products, a great deal can be learned from the services offered by the competition about their strengths and weaknesses, or about how to run similar activities in our own companies. This same activity can be extended to the internal aspect of your business. There are often situations where three or four people from the same company theoretically do the same thing, but in reality, no one knows what the other does, either because they are in different offices or countries or because they simply do not have the habit of making comparisons to learn from each other.

It is not unusual to see two or more people doing more or less the same thing in a large company, but obtaining different results. In these cases, it is useful to have systematic comparisons so that the best methods can be standardized and shared to all.

On the other hand, avoid the "copying blindly" trap. Even what seems to be a straightforward "best practice" often works within the context you are observing based on the leadership, skills, and culture, or the technical process. Blindly copying also kills creativity. The spirit of kaizen is to always try to improve on what you see others do when solving your own internal problems.

Know-how database. Already addressed in a prior section of the book, the know-how database represents a great container of information, and is designed to make access to information easier and more intuitive when needed. All relevant information related to products, processes, guidelines, available checklists, the test results, the performance of existing and new projects, and lessons learned from the past will find a place here. In this case too, however, we always put people on their guard from becoming enamored with the tool rather than the content and especially the process of updating and effective use of the knowledge within it. It is never the brilliant IT solution alone that makes a difference, but the dense network of collaborations and healthy habits that are created around the tools that make the difference.

Problem-solving and A3 Reports focused on learning. Through this type of process, which will be analyzed in detail in the next chapter, a double objective is pursued. On one side, there is the objective of having a standardized method for resolving company problems. On the other hand, there is the objective of capturing the learning on a single A3 page.

Conferences and meetings of project managers and functional managers. Through periodical meetings, once or twice a year, for example, project leaders and managers from different parts of the company can meet to discuss what they have learned from their projects, to compare different implementation methods, and establish any new agreed-upon management standards.

Special Projects Teams. These are cross-functional teams that can do analysis and improvement projects on a specific topic, such as the decision to adopt a new CAD-CAM design tool in the company, or to enter into a particular business, or a new management software, or to explore a new technology that has never been used before. These working groups could even break away from daily activities for several months to focus on the new project. Toyota also has a special category of "business revolution teams." Prius began in a business revolution team.

Skills matrices and career paths for growth. The paths of growth in a Lean company are always a mix of classroom training and *on the job training,* where the role of the mentor is often covered by one's own boss and promotion paths depend on developing and demonstrating the skills. A *skills matrix* can be used to visually show the skills acquired and the gaps in learning for the employee to help them develop expertise over time.

Resident Engineers. Exchanges between suppliers and the company can facilitate integration during the development of complex products and can help to promote the standardization of methods and tools used by both the supplier and customer. Over the long-term, it can also assist in transferring tacit knowledge between organizations.

Hansei. These are moments of structured reflection, simple but very effective. Given its importance to the Lean enterprise, we have devoted Section 4.4 to cover it in more detail.

Summary of KeyPoints in Chapter 3

1. *Jointly sustain productivity and well-being.* At the heart of a company's success is the capacity to involve people deeply, touching on both the emotional, intangible sphere and the rational, tangible one, in the path of innovation and continuous improvement.
2. *Lean Leadership as a model to guide behavior.* Individuals need the passion to self-develop leadership skills which are both technical and social

skills for executing and improving processes. Self-developing leaders then develop others who ultimately lead small work groups in daily kaizen. A well-developed hierarchy of leaders who know how to lead improvement can achieve astonishing aligned objectives. Organizational learning as the cornerstone for the systematic improvement of the entire company.

3. *Ensure a unified vision for the development of new products by choosing strong Project Leaders.* This strategy aims to eliminate waste from hand-offs up and down the leadership chain, lack of synchronization, poor understanding of customer needs, and other transactional wastes during the development and launch of new products. The Project Leader (Chief Engineer) becomes the real "parent" of the project.

4. *Balance technical competency with cross-functional skills in the company.* This strategy is important in order to enable growth and excellence in its own sector, without losing sight of the customer requirements of products and processes necessary for an effective launch of products in the marketplace.

5. *The value of developing deep technical competency.* In a world where everyone seems to try to do everything, knowing how to cultivate top-flight expertise guarantees the ability to design robust products and processes that distinguish themselves from the competition. Remember that the design process influences up to 70% of the entire cost of the product.

6. *Distinguish the different categories of suppliers and choose development partners wisely.* A large part of the value of our products is now "possessed" by our suppliers. It is strategic to ensure we are flanked by the right partners, capable of increasing the value of our products and services.

7. *The culture of organizational learning and continuous improvement.* Know how to value the invisible knowledge residing in our people and suppliers through processes and tools designed to continually help our company grow.

Resource

https://www.lenovys.com/en/blog/emotional-energy/

Notes

1. Kramer S.J., Amabile T.M., 2011.
2. Liker J.K., Convis G., 2012. *The Toyota Way to Lean Leadership*, McGraw-Hill.
3. *The Toyota Way 2001*, Internal Document, Toyota Motor Corporation, Nagoya, Japan.
4. Rother, M., 2009. *Toyota Kata: Managing People for Improvement, Adaptiveness and Superior Results,* N.Y.: McGraw Hill.
5. Morgan J., Liker J.K., 2006.

Chapter 4

Tools for a Lean and Innovative Company

We have emphasized that tools alone do not make great product or process development. Tools do not innovate. Yet tools can be a key enabler. When we think of engineering tools, we often think of sophisticated computer technology for visualization and analysis like solid modeling, rapid prototyping, virtual caves to view the product in 3D, product life cycle management, and the list goes on. These are all remarkable tools, but ultimately they only become remarkable through the creative minds of people. Since computer tools are richly described in many outlets, in this section of the book, we will intentionally focus on simpler tools aimed at enhancing creativity and teamwork; pragmatic tools, which are easy to use but capable of making a profound impact on the performance of product development. In our view, if the organization is incapable of timely design of products and processes that add tremendous value to the customer and provide a competitive edge to the company without dazzling technological tools, the tools themselves will not make a material difference. The tools of an innovative company motivated to achieving superior results with less effort are often simple, correctly sized, and, above all, supporting of their people and processes. These tools are viewed as performance accelerators rather than as technological "anchors" with which processes and people must necessarily comply.

4.1 Criteria for Choosing the Right Tools

> The way to build a complex system that works is to build it from
> very simple systems that work.
>
> **Kevin Kelly**

Nowadays, it is possible to purchase technology and software applications
just like our closest competitor, but this will rarely offer the guarantee of
obtaining superior results. Why? The secret is not in the individual tool, but
in the ability to adapt it to our own processes and people, customizing it
and integrating it into our company's systems so that it becomes unique
in the way it is effectively used. In many businesses, there is a tendency
to hope that the tool of the moment, for example, an innovative piece of
software, will drastically improve performance in the sector for which it
is designed. In fact, when buying such tools, the questions most typically
asked are: How will this software add to our productivity? How can we
justify the purchase? How much money will it save us? How can we obtain
the maximum from this new technology, spending as little as possible? How
many people can it replace? After the purchase of the "latest and greatest" it
is realized that a lot of work is required to modify our processes to obtain
the maximum from the new technology.

A Lean company has done a lot of work before even considering the new
technology. They know that trying to automate a poor process with disen-
gaged people will have a negative effect.

Bill Gates once said:

> The first rule of any technology used in a business is that automa-
> tion applied to an efficient operation will magnify the efficiency.
> The second is that automation applied to an inefficient operation
> will magnify the inefficiency.

This explains why Lean companies invest so much time in the selection
and subsequent customization of software before making it operative. The
reigning conviction is that *efficient processes and well-developed people can
only be helped, never replaced, by tools, in their ongoing journey of continuous improvement.*

In our view, the enormous amount of time spent by many companies
to get new tools, often bought with undue haste, implement them and run

them should make us all reflect. To help us avoid the pitfalls, a few criteria should be considered prior to adopting any new tool or technology.

1. Integration and ease of use;
2. Support of processes;
3. Support people;
4. Reinforce standardization;
5. Enable organizational alignment;
6. Assist organizational learning.

4.1.1 Criteria 1: Integration and Ease of Use

It is always important to ask ourselves if the technology can be easily integrated into our existing processes and systems. Does it interface readily with them? Is it easily accessible to those who will need it? This will facilitate its use by ensuring a reduction in time wasted as a result of having to search for information or changeover between systems on one's own workstation. Think how many software packages that an engineer might use during the development of a new product. These might include software for CAD, simulation, product releases, product standards, change orders, cost estimating, and project management just to name a few. Thinking ahead about the time of the people who will need to use the tools will help us to reduce at the beginning many kinds of waste that only become clear after the implementation.

In many Lean companies, simple tools and complex software coexist in single integrated platforms designed to simplify access and guarantee maximum facility of use.

In Figure 4.1 you will find an example taken from one of our Lean Product and Process Development projects: you can see how the accessibility of the various tools that can be used for the development of a new product for each phase of a development project has been granted. Many tools have been already discussed in prior chapters and others will be discussed later in this chapter. Many of them are simple, non-technological tools which can provide great value in each phase in which they are used.

Often, we carry out full-blown "clean-up" operations of the dozens of tools, big and small, that proliferate the company. It invariably turns out that several are already in use in the company, and just require some optimization, a little standardization, and integration with other existing tools. Others may be missing altogether, but in this case, they are introduced with great

BASIC TOOLS	Phase 1 CONCEPT	Phase 2 KENTOU	Phase 3 DESIGN	Phase 4 ASSEMBLY	Phase 5 TEST	Phase 6 AFTER SALES
Introduction to Lean product Development	Guidelines Concept phase	Guidelines of Kentou phase	Guidelines of Design phase	Guidelines of Assembly phase	Guidelines Test phase	Guidelines After Sales phase
Problem Solving	Reflection (*hansei*)	Reflection (*hansei*)	Reflection (*hansei*)	Reflection (*hansei*)	Reflection (*hansei*)	Final Project Reflection
Diagram of Ishikawa	Concept Paper	Kentou	Fundoshi Scheduling	FMEA Assembly	Final Validation Test	Valid. Customer Report
Analysis of the 5 Why	Project Review System	Tear Down	Enginering Checklist	Assembly Plan	Report Final Test	
Action Plan	Obeya System	Enginering Checklist	Tear Down	Assembly Validation		
Quick Setup	Trade-off Curves	Evaluation Matrix	Design to Cost	Assembly Report		
OEE	VRP Assessment	VRP Assessment	Error Proofing collect.			
List of criticalities	Error Proofing collect.	Progettazione Modulare	FMEA Assembly			
	Market Analysis	Design FMEA	Design For...			
	Target Cost deploym.	Investment Cost Plann.	FMECA			
	Range plan	Target Cost deploym.	Design Review			
	Risk Assessment	Make or Buy				

Figure 4.1 Example of a Product Development Tool Box integrated into the systems of a company.

care, following the six criteria described in this chapter so that they become an effective part of the product development system.

4.1.2 Criteria 2: Support of Processes

Technology must support the process, not control it. Sometimes we are attracted by the sirens of consultants and salespeople anxious to sell us the latest technology "solution" in order to not remain behind the times. But the following two aspects should be considered very carefully.

1. Nowadays, thechnology evolves much faster than the processes themselves. Today's state-of-the-art will be superseded tomorrow. We could renew all the tools and software in a company every year, but whether it is really worth doing it is doubtful.
2. Every time a process is changed in order to pursue a new technology, we can encounter instability, confusion among the people involved, and wasted time and resources. For this reason, it is advisable to seriously evaluate the impact (total cost and time) of introducing any new tool, and usually try a pilot before spreading the tool broadly.

This does not mean that we should not exploit the opportunities offered by technology. Quite the opposite. It means that it might be worth shifting our focus onto the result we want to obtain with the tool, rather than focusing on the tool itself.

If the same result can be obtained with a simpler or even an already existing tool, with a lot less effort, why waste precious energy? Among many possible examples, one that springs to mind is the use of tools for planning and managing projects. Sometimes people opt for complex computer tools, ranging from elaborate spreadsheet files to specialized project management software, even in cases where the result could be achieved much more effectively and with much less effort with simpler methods like the visual management tools described in Section 4.2.

4.1.3 Criteria 3: Support People

In a company guided by the talent and technical competence of its people, technology should be at their service, so as to maximize their value and that talent, while reducing wasted time.

Tools and technology can never replace human competencies, but they can enable people to do more. Often, a lot of reworking in the development of products and processes is due to a lack of synchronization between the people's activities in different departments.

An example of this could be the following one. An engineer changes something in their design, which has an impact on a piece of production equipment or on another person's design, but due to the absence of systems capable of ensuring other colleagues are rapidly informed of the change, it becomes unobserved, only then to require corrective solutions later on, which causes inefficiency and reworking.

On the other hand, a CAD system really designed to support people is based on a parametric design software, so that every time a design is modified, the users of all the other designs connected with it are informed. Colleagues are alerted in real time with color codes about the modification made. This enables a waste reduction due to synchronization and avoidable repetition of activities.

4.1.4 Criteria 4: Reinforce Standardization

On various occasions in this book, we have seen that one of the principles of Lean Thinking is standardization. This principle should apply even to the tools that are used, both to verify that they are coherent and integrated with other existing systems, and to genuinely support the company's efforts of standardization of products, competencies, and processes. Design tools, for instance, should enhance ease of use and sharing within and outside the company, when we collaborate with the resources of suppliers for certain technical activities. For example, we can adopt tools that favor technical standardization, as in case of tools that rapidly find common parts, so an engineer can reuse the knowledge rather than create a new part from scratch.

Other tools can favor the standardization of processes, as in all cases where "process standards" are created. This development of tools can promote standardization of methods ensuring more consistent results and leading towards a common standard that stimulates continuous improvement.

4.1.5 Criteria 5: Enable Organizational Alignment

An important element of any project and organization is to have shared goals and an aligned vision. When these are missing, there will inevitably be enormous amounts of waste deriving from poor communication and a proliferation in the number of different directions taken by individual people. Tools should be clearly evaluated to ensure this does not happen. Some Lean tools and techniques that can help greatly in the process of alignment include:

1. *Concept Paper.* As presented in detail in Section 2.2, in our view, it is an indispensable tool for defining, aligning and structuring a successful project.
2. *Hoshin Kanri.* This is a tool that supports the elaboration and sharing of the company's strategy. It is sometimes called Strategy Deployment. The tool in itself is a simple sheet of A3 paper, on which the following aspects of the company's strategy are cogently summarized and linked together:
   a. The company's strategic goals.
   b. The tactical objectives of the year in progress, with a quantification of expected results
   c. The projects necessary to obtain the expected results
   d. The operative processes and key indicators which allow progress to be monitored
   e. The responsibilities of the individual people involved for each of the projects and objectives
   Generally drawn up every year in Lean companies, this process ensures a strong sharing of goals and overall vision. It is conducted in a "cascade" at the different hierarchical levels of the company and across functions. Personally, we adore this tool, because it can be used by

any size organization from a small entrepreneur to the large multinational. Several companies including Toyota, Ford, Intel, and Proctor and Gamble use this approach.

3. *Obeya System.* We will examine this tool in more detail in Section 4.2. It ensures better alignment and communication between people during a project by making the project's goals and activities more visible.

4.1.6 Criteria 6: Assist Organizational Learning

Many businesses spend a lot of money on Knowledge Management tools, enormous on-line databases that are the state-of-the-art in terms of hardware and software. But despite the massive investments, many continue to have serious difficulties in making organizational learning a genuine and solid source of competitive advantage over rival firms. As discussed in Section 3.6, a key strategic lever in a company consists of its tacit knowledge, the profound know-how possessed by the people working in the company, and their ability to share and re-use it.

When the tool is pursued more than the people involved and processes implemented, the return on investment of these tools in terms of knowledge sharing is quite low. On the contrary, the focus should be on tools that help companies to change the way they work in order to bring out of the people the submerged tacit knowledge.

Below are some examples of tools that can effectively support organizational learning.

1. *Hansei.* We will cover this in detail in Section 4.4. A simple but very powerful organizational and social tool, used to support individuals and working groups in learning and continuous improvement.

2. *A3 Report.* We will look at this in detail in Section 4.3. It is a tool which is emblematic of the whole Lean organization, because it embraces a number of principles at the same time.

3. *Know-how database/Engineering Checklists.* Already mentioned in Section 2.8, this is a system that gathers together and makes available to everyone the layers of knowledge about products and processes that exist in a company. In a Lean business, this database is always built and maintained by the users themselves, who transmit and update the fruits of their knowledge. Subdivision into specific sections helps people to find and reuse the knowledge such as standards, guidelines, manufacturing processes, lists of common parts, etc.

4. *Evaluation Matrix*. This can be used for decision-making during the development of a product or process such as during the Set-Based Concurrent Engineering process. We will see how such matrixes are used in various case studies presented in Chapter 5.

5. *Single-Point Lessons(SPL)*. In classic "A3" style, this involves condensing in a page a very specific topic to teach in any given area of a company. The goal is to reduce the time required to understand the content, using images more than words, and focusing on clear, succinct, and effective messages. Generally, SPLs are positioned near points where they can be useful, such as offices and production plants.

6. *SOP (Standard Operating Procedure)*. A tool that helps to standardize all the processes used in a business: this is a Lean version of traditional procedures. The difference is in the type of processes represented, the aim being to eliminate waste, and in the way they are represented, with the objective of being easy to understand and accessible to anyone who needs them. This tool, therefore, has a dual function: standardization and organizational learning.

4.2 The Obeya

To make yourself understood to the people one must first speak to their eyes.

Napoleon

One of the fundamental instruments used in the management of Lean Innovation projects is the Obeya. "Obeya" is a Japanese word meaning "big room," and it became a common word of the Lean lexicon after Chief Engineer Takeshi Uchiyamada introduced it at the end of the 1990s to indicate the method of communication and alignment adopted in the project for the new Toyota Prius. With this method, Uchiyamada managed to reduce the time it took for various team members involved in the project to highlight issues and communicate with each other. This helped to avoid the typical errors arising from a lack of alignment between goals, priorities, and technical decisions that needed to be made by the work team.

Results were so surprising that Toyota universally adopted the same method, after further refinement and standardization, to all subsequent projects. Methods similar to the Obeya room can also be found in the West. In some cases, they are similar to the Anglo-American-style "war rooms."

What they have in common is that they display the information relevant to the project to every member of the team, besides creating a private, focused working environment where it is possible to optimally integrate different resources to solve problems more quickly.

After having analyzed the Japanese Obeya method and comparing it to other types of rooms used in Western Europe and the United States, we have seen several very good elements which are discussed in the following sections.

4.2.1 The Effectiveness of Different Means of Communication

When we interact with other people, our cerebral activity increases in relation to the degree to which its "communication systems" and the senses are activated simultaneously. As you can see in Figure 4.2, cerebral activation increases according to the type of communication technique we use. When we have to align ourselves with a group of people, emails are the poorest method, because they are one-directional. There is no scope for immediate engagement and clarification with our addressee. We cannot explain all the details in the body of an email without becoming long-winded and inefficient, so it is not always clear what the recipient has understood. Often, we receive unclear, late, or worst of all no feedback, leading to uncertainty of genuine alignment among all stakeholders. In addition, of course, there is the basic drawback of not being able to see with our own eyes the real reactions of the people we are sending the email to. The telephone is more immediate and effective than email, but it is still a "poor" communicative tool for the purposes of alignment within a team, because it is not possible

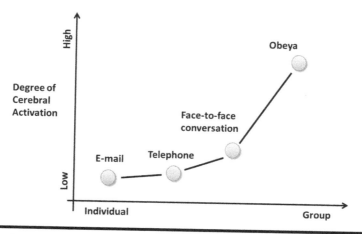

Figure 4.2   Variations in cerebral activation according to the communicative tool.

to see our teammates or to know if they are truly listening or multitasking during the conference call. In face-to-face dialogue, on the other hand, things improve greatly, because there is enormous potential for making alignments easily thanks to direct communication. However, we often have face-to-face discussions with a limited number of people at a time.

With the Obeya approach, we can achieve maximum effectiveness, because it combines the advantages of direct dialogue with the support of a systematic method designed specifically to optimize the entire flow of dialogue within the whole team. With the support of the various physical and visual media available in the room, we are able to gain maximum communication and alignment in a short period of time. Let's look at the method in more detail, because it contains many invaluable ideas that can be applied to any kind of project.

4.2.2 The Importance of Distances

I will start with the importance of communication in an R & D project, and the key factors that can enhance it. Project performance depends directly on the quality of the communication between all the members of the project itself. But the quality of communication depends on the physical distance between the different team members, as was demonstrated back in the preinternet era in important research conducted at the MIT by Thomas Allen and Alan Fusfeld.[1]

This may appear to be an obvious conclusion, but when we observe the real physical conditions in which teams operate or the real spatiotemporal distances between various people in a project's today, we realize that only very rarely are projects organized to favor rapid communication from the beginning, through the elimination of the physical distance among team members. The Obeya is realized taking this concept into consideration. It is a shared space, with a number of "communication accelerators." They are useful for obtaining maximum performance, combining processes and new habits through simple visual tools, designed to support the whole project. The goals of this system are the following ones:

- Guide and accelerate the flow of the project through the product development Value Stream.
- Improve communication and collaboration between all the people involved.
- Quickly highlight the issues (it is the "andon system" of the project).

- Speed up team-based problem-solving.
- Standardize communication within the project team.
- Minimize and simplify reporting to stakeholders.
- Converge toward (and increase) the level of satisfaction of external and internal customers.

The Obeya room becomes a kind of "home-room" where the team can meet, work, and share information: the Chief Engineer, or Project Leader, is generally based in the Obeya room for the duration of the project and meets his or her team members on a regular basis over there. All the team meetings and key activities take place in the Obeya. Meetings with suppliers and customers can also held in the Obeya room, unless there is a specific need for confidentiality. All the information (technical, financial, scheduling, etc.) concerning the project is displayed in the room and it reflects the information contained in the Concept Paper, in order to keep the focus on the project goals. Meetings generally take place standing up, with the project leader and team members walking the walls of the room, discussing issues and exceptions of the project on the given day.

4.2.3 Setting Up an Obeya Room

The Obeya is structured according to a shared idea of the team on how to organize the given space. Figure 4.3 shows an example of a basic layout adopted by one of the many teams we have worked with in recent years. Each team establishes its own standards to satisfy the project requirements, and the structure and layout of the room itself evolve along with the project. Each subgroup of the team has its own section of the room, and is responsible for keeping its content constantly up-to-date.

The system is designed to facilitate the application of other principles discussed in previous sections of this book. For instance, we have described on various occasions the negative effect of wanting to do too many activities all at once. We can see how the Obeya can help us. If we look at the example illustrated in Figure 4.4, the Obeya has already been designed with this kind of problem in mind, and there is a special section devoted to this *week's issues,* in order to focus the team's attention on the few critical problems that need to be solved now, without having on the table more problems than can be actually addressed. Repeating this method, the team gradually trains itself to tackle and solve only a few problems at a time. This visualization of small batches of work helps to focus on the scarce resources of the

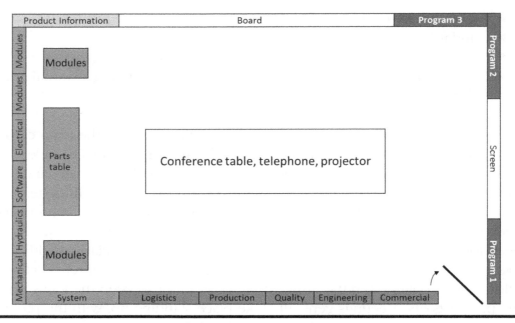

Figure 4.3   Example of a layout design for an Obeya room.

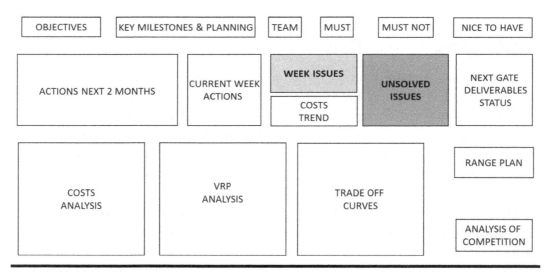

Figure 4.4   Example of subsections in an Obeya room.

team and helps the project to gain speed. In Figure 4.4, you can also see a section devoted to the visual representation of the main parts of the Concept Paper: goals, key milestones and planning, team, must, must not, nice to have—everything needed to keep the team focused on what is value-added to the customer from the start to the end.

4.2.4 Seeing for Yourself

Besides the tangible visualization of data, documents, and work plans, the Obeya room is often used as a place where concrete things can be seen first-hand, instead of having to describe and interpret them, often badly. In other words, an effective Obeya is not just a room full of indicators but it rather helps to visualize not only the project but also the *product*. In one of our projects, the production manager had spent several weeks trying in vain to explain to a designer the non-feasibility of a technical solution produced according to given specifications. This was slowing down the whole project. The suggestion to quickly build a mockup and organize a meeting in the Obeya resolved the matter in a few days, because the engineers were able to "see" the issue better and propose a change even before the meeting got underway. The communicative force of physical objects, visual displays, and real contact is so strong in comparison with all other forms of virtual communication that, through the Obeya method, we try to extend this approach to every possible issue during a project.

Figure 4.5 shows part of an actual Obeya space in action. At the end, simplicity is the key to a successful Obeya. It is not a question of fancy big rooms with the latest gadgets to impress management. Often, moveable panels with sticky notes that can easily be modified

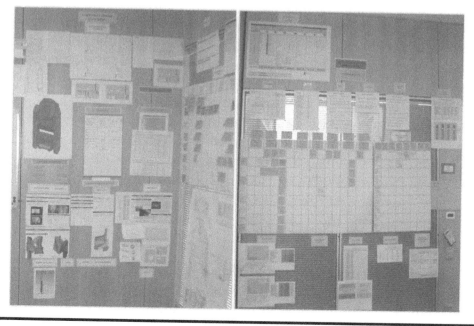

Figure 4.5   Two real cases of an Obeya room.

and shifted around as the project progresses are sufficient. In fact, this approach is more flexible than other technological solutions and it is very cheap!

In the example in Figure 4.5, you can see that project plans and activities were not produced with traditional Project Management tools, even though it was a complex project lasting almost eighteen months. In fact, the team decided to use a quarterly macro plan of activities combined with a detailed ten-day plan, both with large sheets of paper and colored sticky notes to manage their activities and issues.

In the example of Figure 4.5, we can also see another simple but very important Lean tool, the A3 Report, to help us solve problems once they have been identified in Obeya. We will discuss A3 in the following section.

For particularly innovative projects, it is difficult to predict exactly what will happen over a long period of time. So, rather than wasting time trying to work out the details of lots of activities that are difficult to predict with accuracy, it is preferable to fix key future appointments and look with greater attention at short-term activities, periods, using simple, flexible tools such as whiteboards, sheets of paper, and sticky notes.

In fact, for some projects, each team member receives five sticky notes by the Program Manager, to identify the main activities to do in the upcoming period (e.g. the "Top 5" mission critical items for this month). After having negotiated and reached agreement on the activities, the sticky notes are placed on the shared board. After that, they are constantly monitored with red or green color coding to indicate their current status during the month. At the end of the month, the process repeats itself.

Visuals are easy to modify, simple and tactile. They are more than sufficient for the purposes of most projects—this is a further confirmation that it is not the tool we use that determines the success of a team. On the contrary, it is the process that is used in Obeya in conjunction with the high degree of engagement of the team members that leads to superior results. And paradoxically, the more complex the project, the greater the benefits.

4.3 Simplify Communication and Learning with A3

It's better to say little but well rather than a lot but badly.

Anonymous

Imagine how you would feel if you were asked to report on a complex technical challenge, or a status on a large project, or actions being done to resolve a difficult problem, and then you were told that it had to fit in the analysis on a single sheet of paper. Well, this is the essence of Lean Thinking: making the effort to filter and refine your thoughts so they fit onto a single sheet of paper so that anyone who is affected by the particular subject can find their answers just by reading that one sheet. In the Lean terminology, this sheet is now universally known as the "A3 Report."

A3 Reports are a key tool both in the process of communication during projects and in the process of continual learning. For this reason, it can be used in a variety of ways: when we want to communicate the current status of a project, when we want to prepare a proposal for a new opportunity, and when we want to work to solve a problem.

In every case, the true effort that needs to be made is to try to think and represent the topic on a single sheet of A3 paper. Constraining the author to go to the heart of matters, using only the data, facts, and figures to represent the core of the issue, drives a real mental discipline, unlike other tools. Getting everything into one page forces us to be effective in what we think, say, and write, and to make a methodical effort before communicating things to others. For example, arriving at a meeting that has been called to solve a problem or examine the state of progress of a project with an A3 report already drafted up saves lots of time for all the participants and gives them in advance many answers to questions that would crop up in the meeting itself. The meeting can thus move on to a higher level of resolving issues and making sound decisions as a team.

Figure 4.6 illustrates a template of an A3 report used for Problem-Solving.

An A3 Problem Solving Report is used when there is a plan, objective, or standard that is not being achieved. Readers with experience in the automobile manufacturing industry will probably have seen a similar model called "8D," which originated in Ford, or other similar models.

Sometimes we have seen these "one-page reports" used just because people were "forced" to do so by the customers or by their boss, and not because it is really part of the culture of learning and continuous improvement. Once again, it is not the document itself that makes the difference, but the process that lies behind it. The A3 Problem Solving Report is structured in logical steps, to be followed one by one, in order to avoid jumping to the conclusions, as often happens, before having clearly understood what has happened and why it has happened.

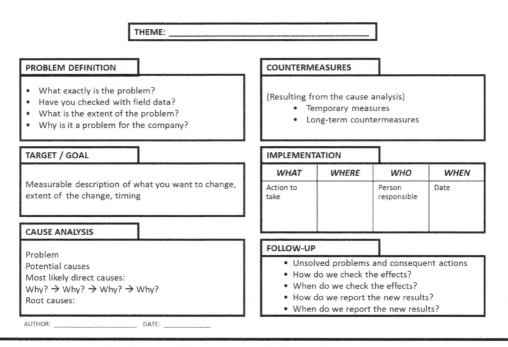

Figure 4.6   Example of a model for an A3 Problem Solving Report.

Every A3 Report always has a single author who is the owner of the process, and the date of the last update. The starting point is the description of the issue encountered and the clear definition of the problem. The first step is to try to gather data and facts for a thorough description of the problem itself, because expressing the problem well is often already part of the solution. The current situation is defined as a standard that has not been met. The extent of the problem is described together with the importance for the company to solve it. After having described the problem thoroughly, the next step is to set the objective in measurable terms. This will involve defining what we want to achieve: what, how much, by when, and how to measure it. The following step moves on to analysis and reasearch of the root cause of the stated problem. Classic problem-solving tools can be used here, such as the "5 whys," the Fishbone diagrams, and more advanced tools in the case of particularly complex problems.

Consequently, the countermeasures will be worked out in relation to the root cause found. In some cases, we may organize alternative countermeasures and evaluate them carefully before making a final choice; in other cases, we may need to have short-term containment measures to meet a pressing customer need and then implement long-term countermeasures in a later phase. After that, there is implementation and the related plan of actions to put the countermeasure(s) in place. Last but not least, in the follow-up section, we will check the effectiveness of the countermeasure versus the objective and act accordingly (e.g. act or adjust). Below in Figure 4.7, we see an example of an A3 Problem Solving report that is in the implementation phase.

When combined with the Obeya, the A3 Report plays an effective role in mechanisms of alignment and sharing, because it speeds up the comprehension and resolution of technical and management problems, and permits the clear communication of proposals arriving from various involved parties. At the same time, it virtually eliminates the need for complex presentations and endless wordsmithing of reports. A3's displayed together with other materials in a given section of the Obeya adds clarity to how issues are being addressed (see Figure 4.8) driving more discussion and input from team members.

Finally, the A3 Report is not only a tool for disciplined thought and an effective means of communication, but it also becomes a fantastic tool for continual learning: with a single sheet of paper we can teach, in a very rapid and concise way, the problem we have solved to our peers.

In Figure 4.9 we see the typical structure of an A3 Proposal Story. This is used when we do not have a plan or goal, but we want to propose a

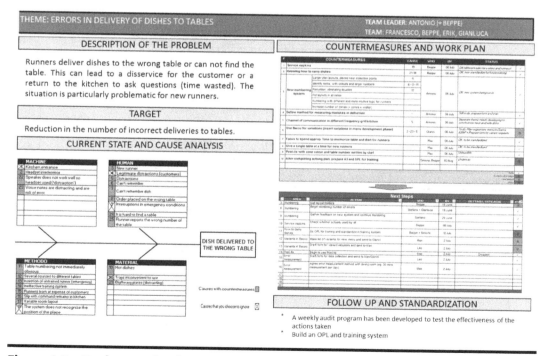

Figure 4.7   Real example of an A3 Problem Solving Report.

Figure 4.8   Example of an A3 Report into the Obeya System in one of our projects.

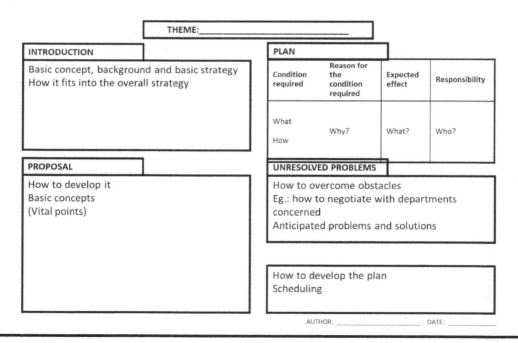

Figure 4.9   Example of an A3 Proposal Story Report.

new initiative, or when a plan or objective existed, but circumstances have changed and a new direction is required.

Other templates can be drawn up using the same criteria and the same basic philosophy. Learning to produce good A3 Reports takes no more than a couple of hours of initial training, but becoming excellent problem-solvers and communicators using them involves a lot of time and a lot of practice alongside someone who has deep experience in using this tool. Once again, the secret of mastering A3 thinking depends more on solid mentoring than on the simple tool itself.

4.3.1 Summary of the Basic Principles of an A3 Report

1. *Discipline of thought*. Applying a standard methodology even when dealing with unfamiliar problems helps us to be more focused and effective.
2. *Effective communication*. Preparing an A3 Report beforehand helps us to drastically reduce the amount of time spent explaining, looking for data, and interpreting issues with others, especially during meetings.
3. *Tool for continual teaching and learning*. The A3 report can be used to train and mentor others and to ensure that valuable accumulated knowledge is shared.

4.4 Systematic Reflection in Order to Learn from Experience

> A pessimist sees the difficulty in every opportunity; an optimist sees the opportunity in every difficulty.

Winston Churchill

A key concept in Japanese culture is *hansei,* which literally translated means "self-reflection." Its meaning relates to the idea of understanding the reasons for errors made in the past in order to improve in the future. In a business context, they are simply structured moments of conscious reflection: an effort is made to understand whether and at which level established goals have been achieved, and what to do to improve the situation, whatever it may be.

The focus is both on the results and on the process being used to achieve them. The typical phases of a *hansei* are the following.

1. *What did we set out to do?* This initial phase involves refocusing on objectives and results we reached or should have reached.
2. *What actually happened?* Reflecting on the actual achievements versus the pre-established objectives.
3. *Why did it happen?* Analyzing the causes of the gaps (positive and negative) between the expected outcomes and actual outcomes.
4. *What are we going to do next time?* The final phase, the most important of all, is devoted to thinking constructively about the future and to developing a structured action plan to address the root causes of the gaps that were discovered.

The time dedicated to each of the four phases should *not* be the same. A best practice is to spend about half of the available time on doing the fourth phase well; use a quarter of the time to really understand the causes (the third phase), while the remaining time should be sufficient to deal with the first two questions. You may not believe it, but sometimes the first difficulty we encounter when we do *hansei workshops* with various clients is obtaining a clear and unambiguous outline of the initial goals toward which the people were working. During a *hansei* done in 2008 in a very well-known Italian company, the greatest difficulty in the whole workshop was to achieve a shared definition of what the objectives of the team were (or should have been). Everyone had a similar, but not identical, interpretation of the goal, and in some areas of the project, there were not even precise measures about what was done. The team had already been working for almost a year on a new family of products, but it effectively took almost an entire day to produce a clear and agreed-upon point-by-point definition of objectives that should have been clear from the very beginning of the project. This is another confirmation that in many companies there is still a widespread tendency to swing into action before having decided precisely what to do and in which exact direction to go. The *hansei* is a great way to surface wastes throughout a project and help the team stay focused on their goals and meeting the customer needs.

4.4.1 When Do We Do It? And Who Should Do It?

Hansei can be applied to various issues within a company, from a technical problem to a management issue, from team issues to individual ones.

What's more, getting used to practicing it helps people to communicate with more and more focus on facts, figures, and results.

Hansei can be introduced at various levels of the business. When associated with the running of a project, *hansei* sessions should be held at the beginning of the project, at key milestones/learning points during the project, and at the end.

It can also be done individually, where the main aim is constructive personal reflection. This can be particularly useful prior to a performance review with your boss so you may objectively see how you have progressed and see what gaps you still need to address.

Hansei may even be used in product strategy for making major changes related to the direction of the company.

The example in Figure 4.10 features part of a *hansei* used in a project to review and led to several systemic changes in R & D in a well-known Italian company. In this case, we inserted a few *hansei* sessions into the mapping of the current state of R & D processes (Value Stream Map) to deeper probe the wastes found and used the findings to help better define the future state map.

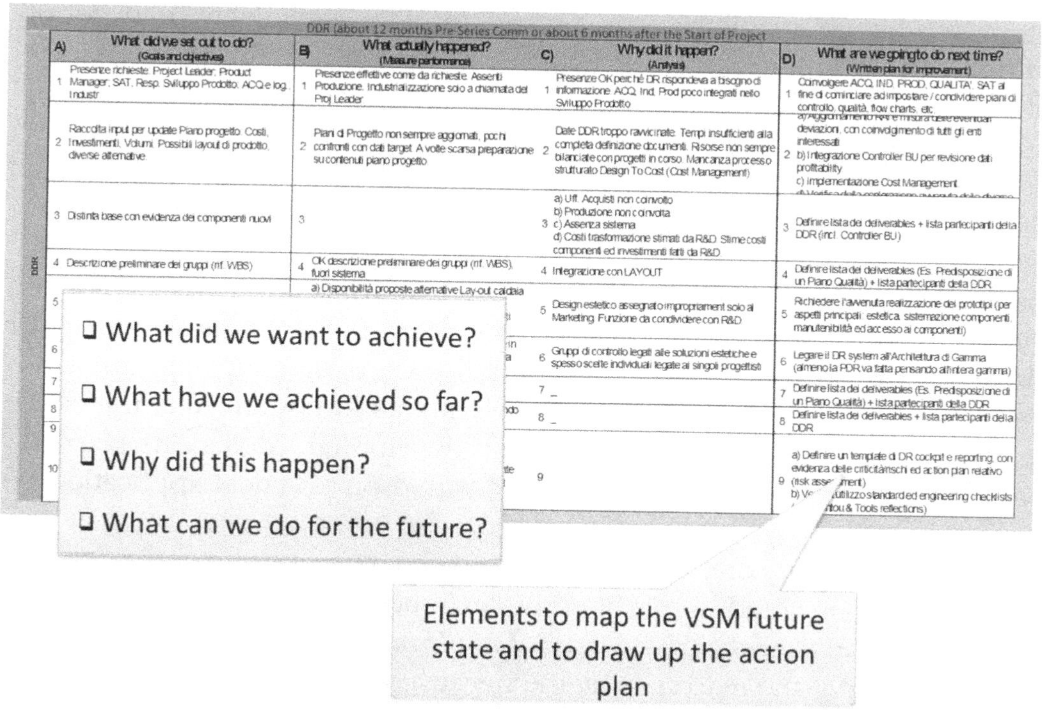

Figure 4.10 Example of *hansei* preliminary to a Value Stream Map future state.

In our experience, as shown in the example above, it is important to have a skilled facilitator who can guide the team through the process and can ask the right questions to harvest the learnings.

When working on very long product innovation and development projects, we recommend conducting a *hansei* every three months, because there may be various kinds of problems, more or less hidden, that can be questioned. It also allows us to routinely identify, capture and share learnings with the rest of the organization.

In essence, *hansei* becomes a subtle mechanism for calibrating our actions continually and precisely, enabling us to learn from the recent past and to achieve a better focus on what to do in the near future.

4.4.2 What Is the Difference between Hansei and Lessons Learned?

Sometimes we are asked whether *hansei* is the same as lessons learned sessions used by many companies. Answer: yes and no. For example, one the authors once took part in an enterprise lessons learned program in a big company. He was amazed how, in a relatively brief period of time, an enormous database had been built up containing thousands of lessons learned, with long prescriptive lists of what should or should not be done on the basis of evidence gathered from dozens of projects. Technically speaking, this database was organized very well: all you had to do was type in a key word and the database generated hundreds of references and recommendations for users. In your opinion, how much was this fantastic database really used by everyone? After having spent a lot of time and money developing it, the degree of use was so low that it created some embarrassment initially, followed by management preaching and coercion to use it and ultimately it was forgotten. Again, technology prevailed over the process when developing the lessons learned program where input and searching prevailed on practical application of learnings.

The point is that companies often issue recommendations of the "don't do this and you should to that" but the real question to be asked is this: *what can we do to make what we want really happen?* Without a deep understanding of the reasons why the negative (or positive) things happen, and without a careful appraisal of what can be practically done in the future, these lessons learned mostly remain "lessons" without being turned into true knowledge that can be applied. *Hansei* helps to take data and facts, analyze them and turn the learnings into actionable items for future projects.

In our view, therefore, it is a good idea not to have masses of "lessons learned," but to learn to be more focused on a few things that can be put into practice. Rather than the twelve-thousand lessons learned, it is better to have five or ten at a time, but to deeply understand them and to put into practice what has been learned, instead of creating a white elephant that no one will use.

4.4.3 Some Practical Examples

In Figures 4.11 and 4.12 you can see two excerpts from *hansei's* relating to product development projects.

In the example in Figure 4.11, the team was focusing on a knowledge "dispersion" problem concerning issues faced and solved by installation and maintenance technicians working on site with the client. The company had been unable to implement effective feedback to the designers so that certain design aspects of the new product could be improved and old errors avoided. Having done the *hansei* before starting the new project, the action plan coming out of the event made it possible to improve certain processes of the new project, and to immediately put into practice what needed to be done to close the gap that was discovered.

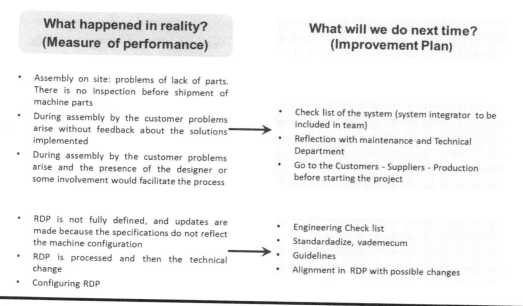

What happened in reality? (Measure of performance)	**What will we do next time?** (Improvement Plan)
• Assembly on site: problems of lack of parts. There is no inspection before shipment of machine parts	
• During assembly by the customer problems arise without feedback about the solutions implemented	• Check list of the system (system integrator to be included in team)
• During assembly by the customer problems arise and the presence of the designer or some involvement would facilitate the process	• Reflection with maintenance and Technical Department
	• Go to the Customers - Suppliers - Production before starting the project
• RDP is not fully defined, and updates are made because the specifications do not reflect the machine configuration	• Engineering Check list
• RDP is processed and then the technical change	• Standardadize, vademecum
	• Guidelines
• Configuring RDP	• Alignment in RDP with possible changes

Figure 4.11   Example of *hansei* to address organizational problems.

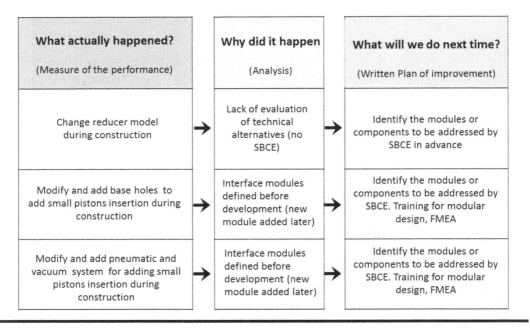

Figure 4.12 Example of *hansei* for the management of modifications.

In the example in 4.12, the purpose of the *hansei* was to understand the causes and to devise feasible actions to deal with the excessive and recurrent number of modifications that occurred following the launch of a new product.

By analyzing the individual modifications done to the pneumatic system while ramping up production, the team achieved a genuine understanding of the impacts—not only financial but also in terms of design, materials, production, and the negative consequences of schedule delays—of a "rushed" choice that had been done in design phase and the lack of a modular approach to the design. As a result of the *hansei*, the team decided to introduce into the next project the Lean methodologies of Set-Based Concurrent Engineering and modular design.

Both examples above illustrate the broad applicability of *hansei*. As we have seen, it is a simple technique that can bring out great insights that can help executives, project teams and team members to better achieve their goals in the short and longer term.

4.5 Summary of Chapter 4

1. *Choose the right tools to support processes and people.* In a Lean company engaged in innovation, the first step is always to reduce waste in processes. Tools should be evaluated based on the six criteria: integration and ease of use, support for processes, support for people, reinforce standardization, enable organizational alignment, and assist in organizational learning.

2. *Visually align and manage the entire project team.* The Obeya Alignment System is the key tool for realizing this strategy. It simplifies project management by making it visual and it facilitates on-going collaboration.

3. *Simplify all communication with the A3 methodology.* This makes it possible to achieve discipline of thought, by using a tool that is also useful for sharing information, conducting structured problem-solving and driving continuous learning.

4. *Structured reflection in order to learn from experience. Hansei* conditions people to have moments of systematic reflection, at both an individual and group level, in order to continually improve their processes and products.

Resources

https://www.lenovys.com/en/case-history/mahle/
https://www.lenovys.com/en/blog/tco/

Note

1. Allen T.J., Fusfeld A.R., 1974.

Chapter 5

Companies That Have Successfully Streamlined and Innovated Their Product Development

This chapter looks at different cases involving Lean innovation projects. In the two Sacmi case studies, new products were designed from scratch facing an important change management activity due to the complete implementation of Lean product and process development principles, for the first time in the company's life. The Laika case study examines the innovative path taken by a company in the face of a drastic reduction in its traditional markets. The Continental case deals with the development of a new and innovative production technology using various strategies such as the standardization of testing activities and Set-Based Concurrent Engineering. The latter strategy was also employed in the Peugeot Citroën project pursued with John Drogosz. This was an important case because it marked a decisive move in the direction of Lean Innovation on the part of the well-known French automobile manufacturer. The case history of Natuzzi is a very interesting business case of a company re-building, after a dark period of recession, focused on a Lean Product and Process Development including Modularity and Industrial Complexity reduction. Natuzzi, listed on New York Stock Exchange, designs, produces, and markets sofas, armchairs, and living room accessories. The end of the chapter describes a project developed in Lamborghini, famous around the world for having made its ability for product innovation an indisputable strategic competitive weapon.

5.1 Sacmi Ceramics

5.1.1 Mature Technology and Market Leadership. The Quest for Continuous Improvement and Growth

Sacmi is a world-leading international group that manufactures machinery for the ceramics industry, for the beverages and packaging sector, and for food and plastics processing. With 4,239 employees and annual sales of about 1.4 billion euros, the company has distinguished itself by developing innovative solutions in the various sectors in which it operates. The Ceramics Division, with 2,337 employees and annual sales of 881 million euros,[1] occupies a prominent position in the world of machines and plants for the manufacturing of tiles, bathroom fixtures, plates, firebricks, and standard bricks.

The Sacmi Lean Innovation Ceramics project began with very ambitious goals, when General Director Pietro Cassani agreed with his team on the need to develop an entirely new product with lower costs, a shorter time to market, and, above all, improving performance of current processes. The point of departure was a consolidated, long-established product, a press for producing ceramic tiles that had been on the market for several years.

The project started with the formation of a steering committee, the choice of a team leader, the selection of the team members, and discussion regarding everything that would be needed to overcome the current status quo in terms of project performance and company culture. The first sessions consisted of basic training in the key concepts of Lean Product Development and Innovation. This was quickly followed by the definition of the product scope, the perceived challenges to overcome, and a rough plan to roll out the Lean principles into the project.

5.1.2 Value Stream Mapping—Current State

The first activity done with the team was to do an assessment of the current capabilities of their product development process to gain an understanding of the opportunities that were present. To analyze the current situation, the team applied the Value Stream Mapping methodology for Product Development developed by Morgan and Liker.

The team chose the latest generation press as their reference when mapping the current state, considering everything that had been done to develop one of the most recent machines brought out onto the market, the so-called

Imola series. In the Value Stream workshops, we pieced together the history and the ways in which the team had worked, going right back to the moment in which this earlier machine had been defined, and examining the initial documents which formalized the decision to launch the production. A total of fourteen groups within the company were involved in the various activities of product development and participated in creating and analyzing the current state map. They mapped all their activities and interactions, which generated fourteen different sub-Value Streams, including the design, purchasing, logistics, industrialization, commercial, and marketing departments. In building up a timeline of the activities, the team indicated the initial estimates that were made for the various activities and milestones in the official documents drawn up at the beginning of the project, and then represented the actual duration of the same activities, indicating the point when the milestones were achieved.

It was a very "enlightening" experience for the people involved to reconstruct and map their activities, and above all, to see objectively the difference between their perception about the process and its duration and what actually happened (see Figure 5.1).

In particular, the team was shocked by the frequent iterations of the same activities and the repetition of the same milestones in the course of the product's development. The team highlighted every time an activity was repeated; where someone had to wait for information, documents, drawings, or semi-finished parts from someone else; and any critical issues which impeded the work of others. The map of processes was extremely useful in

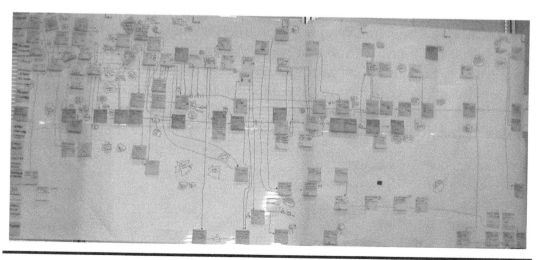

Figure 5.1   Current State Value Stream Map.

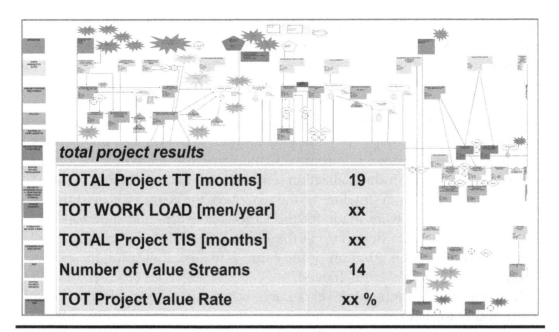

Figure 5.2   Quantification of performance in the VSM analysis.

identifying the opportunities for improvement such as—poorly synchronized activities, rework, modifications, Stop and Go, waiting. Figure 5.2 shows the completed map in electronic format with some quantification of the current state performance of the process.

During the mapping workshop, a new awareness began to emerge, and it was amazing to see the change in the attitude of the team members in describing their everyday processes using sticky notes, and crude printouts pinned to a large wall. After some initial denial, the seed of doubt began to grow in the group, and people began to entertain the idea that several things could be improved and that some old ways of doing things should be completely rethought. It had become evident that there were certain social and organizational dysfunctions, combined with several technical problems, that had become commonplace over the years. The following is a list of the wastes the team decided to work on for the new project:

■ Unsynchronized activities
■ Large number of hand-overs
■ Communication barriers
■ Waiting and delays
■ Numerous instances of reworking and modifications in all the groups
■ Unexploited and poorly structured knowledge: decisions based on sometimes inadequate data and with few existing standards

- Variability in the duration of processes and expected outputs
- Absence of "discipline" to timelines

For every identified area of waste, they tried to identify the root cause and define a possible countermeasure that could be adopted in the new project. Below are examples (from Figures 5.3 to 5.6) summarizing the identified areas of waste, together with the appropriate countermeasures.

5.1.3 Hansei

The next phase after the Value Stream Current State Mapping workshop was the *hansei* sessions. These moments of group reflection dealt with a number of different issues identified in the Current State Map, including planning, monitoring of costs, and the conducting of the Design Review. For each of them, the group followed the typical *hansei* approach discussed in Chapter 4. They were asked to consider what objectives had been set at the beginning of the previous project, what results had been achieved (or not), what were the causes for any of the deviations (negative or positive) between goals set and results achieved, and what actions could be implemented in designing the new product to avoid poor performance seen in the past.

The *hansei* sessions yielded a series of solutions to various critical issues found within the product development processes. In these sessions, as in the earlier Value Stream Mapping, the coach–consultant's task was simply to facilitate the discussion in a wholly impartial manner, and to highlight, on a

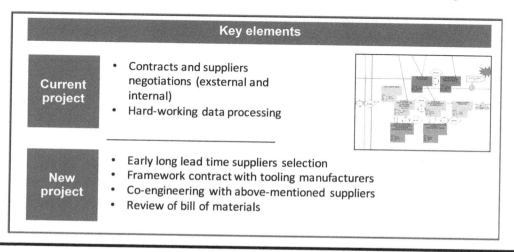

Figure 5.3   Example of an area of waste and relative countermeasures.

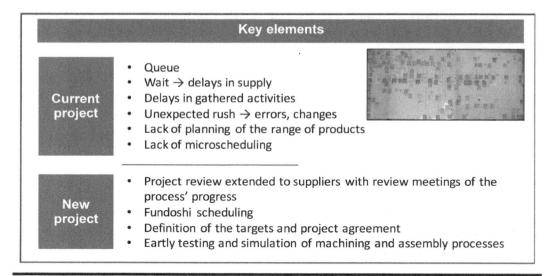

Figure 5.4   Example of an area of waste and relative countermeasures.

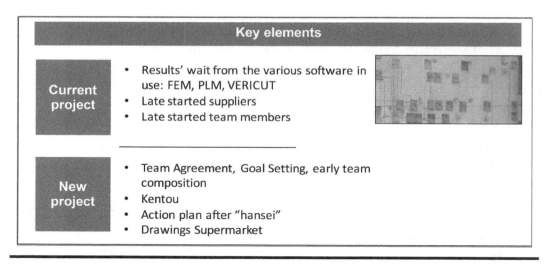

Figure 5.5   Example of an area of waste and relative countermeasures.

case-by-case and problem-by-problem basis, possible solutions adopted by other companies in similar circumstances. However, no solution was ever imposed. It was left up to the team to find, adapt, or choose the solutions and specific actions deemed most suitable for their own project.

Figures 5.7 and 5.8 illustrate the output of two of the *hansei* sessions.

An important aspect of this phase of the work was that the team became more aware and focused in the search for innovative ways of dealing with historic problems that they had come to accept as unavoidable parts of their development process.

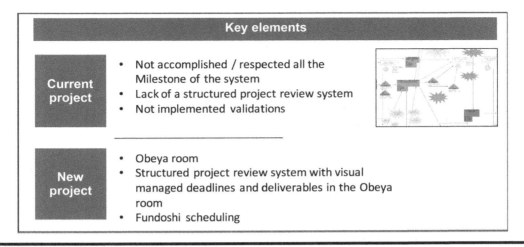

Figure 5.6   Example of an area of waste and relative countermeasures.

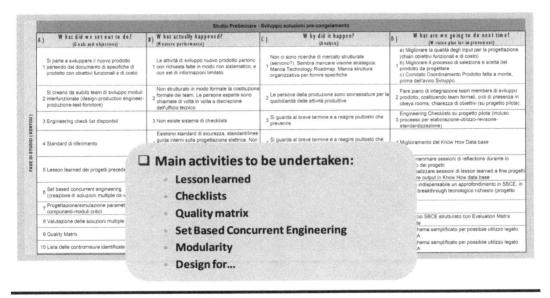

Figure 5.7   Excerpt from a *hansei* session.

5.1.4 Value Stream Mapping—Future State

The following step for the team was to draw up the Future State Value Stream Map to represent the processes to follow for future projects. Combining the countermeasures that had emerged as a result of the Current State Value Stream Map and the actions defined in the *hansei* sessions, the team outlined a proposed new product development process in which the activities were remodeled to address earlier problems of synchronization,

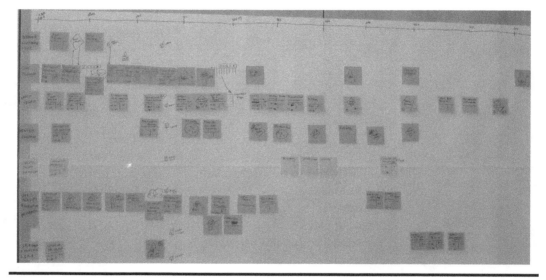

	COMUNICAZIONE E ALLINEAMENTO DELL'ORGANIZZAZIONE			
A) What did we set out to do? (Goals and objectives)	B) What actually happened? (Measure performance)	C) Why did it happen? (Analysis)	D) What are we going to do next time? (Written plan for improvement)
1 Strumenti standard di Comunicazione verso il Management	1 Non ci sono standard	1 Non sentito come problema	1
2 Obeya room (stanza fisica del progetto)	2 Non c'è	2 Non sentito come problema	2 Lanciare strumento in progetto pilota
3 A3 reports	3 Non si usano	3 Manca cultura	3 Lanciare strumento in progetto pilota
4 Sistema Key Performance Indicators e deployment/monitoring obiettivi	4 Non c'è	4 La motivazione al miglioramento è insita nelle persone, anche se non strutturata attraverso metriche di miglioramento	4 Definire un sistema di KPI ed obiettivi nel progetto pilota (+ sistema premiante)
5 Statuto del progetto			

❑ Main activities to be undertaken :

- Obeya room
- A3 Reports
- Know How data base
- Standardization
- Key Performance Indicators System

A) What did we set out to (Goals and objectives)			next time? (rement)
1 Standardizzazione dei comp diverse macchine			ll'introduzione di
2 Know How data base (incl. L			

Figure 5.8   Excerpt from a *hansei* session.

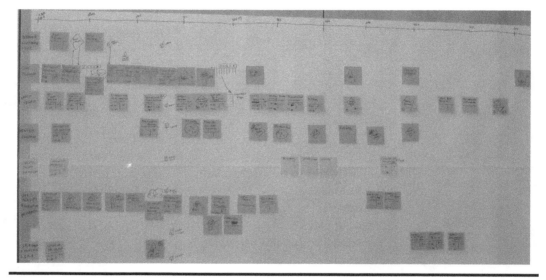

Figure 5.9   Future State VSM.

difficulties in communication, and the need to avoid endless modifications (Figure 5.9).

While drawing the Future State Map, it became clear that some activities, if introduced at the appropriate time, could not only reduce the overall duration of the project, but also increase the final quality of the product, responding better to the market's and manufacturing's needs. Some examples were the project preparation phases, the defining of the Concept Paper, and goal-setting, together with a greater emphasis on getting the project team truly involved in the very early stages of the project (Figure 5.10).

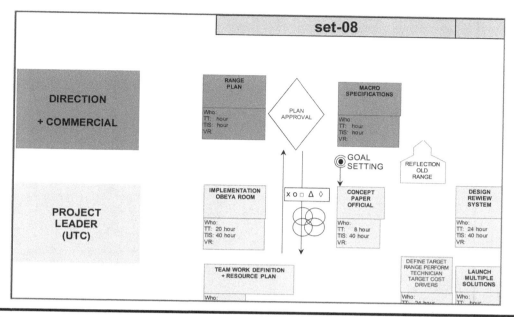

Figure 5.10 Detail of the future state process: the start phase of the project.

Another significant change introduced into the new product development flow was the early involvement of suppliers with long lead times, such as the foundries for the cast-iron bases, and those supplying very expensive components, effectively incorporating these suppliers into the co-design needed to meet the cost reduction goals of the project. (Figure 5.11). In this case, the purchasing department was to play a key role in the choice of the supplier-partner to involve in the early concept phase, well before the traditional purchase order would have typically been placed. The only condition that had to be carefully respected was the importance of not changing supplier partway through the project in order to avoid wasting the great efforts made by the company's designers and their counterparts at the suppliers.

Another major change in the new process's development was the complete reorganization of the product concept and design phases, with the systematic incorporation of the techniques of Set-Based Concurrent Engineering for those parts of the product with greatest added value for the client and greatest cost for the company (Figure 5.12).

5.1.5 Project Start: The Concept Paper

Once the new future state map had been defined, the project execution proceeded with incorporating the first Lean technique: the Concept Paper.

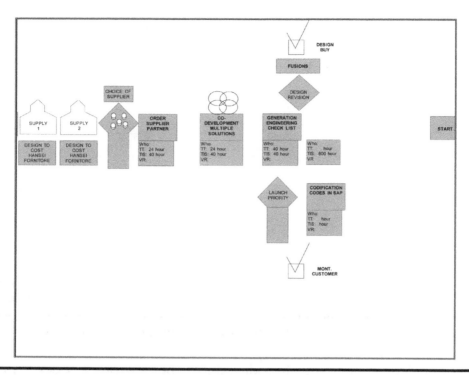

Figure 5.11   Detail of future state process: selection, co-design and management of key suppliers.

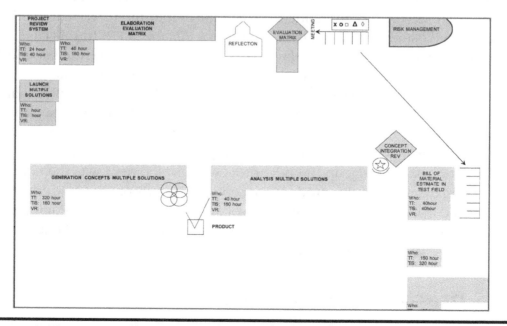

Figure 5.12   Detail of future state process: conceptual pre-study and Set-Based Concurrent Engineering phase.

During this phase of the project, the team conducted a careful analysis of the performance and cost drivers of the new product (i.e. the stamped concrete press) as viewed by their customers and by benchmarking the competition. The former was carried out in conjunction with the commercial managers, doing on-site visits with customers, and direct contact with end-users and technicians who maintained the machines. The Concept Paper phase lasted longer than expected; various conflicts were identified and deliberately made to emerge in order to demonstrate how important it is to "force" team members to reach consensus in the early phases of the project, rather than waiting for conflicts to reemerge when the designs have nearly been finalized. For example, as the Concept Paper was being prepared, it emerged that the team's principal motive for innovating the product was to avoid its rapid obsolescence, which could have led to a loss in market share and/or reduced margins.

As the market needs were thoroughly explored, the team gradually focused on the areas of the product where it would be possible to improve customer satisfaction. These areas included:

- User-friendly computer interface
- Troubleshooting carried out in the computer on the machine itself
- Improvement of the mechanical devices.

Different degrees of priority ("must," "must not," and "nice to have") were identified for the various needs of the product.

Here are some examples of "must-haves" of the product:

- Preloaded structure
- Use of castings
- Use of capacity and pressure multiplier
- Use of variable capacity pump
- New computer interface.

The following were "nice to have" items:

- Binding
- Power supply management of die temperature
- Inductive safety micros
- Inputs for the management of external equipment signals and software configuration for these inputs

- Optional integrated device to facilitate the change of die/buffer
- Sacmi structural proportional logic elements
- Detector device for the level of oil contamination
- Visual oil level indicator.

And finally, below was a "must not" for the new product definition:

- Switchboard.

Trade-off curves were defined to aid in the understanding and analysis of the major cost drivers of the product. The technical and financial data relating to various types of machine were plotted and compared. What emerged most evidently was a known driver, namely weight, and its influence on overall cost was quantified according to the different models of the machine itself (Figure 5.13).

This insight from the trade-off curves led the project team to later use the latest generation finite element method (FEM) for topological optimization in order to find the best technical solution for the cast-iron load-bearing structure; combining structural solidity with the need to keep weight to a strict minimum to achieve the product cost target.

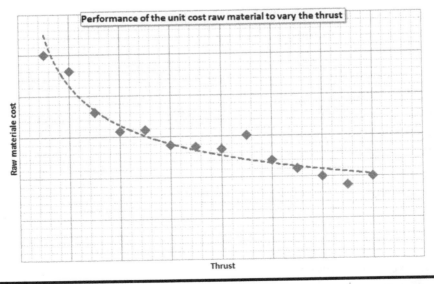

Figure 5.13   Example of a trade-off curve. (The numerical values have been removed for reasons of confidentiality.)

5.1.6 Kentou

As soon as the Concept Paper was completed, the team began the concept phase by exploring many design alternatives. This proved to be a particularly laborious process, because the degree of innovation needed was very high based on the requirements set in the Concept Paper. For example, the team produced over twenty-five different product architecture solutions, which were then narrowed down through numerical methods and qualitative evaluation. Before being formally "designed," each solution was vetted in the "old-fashioned" way, using paper, pencil, and brains. In Figures 5.14 through 5.16, you can see some examples of the range of solutions for various parts of the machine.

The team considered the data, facts, and analyses provided by suppliers, in-house assemblers, and all the other staff involved when preparing an evaluation matrix (Figure 5.17), which enabled them to whittle down the initial twenty-five solutions to just four in a relatively short period of time. The remaining four contenders were then developed in parallel through to the point at which just two were chosen after prototyping. One was more promising in terms of costs and performance, but also more innovative and risky, while the other was a little less performing and less innovative, but had less technical risk, and was therefore chosen as a backup solution thus applying to the letter one of the basic principles of Set-Based Concurrent Engineering.

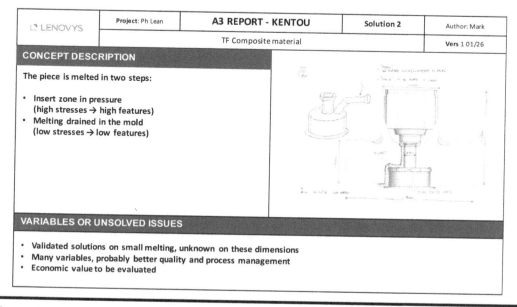

Figure 5.14   **Example of conceptual solution developed in the Kentou phase.**

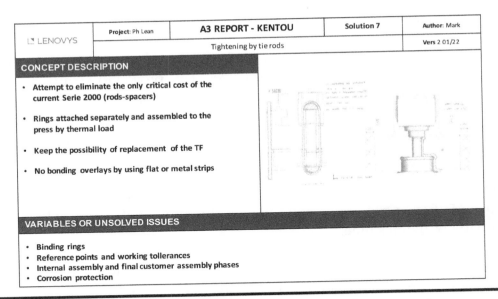

Figure 5.15   Example of conceptual solution developed in the Kentou phase.

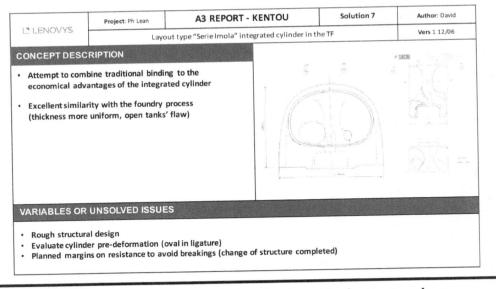

Figure 5.16   Example of conceptual solution developed in the Kentou phase.

More trade-off curves were generated to compare and evaluate the different solutions and took into account various critical factors including indexes of quality, cost, lead time, maintainability, logistics, etc. Some examples can be seen in Figure 5.18.

The more analysis that was done upfront, the more it became apparent how many things had historically gone unobserved or untreated until

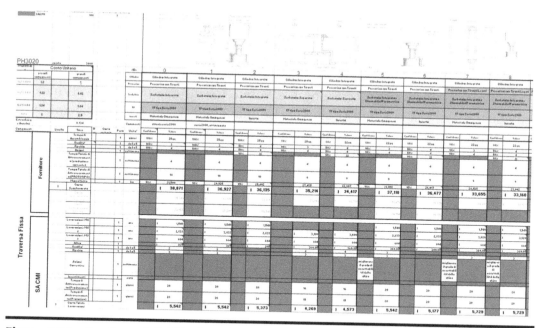

Figure 5.17   Section of the final evaluation matrix.

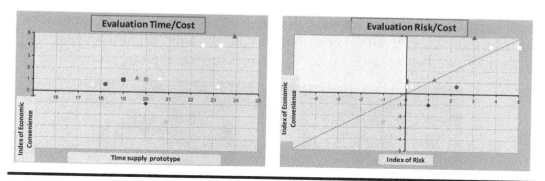

Figure 5.18   Example of trade-off curves produced for the final evaluation in the Kentou phase.

much later in the project. Many factors did not seem critical at first until they analyzed them in depth. People realized how many times lots of problems could have been avoided in the past if more time had been devoted to preventing them and to looking for alternatives at the appropriate moment. By bearing in mind critical factors such as the prototype supply time, the supplier cost variances, and various critical in-house production operations, it became possible to produce better comparative risk evaluations that cast a different light on each of the alternatives being considered during the kentou phase.

5.1.7 Managing the Project: The Obeya System

The whole project was managed through the Obeya System (Figure 5.19). The large, well-equipped room grew and changed appearance several times as the work progressed, becoming the venue for all meetings and all major activities. As it was the first project to be managed in this way at Sacmi, it was also used as a point of reference for other working groups that would subsequently embark on their own Lean projects. Avoiding long-winded explanations, it was sufficient to take other project teams to the Obeya for half an hour or so to walk the walls and observe a meeting, and they were able to quickly grasp the principles of the system and how it had been applied in the Ceramics Lean Innovation Team.

5.1.8 The "Quick Die Change" Subgroup—Adding Customer Value

An optional integrated device to make it easier to change the die was defined in the Concept Paper phase as a "nice to have" that would improve customer satisfaction with the machine. Based on the difficulty encountered by many clients in changing the die to switch from one tile model to another, the project team, in conjunction with the sales department, decided to set up a parallel working group to address this customer challenge.

Figure 5.19 The Obeya room of the project.

The first step was to devise the "set-up matrix," in order to identify the different possible types of die changes. This was immediately followed by the filming of a set-up at a customer's factory. The time it took to change the dye amounted to about seven hours. Interviews conducted with other customers revealed that the best case of a die change for a well-organized team was not less than five hours. The team clearly saw the value proposition to the client of reducing the changeover time and consequently set an aggressive target for the new machine: to reduce the die change time from seven hours to just thirty minutes, thanks to the redesign of the machine mechanisms

Analysis of the video (Figure 5.20) first made it possible to see the wastes in the current machine changeover and to establish the requirements and new specifications for the new press.

The project for the optional quick die change device was conducted by applying the same basic methodology used for the overall project, as can be seen in summary form in Figure 5.21.

5.1.9 Conclusions

In September 2010, the new Sacmi PH 3200 machine, complete with the quick die change device, was presented at Tecnargilla, the most important trade fair in the world for supplies to the ceramics and brick industry.

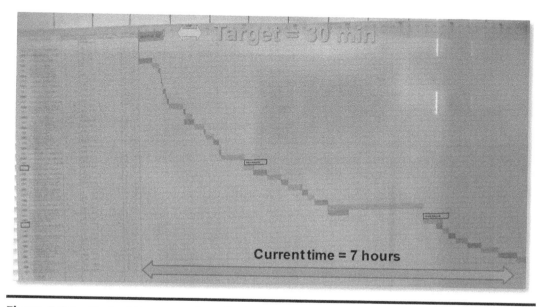

Figure 5.20   Part of the map of preliminary activities in the die change process.

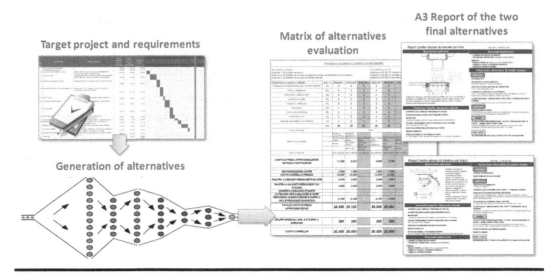

Figure 5.21 Summary of the working method for the "quick die change" subgroup.

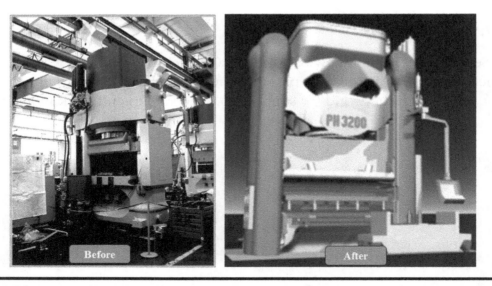

Figure 5.22 Comparison of the machines before and after the project.

The fair was an ideal opportunity to demonstrate to the market the unique thirty-minute quick dye change device and the innovative, attractively designed machine (Figure 5.22), confirming Sacmi's world leadership in the ceramics sector.

Discussing the company's line of presses and efforts to achieve "maximum flexibility and the capacity to create products with high added value," Sacmi's Annual Report comments:[2]

Regarding the pressing, the positive performance of the latest presses released on the market—the PH10.000 and PH3200 Lean—should also be pointed out.
The innovation of fast die changeover has won widespread approval from the ceramic world as it constitutes another step toward achieving ever more flexible production lines.

In the end, both the innovative solution and even the second backup solution were produced. The team managed to reduce the time it took to complete the whole project of a completely new innovative machine by 30% over prior projects and, in reality, launching two final products simultaneously. The innovative quick die change solution was undoubtedly the most noteworthy, but other significant improvements were realized:

■ Better machine diagnostics
■ Higher speed
■ Better operator ergonomics
■ Revolutionary design of the fixed transverse
■ A new method of structural clamping
■ A new and more functional oil-pressure system.

All this was made possible by a group of people—designers, sales staff, technicians, maintenance people, assemblers—led by an expert project leader, who could see the potential benefits of applying Lean techniques in product development. In addition, Sacmi had a leadership team who had the courage to allow their employees to challenge the company's own practices that had served them well over the years. Through the first Lean Innovation project, Sacmi managed to channel the competence and skills of their people into a true strategic competitive advantage in their marketplace.

5.2 Laika

5.2.1 Innovation and Lean Leadership as a Reaction to Economic Crisis

The Laika project is quite a particular example of Lean Innovation and Product Development, implemented in a period of deep economic crisis—an example showing courage, strength, resolve, and intuition in a time of fear and uncertainty.

The leading motorhome manufacturer in Italy, Laika, was founded in 1964 at Tavernelle Val di Pesa, about thirty kilometers from Florence, Italy, and the company is still based there today. The founder, Giovambattista Moscardini, was fascinated by travel and the new human adventures happening with the exploration of space, which were opening up exciting new horizons. That's why he decided to name the company after the first dog to be sent into space and chose as its logo, a red greyhound with wings, which is still present as a powerful brand on all the company's vehicles. The year of the company's founding, 1964, was also the year of its first caravan model, the tiny 500 (Figure 5.23), which was so small that it could be towed by a Fiat 500.

Laika is owned since 2000 by ERWIN HYMER, the German group that unifies Europe's leading caravan and motor home manufacturers, approximately 50,000 vehicles sold, with a total turnover of 1.9 billion euros and approximately 5,500 employees.

The company, the premium brand manufacturer of the German Group, embarked on its Lean innovation journey at a time when the storm of the economic crisis was just beginning, as can be seen from the graph of sales in Europe in Figure 5.24.

The European market dipped sharply from 88,000 vehicles to just 65,000 in less than two years, while the situation in Italy was even worse, with sales falling from 15,000 to 8,000 in the same period. In a sector accustomed to steady continual growth and to working with large stocks both at dealers and manufacturers, this sharp drop in sales caused very serious problems, putting the survival of many companies at risk. Despite the gravity of the

Figure 5.23   The Laika 500, the first caravan produced in Italy.

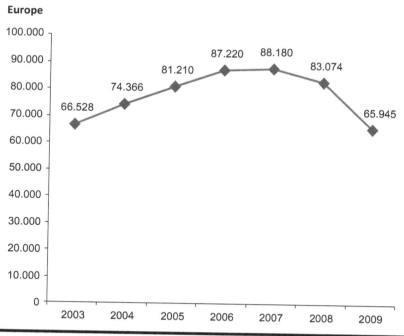

Figure 5.24   Sales in Europe, 2003–2009.

situation, together with Laika management, we helped organize a project with the goal of capitalizing on all the strategic opportunities offered by the moment, rather than simply limiting ourselves to cutting costs in the face of a drastic fall in sales.

Convinced that it would be extremely risky to stake everything on traditional forms of cost reduction, the team prepared two lines of action, one focusing on efficiency, the other one on effectiveness. For the first aspect, we tried to make the company more streamlined and flexible, while from an effectivness point of view, we endeavored to increase the company's position in the marketplace. This was achieved by exploring new ideas on various fronts, ranging from new products to new markets, in addition to a wide range of innovations along the entire value chain. The two projects' goals were as follows:

1. *Efficiency: reduction of waste and lower costs*
   - Reduction of inventories along the entire value chain
   - Reduction in production capacity
   - Reduction in general costs
   - Reduction in staff costs
   - Reduction in production batches/increased flexibility.

2. *Effectiveness: increase customer value and grow sales*
   - New, top-of-the-line products
   - Invest in products for new foreign markets
   - Invest in new sales networks and Lean Sales Organization
   - Enlarge the dealer network
   - Invest in marketing and post-sales
   - New products with higher value and lower costs in their price ranges.

It was necessary to take a different approach to these projects versus other improvement activities undertaken by the company in the past. With the signs of an economic crisis from outside and a wave of frustration on the inside, there were clear signs of a demoralized workforce at every level in the company. In some departments, for instance, the rate of absenteeism was close to 10%, a discouraging sign for obtaining everyone's positive involvement in a time requiring radical change. For this reason, one of the projects' clear goals was to put people at the center of the renewal process. The Lean transformation included various areas, from the supply chain to vehicle assembly, design, and post-sales. Strong emphasis was placed on aspects of leadership, the management involvement, and engagement of the entire workforce, so that the improvement could be rapidly accepted, thus making the people the real drivers of sustainable change along the entire value chain using cross-functional teams (Figure 5.25). In a little less than two years, absenteeism fell to almost zero, a clear demonstration of the effectiveness of the steps taken to involve people in the project.

The company's top management backed the approach. One of the greatest supporters was the chief executive, Jan De Haas, a German who has been in Italy for many years. As he was involved firsthand in the process of profound transformation, we asked him to describe his thoughts on the project, and to give an overview of the transformation in relation to the difficult period the company went through. This is what he said about the Lean Innovation projects in Laika:

> Italy represented 70% of Laika's overall sales, and in two years the market fell by almost 50%. Speaking in terms of inventory, this created some really worrying moments for us, for our manufacturers and for our dealers. And so began our journey into the lean world, which meant, first of all, reducing inventory in order to obtain current assets that would otherwise have been tied up in

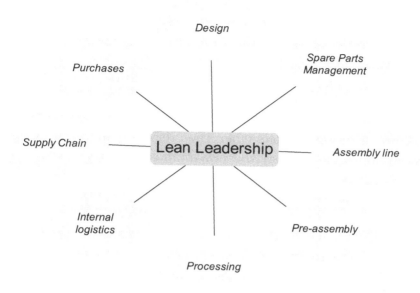

Figure 5.25 The model of Lean Innovation in Laika: putting people at the center of the program.

the unsold inventories; then production was reduced by 40% in the space of a few months. To avoid errors made in the past, we reduced production batches to just five vehicles. Accustomed as we were to producing as many as 40 vehicles of the same model at the same time, switching to producing just the vehicles that had been ordered required a great effort. Obviously, this contraction in production also led to staff reductions, and we resorted to tools such as the wages guarantee fund, staff transfers, and early retirement, giving great attention to every single cost. It was immediately obvious that the crisis would not be short and that the market would not return to its previous levels. We therefore chose to invest heavily to get through the crisis and we realized that growth could not be achieved by increasing the volume of production, as had once been the case, but that this time we would quickly need to learn to "take" market share from our competitors. We decided to invest, then, in top-range products in order to win customers with a high spending capacity; and in new models with higher performance, greater value, and less cost in the other ranges as well. We invested in the sales network, increasing the number of salespeople and upping the number of dealers by 32. We invested in marketing and post-sales, trying to obtain efficiency and transparency. In other words, we tried to be lean not only in production, but also at the very heart of our product and along the whole value chain. The most difficult year for us was 2008–2009 (the tax year for us runs from September to August). This year, 2010–2011, although the markets are still dropping, we have had a 22% increase in sales over the previous year. We have invested a lot in innovation: we had 26 motorhome models when the crisis began, and now we have 40, in order to satisfy the new markets we have expanded into. On the one hand this has meant reducing production batches and optimizing the whole value chain, from the supplier through to delivery of the vehicle; on the other, it has created a more complex situation to manage. The company must be ready to react with an "on-off" approach, and we have chosen a Lean Innovation project suitable for reaching this goal. Staff training was fundamental: for about 46 years, people have ridden the wave of success, and so they were mentally ill-disposed to change, also because they were not used to pinpointing what was exactly wrong in their processes. We began, then, with lean training, starting from the top, because "the fish always stinks from the head down," gradually extending the program to include every staff member. Each of us found ourselves learning to recognize waste in our own particular area, before taking steps to improve others' processes. This adventure was a great lesson for me. Even if we now have strong signals of positive growth, we do not know in reality how long this crisis will last. But I think that what we have learned and applied will be useful for us in readapting once again whenever situations of this kind occur again and whenever the need arises.

5.2.2 The New Kreos Motorhome Project

The Kreos Motorhome project was one of the first steps taken toward the adoption of a complete Lean Product and Process Development methodology at Laika. This methodology was deemed necessary for ensuring a reduction in development time and in costs, while increasing quality and customer satisfaction. The study phase of the project began in June 2009, and the established goals were very ambitious. Three key areas for improvement were identified: *style, quality, and weight reduction*. Previous experiences had not been shining examples of collaboration between the production and design departments. For this reason, the team decided to tackle the research and development process with a *total design* approach, that is to say, to ensure that the styling did not compromise the production process, and that design choices were geared from the outset to achieve the goal of minimum overall cost. This led to intense collaboration between designers and production engineers—often worlds apart—in order to be able to produce an attractive new motorhome with high levels of safety, avant-garde quality, reduced weight, and at a lower cost than previous models.

Compared to Laika's traditional approach, eight new approaches were introduced.

1. Choice of a single project leader to see the project through from start to finish.
2. Extended project team that includes, from the very outset, people with expertise in manufacturing.
3. Careful, jointly agreed-upon project specifications, giving due attention to marketing, design, engineering, and production considerations from the very start.
4. Exploration of many different conceptual design alternatives, with evaluations by all the team members, including early participation of key suppliers.
5. Direct elimination of the most frequent problems of quality in production through technical countermeasures being directly designed into the product.
6. Reduction in assembly time, with the definition of kitting assembly to be done line-side and pre-assembled subsystems delivered directly to the line.
7. Use of frequent cross-functional Design Reviews with the participation of marketing, engineering, and production people during the concept and design phases.
8. Construction of the first prototype under the direct supervision of the future production manager, together with a dedicated designer.

In the months following the official start of the project, numerous meetings took place to shape up and redefine the various aspects of the product design with the engineering and production personnel. Exploration alternative concepts resulted in innovative solutions arising from the juxtaposition of styling, aesthetic, technical, and production points of view.

One example is the fundamental requirement to give resistance to the load-bearing element of the cab and to attach the front windscreen to it. This was obtained by a single fiberglass unit produced with RTM technology (Resin Transfer Molding) rather than hand-layered, because it had to be lighter while ensuring dimensional stability. The technology involved is a particular fiberglass production technique, which yields pieces with superior mechanical properties to those obtained with the traditional method, weigh less (all mechanical characteristics being equal), have a uniform thickness, and a lower manufacturing cost.

Around this structural, load-bearing element, the designers and technicians produced what became familiarly known as the "dress." Here too, the dual objective to obtain attractive forms with the minimum industrial cost resulted in a truly innovative solution, from both the stylistic and manufacturing points of view. The technicians opted to build the carters in thermally molded plastic.

These solutions reduced the weight and improved quality, because the most critical components were made directly from the colored sheet and did not need to be painted—an aspect of fundamental importance, given the innumerable problems that had always arisen as a result of the need to paint fiberglass elements during production. The guidelines provided by the marketing department envisioned a vehicle capable of conveying a sense of innovation while at the same time retaining a classic image. To meet this need, it was decided, very appreciated by the marketing leads, to opt for an enormous windshield that was integrated with the side windows (Figure 5.26).

The choice of headlights was crucial for modeling the bodywork components in plastic (Figure 5.27). In this case, adopting solutions from the

Figure 5.26   One of the first sketches of the new Laika Kreos.

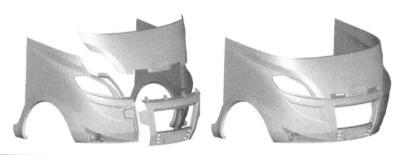

Figure 5.27   Final solution for the new integrated frontal area.

automotive sector was a winner, because for the first time Laika was able to fit lights totally integrated with the bodywork, thereby obtaining various advantages: this created efficiency and enhanced customer value, in that the new lighting system made nighttime driving less tiring, thus increasing both comfort and safety.

Various problems arose but were promptly resolved in the frequent Design Reviews, without having to wait for the traditional feedback from the field once the vehicle was complete. For example, the large windshield solution initially created problems of thermal insulation. For this reason the plant technicians developed forced air solutions to avoid condensation and cold points in the area near the glass (Figure 5.28), especially in view of the fact that the large "mobile" top bed, another great feature of the new motorhome, was just behind the cabin windshield.

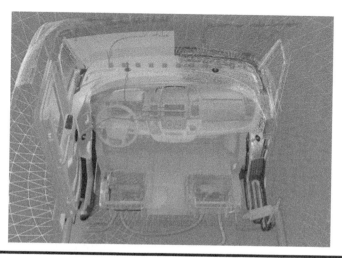

Figure 5.28   Plant solution to solve the issue of thermal insulation at the "drawing board."

The 3D modeling of the cabin was completed in February 2010. It then took another three months to produce the prototype molds and the first sample pieces in order to build a prototype of the vehicle, necessary for obtaining final approval from Sales and Marketing. In this period, there was an ongoing discussion between the various departments in order to solve production and quality issues, because, quite aside from the aesthetics, it was important to meet production cost targets. This upfront effort led to a significant reduction in the number of modifications after the prototype phase.

The prototype was finished in June 2010 and met the all the requirements set at the beginning of the project: soft, elegant lines combined with a dynamic form, and the resolution of chronic past production problems. The satisfaction on the faces of the marketing managers was the response everyone was hoping for, namely a green light to move on to manufacturing of the production molds. Below is a summary of the main results achieved in the Lean Innovation project:

1. Reduction of the cabin weight by about fifteen kg, 5% of the total.
2. Total elimination of paint problems regarding fiberglass parts.
3. Reduction in the number of cabin components.
4. Reduction in the cost of the cabin by about 10%.
5. Reduction in the total project time, from idea to prototype, by about 25% compared to past projects.
6. Reduction in the total number of modifications required after the first prototype.
7. Reduction in production line assembly time by approximately 20%.

The project also relied strongly on the production departments: from the woodworking to the mechanical processing of the furniture, from the line-side assembly of units to the final assembly of the vehicle, and from the primary materials warehouse to suppliers. The final product is shown in Figure 5.29.

Although we are not focusing, in this book, on the specific Lean production innovation, we would like to provide a brief sketch of the activities that were carried out insofar as they were linked to the important process of the overall transformation.

We tried to involve people in the process of introducing improvements right from the beginning, partly because they have a great deal of know-how, and also to dispel the frustrating "crisis syndrome" that was hanging

Figure 5.29   Final vehicle.

heavily in the air at the start of the project. The following, in short, is a list of the activities carried out and still underway:

1. *Efficiency in production*
   a. Improvement of material flow in departments
   b. Creation of a single "mixed model" assembly line to replace the current lines
   c. System of planning, management, and process checks, with the introduction of production leveling techniques
   d. Improvement of individual work stations, from ergonomics to standardization
   e. Reduction of changeover and set-up times, both for numerically controlled machines and in the assembly areas
   f. Extension of Visual Management to every department
   g. Increases in Overall Equipment Effectiveness
2. *Quality improvement*
   a. Reduction in scrap on the production line
   b. Reduction in scrap at the suppliers' sites
   c. Reduction of complaints by dealers and end customers
3. *Optimization of Supply Chain*
   a. Reduction in supplier lead times
   b. Reduction in total lead time in the factory
   c. Introduction of an integrated Vendor Rating system

    d. Reduction in the total transport and handling costs for components

    e. Reduction in the amount of occupied space and the quantity of materials in the warehouse

4. *Integrated performance control system*

    a. Definition of Key Performance Indicators (KPI) for each level in the company

    b. Introduction of a KPI management and control system

5.2.3 Coaching and Training

The project at Laika was accompanied by a training path focusing both on technical matters and on social, relational, and motivational issues. We organized a strategic program designed to activate a self-generating system of continuous improvement, the objective being to achieve challenging goals while respecting people. The coaching program has included the optimization of working methods, the adoption of effective relational strategies in management, personal, and professional growth, and the on-going development of the skills of all employees.

One area of focus was to reinforce the sense of loyalty to the company, creating a team in which each member could work together but also autonomously, with respect to clearly defined and agreed objectives, valuing their individual contribution as well as their contribution to the team. The result has been a marked improvement in employee morale and a motivated management team that challenges and empowers its employees.

5.2.4 Next Steps

The Laika activities are currently in full swing: new efforts are underway to consolidate Lean Development methodologies and to extend them to the whole family of products (Figure 5.30); a new plant is being designed with the goal of becoming a model in Europe for the whole motorhome sector. Lean Manufacturing activities continue to be expanded in all the production departments and now with suppliers. Having successfully overcome the perilous period of the economic crisis, Laika has actually strengthened itself using technology and innovation as a strategic lever for success. In fact, it is no coincidence that the new program has the symbolic name of "Fortemente Laika," aka, "Strongly Laika."

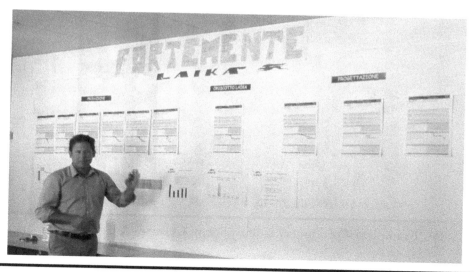

Figure 5.30 The CEO of Laika S.p.A., Jan De Haas, at the opening session of new program.

5.3 Sacmi Closures

5.3.1 Cut Costs or Earn More?

Sacmi's Closures & Containers Division, which employs 365 staff and has annual sales of around 170 million euros,[3] produces individual machines and complete manufacturing systems for the beverage industry. The product range includes equipment for the manufacturing of containers, for bottling and labeling, and for the handling of the finished product. Figure 5.31 shows some of the finished products made by the Sacmi machines.

In this project, we dealt with the development of a new machine to produce plastic bottle caps with "compression" technology (Figure 5.32). The first time we saw this machine we felt overwhelmed by its complexity. It had more than seven-thousand components and required an incredible number of different technologies to manufacture the machine: from the casting of the cast-iron base to electronic micrometers for the precision control of the die position, from rough-and-ready carpentry to mechanical processes accurate down to one hundredth of a millimeter, from granules of plastic to the melting and automatic transportation of boiling drops of molten plastic into steel dies, ready to open and close with impressive rapid synchronization. Now imagine an enormous disc one to two meters wide, about one-meter high, with the number of cavities ranging from twenty-four to eighty according to the model, in which the dies are housed. The disc turns at such a high

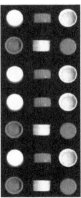

Figure 5.31 Examples of products made by Sacmi Closures & Containers machines.

Figure 5.32 The existing machine at the start of the project.

rate that it is impossible to see what is happening inside or to distinguish between the opening and closing of the dies. Imagine seeing the machine spewing out ten to thirty-five plastic tops per second, all 100% checked for quality, weight, and size. It is an amazing machine to watch in action.

5.3.2 Current State Value Stream Mapping

When we started, the time required to design such a complex machine ranged from twenty-four to forty-eight months, depending on the features required in the machine.

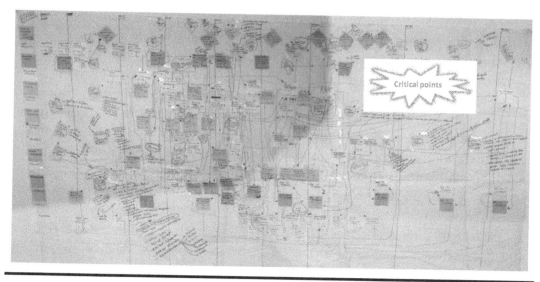

Figure 5.33   Present State Value Stream Map.

Figure 5.33 shows the complete map of product development processes mapped in the initial workshops. It was an extremely valuable exercise, because it enabled an understanding of the technical and social interactions occurring across the company over the almost four years of development. On the vertical axis are the titles of the people or groups involved such as logistics, production, tooling, engineering, simulation, etc. Along the horizontal axis is the timeline of the past project. During the session, we witnessed an interesting phenomenon: a growing perception of the real duration of the project by the people involved, on the basis of real data as they were gathered. At the beginning, there was no emphasis on the duration of the projects by project teams and management. Projects were regarded as "finished" when the first machine was released into the market, even though a team continued to make various modifications and adjustments for the following *eighteen* months. The detailed reconstruction of the flow of the project allowed many lessons to be learned, which were then transformed into various improvement actions. The main problems discovered were the following:

1. *Communication barriers.* The team clearly saw the effect of communications barriers and of the lack of involvement by some members in the early phases of the project. For example, seeing that a colleague downstream repeated the same activity three times due to inadequate communications upfront. This helped facilitate the first changes in attitudes among

the new project team regarding the importance to truly collaborate at the right time versus simply pushing data whenever it was available.

2. *Numerous modifications by all the working groups.* People were so accustomed to making modifications in every phase of the project (including after launch) that they confused modifications with normal activities. We quantified the real impact of modifications, making them one of the most critical areas to work on.

3. *Unexploited and poorly structured knowledge.* This sometimes led to decisions being made rapidly with insufficient data. We are talking here of a group of knowledgeable people accustomed to making quick decisions based on experience and "gut feel" that has made them world leaders in their technologies. However, when they evaluated the real effect of decisions taken in the past and saw the rework it often caused later, it became apparent that sometimes, in order to go faster on the overall project, it is better to slow down.

4. *Variability in the duration of processes and expected outputs.* The same activity sometimes took a month and at other times three months depending on who did the task. This finding led to a better understanding by the team of why the standardization of products, processes and competencies is important.

5. *Impact of trade fairs on the development of a new product.* The company must attend all the top trade fairs in their industry, especially when launching new products. However, this can lead to problems during the product development cycle. The failure to manage this need brought development activities to a standstill in order to give priority to the upcoming fair. When a product or a prototype needed a modification to meet the timing of the fair, the development activities halted. One of the ideas implemented was to increase the number of prototypes to be built from two to three. The idea was to use one of these for fairs, thereby maintaining distinct flows of activities (a difficult decision that it has not always been possible to implement). Even if it was costly from a prototype standpoint, it turned out to be less costly for the overall development project. At Sacmi, people began to realize that saving time and money cost more at the beginning.

5.3.3 Hansei and the Future State Value Stream Map

The next steps for the team were to gain a deeper understanding of why the critical issues identified in the current state map had occurred in the past.

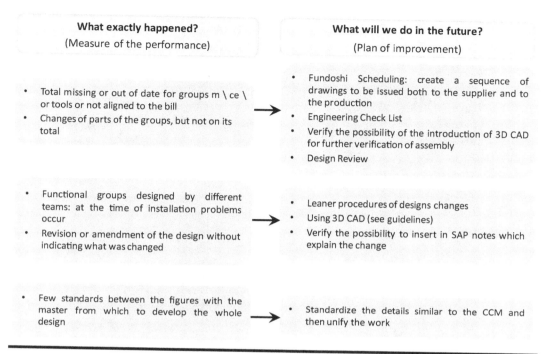

What exactly happened? (Measure of the performance)	**What will we do in the future?** (Plan of improvement)
• Total missing or out of date for groups m \ ce \ or tools or not aligned to the bill • Changes of parts of the groups, but not on its total	• Fundoshi Scheduling: create a sequence of drawings to be issued both to the supplier and to the production • Engineering Check List • Verify the possibility of the introduction of 3D CAD for further verification of assembly • Design Review
• Functional groups designed by different teams: at the time of installation problems occur • Revision or amendment of the design without indicating what was changed	• Leaner procedures of designs changes • Using 3D CAD (see guidelines) • Verify the possibility to insert in SAP notes which explain the change
• Few standards between the figures with the master from which to develop the whole design	• Standardize the details similar to the CCM and then unify the work

Figure 5.34   Excerpt from the *hansei* activity.

Figure 5.34 shows an excerpt from a *hansei* session, in which a number of causes and countermeasures were devised. These were later adopted in the course of the new project. Two examples of major causes for longer lead times were the interaction between design and production in the development phase, while the other was the excessive number of modifications made after the first official release of the machine into the market.

Regarding the multitude of late modifications, the initial belief of the team was that many changes made were primarily due to changes in requirements by the external customer being transmitted via the salesperson. To analyze this problem more thoroughly, the team opened an A3 Problem-Solving Report to examine modifications made between 2004 and 2008. As a result, a very different picture emerged. In fact, the real sources of the modifications were much more widely distributed: some had originated from the technical office itself; a significant proportion came from the assembly and still, others came from the suppliers' quality control departments. Only a fraction came from changes in specifications. Here too, the team, having become aware of the problem thanks to analysis of the data and figures, devised suitable countermeasures for the future project.

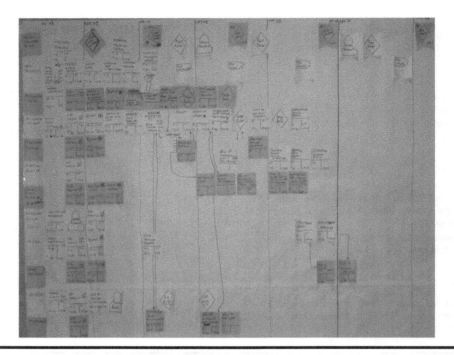

Figure 5.35   Future State Value Stream Map.

When the team defined the new processes in the Future State Value Stream Map (Figure 5.35) for the new machine project, they tried to introduce some Lean principles to deal with the main obstacles.

The Lean principles selected included:

- Regular work cadence and team meetings. Pre-established structured weekly meetings, with rules known to every team member.
- Separation of the sub-flows of work of the various groups, with a clear definition of necessary input and output for each. The machine was divided into modules around a common architecture/platform.
- More front-loading, giving more time to the "thinking" phase of the project than in the past, leaving much more time for elaborating the Concept Paper. Then giving the emerging team more time during the Kentou, the phase of greatest creativity, during which various possible concepts were analyzed and explored in order to obtain the best solution for the overall machine (Figure 5.36).
- We set a target of reducing the overall development time by about 35%–40%, based on the proposed improvements stemming from our reflection on past experiences and incorporating Lean principles (Figure 5.36).

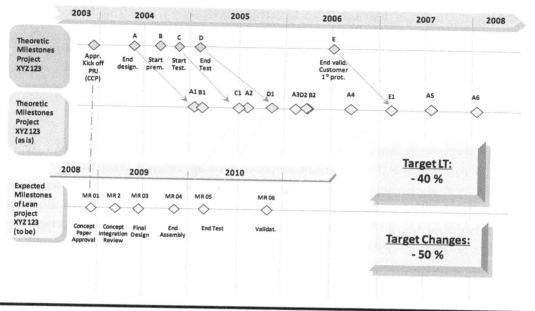

Figure 5.36 **Calculating the lead time and number-of-modifications targets for the new project.**

■ We set a target of reducing the number of modifications by 50%, in order to immediately address the causes identified during the current state analysis (Figure 5.36).

5.3.4 Concept Paper

The Concept Paper for this machine was one of the best we have seen in recent years. It took two months to complete the formal paper condensed into a document of about sixteen pages and agreed upon by all. The work that was done was a truly unique example in terms of creativity, process discipline, and professionalism. After the general overview, a great deal of discussion was devoted to the following key points:

■ Product platform rather than focusing on a particular model to launch.
■ Overview of the product's use was conducted with great attention toward existing competition, including the different technologies applied to similar products.
■ Historic analysis tracing the evolution of the technology and machine performance. Key performance trade-off curves and projections of future performance expected by the market were also included.

■ Direct customer feedback on features, technology, and machine concepts.
■ Deep analysis of the market segments, the motivations underlying such differentiation, and the number of products made according to customer type, along with sales estimates and assumptions for each segment of the market.

After the two months to do the key selling points, the challenges of the project were understood by all and everyone was aligned with the scope and goals of the project. Most importantly, everyone now had real ownership in the project and a stake in its success. The time spent was a valuable investment that involved the whole project team and not just the marketing, design, and salespeople. The document became the "Bible" of the project and posted in the Obeya. Many questions and wasted time were avoided throughout the project thanks to the great work done upfront.

5.3.5 *From Efficiency to Effectiveness*

The competitive analysis was carried out using the main performance criteria to focus the team's attention not only on how to close certain gaps but also how to make the new product stand out. The latter was done using SWOT analysis, a matrix highlighting strengths, weaknesses, opportunities, and threats. The characteristics to obtain in the new project were then condensed into a list of must-haves, nice to have, and not needed.

The team then prepared a large table of goals in the Obeya, subdividing them into three different categories: performance, cost, and product characteristics/features. For each goal, the following data were set: the current value, the target value, the impact on EBIT, and a "confidence to achieve" index.

This project was initially set up to reduce costs, but at the end of the two months spent working on the Concept Paper, the team had the courage to do something more than what had been asked to them. In fact, thanks to the robust interaction between production, design, and sales, and by *asking the right questions,* it became clear that what the market was asking for was not simply a lower cost machine but the introduction of "intelligent" improvements that would help customers to use the machine better in the field. In some cases, they made choices that determined a higher cost for some parts of the machine, but a greater customer value and profitability for the company.

The great value of having different points of view represented around the same table to make decisions was confirmed by the unexpected solutions which came out before startig the project. No one had thought to increase the cost of some parts of the machine until the sales manager understood to focus not only on cost, but on producing an answer to the following question. What do you really need to sell more machines in the future? For example, one of the most important measures to successfully sell a machine was the index of machine productivity, measured in euros per capsule produced in a unit of time.

The reflection arising from this drew attention to the reasons why the company had lost out to competitors on some previous bids, and on the reasons why it had been unable to sell any machines in certain areas and to certain clients in particular. It was not only cost but rather *value* that was missing

By changing point of view, then, the team moved on from a simple quest for cost/efficiency to the search for value/effectiveness.

Once again, it is worth repeating that it is not the document or tool as that made the difference, but the social process which involved the team to reach consensus on what was truly value added for the customer.

5.3.6 *The Project Review System and Management of the Project*

This project was also managed using tools of the Project Review System. We encountered a particular difficulty compared to other projects if we were to achieve the 40% reduction in lead time. Namely, how to keep a steady cadence in the various project activities. Getting a group that had sometimes a core team of more than twenty people to harmonize their activities and deliver their part at the right time was critical. First of all, the project was divided into seven phases and a key date was set for each of the seven phases (Figure 5.37). For each group, key items to deliver were identified. The activities that had to be done to realize those key deliverables were inserted into detailed planning sheets produced directly by the individuals responsible for each deliverable. The progress status of each element was indicated in order to obtain visual control of the whole project on a single sheet of A3 paper.

Finally, the group imposed upon itself a number of team norms for the shared management of the project:

1. Plan meetings in advance, define goals and fixed duration.

Figure 5.37   Part of the Project Review System.

The table is titled **PROJECT REVIEW SYSTEM per NUOVA CCM 48 SB LEAN** and is organized into seven phases for the Project Team / Steering levels with Key Deliverables and Key Dates:

Phase	Project Team / Steering	Key Deliverables (with responsible codes)
Phase 1	Project Scheduling & Concept Paper Agreement — MR1	Concept Paper Approvato (ALL); Reflection Criticità Attuali Produzione (UTT, UACT, RICT, MT); Reflection Criticità Attuali Clienti (UTT, UACT, RICT); Target Cost Deployment (UAT); Definizione VRP (variation reduction program) (UTT); Analisi Mercato (UCT); Piano di gamma (UTT, UCT); Planning macro di progetto (ALL); Macro Risk Assessment Preliminare (ALL); Obeya Room avviata (ALL)
Phase 2	Concept Phase / Kentou — MR2	Engineering Check List (ALL); Elenco soluzioni Kentou Macchine & Stampi (ALL); Specifiche tecniche Macchine & Stampi (UTTC, UTTP); Evaluation Matrix Soluzioni Macchine & Stampi (UTTC, UTTP); Project Reflection (ALL); Planning dettagliato dei membri del team di progetto (ALL); Criteri guida VRP (Lista di tutte le interfacce e dei vincoli) (UTTC, UTTP); Scelta Fornitori per co-sviluppo (UTTC, STPR); Impostazione della riduzione costi distinta dettagliata (tear down) (UTTC, UTTP, UTE, UAT); Investment / Costs planning (CAPO PROGETTO); Design FMEA Macchine e Stampi (UTT, UTEP)
Phase 3	System & Long Lead Time Components Design — MR3 (Sub-Phases)	Risk assesment update (ALL); Project Review & Planning update (ALL); Design & Drawing Review (ALL); Distinta base provvisoria (UTT); Project Reflection (ALL); Lista Lead Time Componenti (UPOT); Schedulazione della consegna dei disegni (UTT, UTTP); VRP Assessment (UTT, UTTP); Lancio acquisto materiali a lungo tempo di consegna (UAC); Aggiornamento della riduzione costi distinta dettagliata (tear down) (UTTC, UTTP, UTE, UTE); Disegni dettaglio 3 soluzioni Stampi (UTTP); Aggiornamento Specifiche tecniche Macchine & Stampi, inclusi input elettrici (UTTC, UTE); Risultati parziali prima soluzione stampi (UTTP); Investment / Costs update (CAPO PROGETTO); FMEA montaggio (MT, DPV); Design FMEA Macchine e Stampi update (UTT, UTEP); Scelta cliente e definizione capsula per macchina prototipo (UCT)
Phase 4	Components Detail Design — MR4	Risk assesment update (ALL); Project Review & Planning update (ALL); Design & Drawing Review (ALL); Investment / Costs update (CAPO PROGETTO); Project Reflection (ALL); Disegni (particolari + assiemi) e distinte (UTTC, UTE); VRP Assessment update (UTT, UTEP); Codifica codici in SAP (UTT, SI); FMEA montaggio update (MT, DPV); RCM - FMEA (DPV); Report CQ (CQ); Conclusione della riduzione costi distinta dettagliata (tear down) (UTTC, UTTP, UTE, STPR); Risultati parziali tre soluzioni stampi (UTTP); Lancio set stampi prima soluzione (UTTP); Dati di Stabilimento per macchina prototipo cliente (UCT); Lancio parti meccaniche + elettriche (UPOT)
Phase 5	Montaggio — MR5	Risk assesment update (ALL); Project Review & Planning update (ALL); Design & Drawing Review (ALL); Investment / Costs update (CAPO PROGETTO); Project Reflection (ALL); FMEA montaggio update (MT, DPV); Software (UTE); Report montaggio (MT); Validazione montaggio (MT); Validazione prototipazione soluzioni 2 e 3 stampi (UTTP)
Phase 6	Test — MR6	Risk assesment update (ALL); Project Review & Planning update (ALL); Design & Drawing Review (ALL); Investment / Costs update (CAPO PROGETTO); Project Reflection (ALL); FMEA montaggio update (MT, DPV); Spedizione prototipo (SLOG); Report collaudo (MT, RST); Validazione collaudo (CAPO PROGETTO)
Phase 7	Feedback / After Sales — MR7	Risk assesment update (ALL); RCM - FMEA update (DPV); Final Design & Drawing Review (ALL); Investment / Costs update (CAPO PROGETTO); Final Project Reflection incluso After Sales (ALL); Report / Validazione prototipo (CAPO PROGETTO)

Key Dates: 28.02.09 | 30.04.09 | 30.06.09 | 30.09.09 | 28.02.10 | 30.06.10 | 28.02.11

2. Arrive at meetings punctually and with all relevant data already prepared in the form of an A3 Report.

3. For the core team: hold meetings regularly, meeting once a week on the same day and at the same time. Attendance is mandatory for all. Inform the other group members in the event of an emergency and you cannot attend.

4. Members of the module groups who need to discuss specific issues will meet more than once a week as required in order to report back to the weekly core team.

5. Define action plans (what, who, when) to address open items before ending the meeting.

6. The group will explore feasibility and risks during the Kentou phase and follow structured Design Reviews in the design phase.

7. The group undertakes to use the Engineering Checklists/standards prevent errors, to conduct FMEA analysis, and to deal with critical issues relating to final assembly.

5.3.7 The Kentou Phase and the Design Execution Phase

From the beginning of the project, a number of different issues needed to be tackled, including the ones listed below.

- Rationalization of similar machines in order to benefit from increased product standardization. An internal benchmarking was carried out to adopt the existing in-house best solutions with regards to cost and performance.
- Rationalization of the dies to increase the number of parts common to the whole product range.
- Identification of technical solutions to reduce cycle times.
- Identification of technical solutions to broaden the mix of capsules producible by the same machine.
- Resolution of certain known technical problems with the existing machine.
- Consolidation of the degree of modularity of the machine.
- Find technical solutions to reduce assembly time.
- Find technical solutions to simplify the on-going maintenance of the new machine
- Reduce the cost of components via standardization, part count reduction, and design simplification (Figure 5.38).

The team split up into different subgroups, each dedicated to one or more of the modules: base, die wheel, extruder, oil-pressure system, electric plant, insertion wheel, dies. The team leader performed both system

Figure 5.38   The project's Obeya room.

integration and program management tasks, with a profile very similar to the one of the Chief Engineer outlined in Chapter 3.

All the subgroups developed their own technical solutions, applying the Set-Based Concurrent Engineering methodology for each critical area of the design. They created their own Engineering Checklists and recruited into their groups the people they needed, including maintenance technicians, assemblers, process engineers, and key component suppliers.

These expanded teams contributed both to generate a multitude of potential solutions and provided vital input into the evaluation of each idea. The criteria for choosing among different solutions were adapted according to particular internal and external customer needs. When possible, trade-off curves were used to have more objective data in evaluating potential solutions. Figure 5.39 shows the design space in which the four final solutions for the "wheel" were evaluated.

The suppliers of critical parts were selected and involved much earlier than usual. In particular, the suppliers of the wheel, base, and coupling, three of the most important components in the whole machine were involved from the early stages of Kentou. The joint design led to great improvements in terms of ease of maintenance, reliability, and ease of assembly. For example, the oil-pressure unit was kept separate and positioned outside the body of the machine, making it easier to carry out maintenance and to actually mount the unit. It was entertaining to watch designers and assemblers debating in front of large monitors in the Obeya

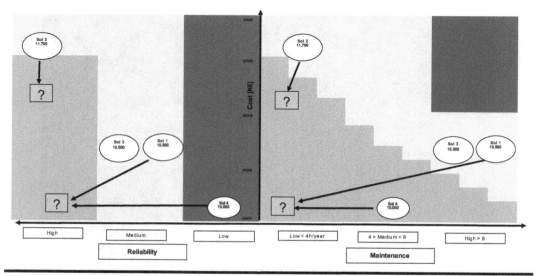

Figure 5.39   Trade-off curve for the choice of wheel solution.

room about the position of a junction or tube and being able to quickly change the position of that junction or tube with a few clicks on a mouse, rather than seeing them arguing in the plant when the pieces had already been made and they had clearance issues as used to happen in the past.

5.3.8 Modifications: Are We Sure We Know the Causes?

During the project, one of the main problems we had to address was the historically high number of design modifications made during the project, especially after the design phase that had supposedly been completed. The most common reason given was: "Yes, the sales people always change the specifications. They're always shifting the ground beneath us."

As a starting point, we examined the previous one hundred modifications in chronological order, analyzing the reasons for making the changes, measuring the effects they had, and came up with solutions for each issue. Of the hundred modifications, we found only a very small number turned out to be associated with the external market—neither the salespeople nor the customers had actually asked for the majority of changes.

In most cases, the causes were much simpler, internal deviations or mix-ups due to an inadequate exchange of information between groups. For example, a paint application not clearly indicated on the design and therefore poorly executed, or the impossibility of fixing two parts together because one of them lacked a hole. The objective reality, backed up by facts and figures, helped us to focus our attention where it was needed, rather than chasing issues based on past perceptions.

5.3.9 The Assembly of the Prototype

There were a number of "rough patches" in the design phase, due to various organizational, workload, and technical problems, but the team always managed to pull together and to keep on track toward the objectives. The assembly of the first prototype began in July 2010. Unlike what traditionally would have happened, a number of important new steps were introduced to improve the prototype which included:

1. A designer from the technical office always on-site throughout the whole assembly process.
2. The Obeya was moved to the production area and adapted to meet the needs for this phase of the project.

3. The periodic team meetings took place in the production area, with the machine on one side and the Obeya on the other, as shown in Figure 5.40.
4. Two specialist assemblers were chosen to do the whole assembly, but they were asked to do so with a critical eye and to point out straight-away any problem or anomalies, so the team could address them prior to the production launch.
5. A visual system was set up to monitor every step of the assembly process, comparing the time actually spent with what had been predicted, noting the differences and brainstorming countermeasures when needed.
6. Each major problem was managed with the A3 methodology and discussed in the Obeya.
7. Every anomaly in the components was immediately jotted down on a special chart in full view in the Obeya, so temporary measures could be taken for the construction of the prototype and permanent ones addressed with the suppliers.
8. The pace of the assembly was monitored constantly and visualized directly on the chart in front of the machine. Anyone walking by could see the prototype build status at a glance.
9. The action plans of the whole team were visualized on a large chart using colored sticky notes for different types of issues.
10. The full action list status was reviewed in the team's daily meeting out on the shop floor.

Figure 5.40   Photo of a progress meeting during the assembly of the prototype.

"Finally, someone from design group who is in the production department for the whole duration of the assembly and testing phase," was the comment that emerged as one of the many positive aspects of the experience during the end-of-project *hansei* meeting. The close collaboration that took place during the building of the prototype enabled the rapid resolution of the problems that arose, and the gathering of very precise and specific feedback useful for clearly defining all the modifications that needed to be made to the pre-series machine. It also made possible to drastically reduce the late changes that had plagued previous projects.

The sharing of information from the very start of the project was extremely important, enabling the issues and risks of the project to become immediately obvious before the pieces were designed and built. Obviously, all of the activities were not simple. For example, various team members stressed the difficulty of keeping resources focused, completely or in part, to the project, as they were frequently "snatched" for other activities. But making the management of the whole project completely open and transparent meant that even resource problems did not remain hidden for long. Rather, they came to the surface and were solved promptly.

5.3.10 Conclusions

After the assembly and testing phases were completed on schedule, the CCM48SB Lean was presented at Interpack 2011 fair in Düsseldorf, Germany, where it was a great success. In Figure 5.41, you can see the machine unveiled.

"Cycle time 1.8 sec," is prominently displayed on the machine to market a key selling point of the new series. When the team leader was asked about the state of the project in June 2011, he said:

> The main goals of the project have been fully achieved: cycle time (we've managed to exceed the target speed without difficulty), energy consumption (we have reduced energy consumption at high speeds as well, and by a higher percentage than predicted), cost (current estimates suggest the cost will be close to the target figure). It remains to be seen in the field whether we will meet the other objectives, but at the moment we are confident of doing so. Besides the project goals, I sense there is a positive attitude to the machine as a whole, both from the operators who use it and from the sales people and managers who have to sell it to the market.[4]

Figure 5.41   The new machine on display at Interpack 2011, Düsseldorf, Germany.

In the section about the group's Beverage Division, the Sacmi 2010 Annual Report states:[5]

> Despite a world economy that is going to return to pre-recession levels, sales posted by the CLOSURES & CONTAINERS division exceeded 171 million Euros, an increase on the previous year of just under 12%. [...] the fact remains that our machines are sold world-wide and are currently used in over 60 nations on five continents. The year 2010 also saw the delivery of the 1000th compression machine to one of our most important Taiwanese customers (THC). A leadership like this is maintened only with a development: the near-completion of the new CCM48SB, developed by applying Lean manufacturing methods to our compression machines, is an example. If results are in line with expectations, the same process will gradually be applied to our entire machine range.

The results to date have exceeded everyone's expectations, thanks to an excellent, close-knit team guided by visionary managers.

> And now? [...] And now we carry on! Another fair, the machine to be installed for field monitoring with clients .... New projects in the pipeline for the CCMs ... the work goes on.

Another continuous improvement cycle begins...stay tuned!

5.4 Continental

5.4.1 Not Enough Time to Develop a New Technology?

Continental is a German company, leader in the automotive tires manufacturing and sales. Based in Hanover and founded back in 1871, it is also
one of the world's five biggest automotive suppliers. Continental employs
approximately 212,000 people in fifty-one countries, with over 39€ billion
of sales recorded in 2016. One of its six divisions, the Powertrain
Division, has a plant in Pisa, Italy, which employs over one-thousand
workers.

The project we developed with a group of engineers at Continental in
Pisa involved a specific application of Lean Innovation principles to the
development of a new production technology. Even if numerical data and
figures have been omitted for confidentiality reasons, the case is quite interesting, because it demonstrates how it is possible to adapt Lean principles to
industrial technology projects and the benefits that can be obtained in terms
of efficiency and overall cost.

5.4.2 The Problem

The Continental plant in Pisa is a leader in the design and production of
fuel injectors for the automotive industry, which can serve world-class clients like Porsche, Audi, BMW, Mercedes, and PSA. The company was facing
higher costs than expected for one of its most critical components, the high-
pressure fuel injectors. The component is a casing, through which gasoline
is nebulized directly into the engine cylinder. To ensure a regular flow,
together with the geometric and fluid dynamic characteristics, the quality
of the holes has to be so precise that it is necessary to use expensive high-
precision technology. The technology used at the beginning of the project
was Electrical Discharge Machining (EDM). EDM is a production process
for obtaining the desired shape by using specific electrical discharges. The
material is removed from the piece through a series of alternating, high-
frequency current discharges between two electrodes, separated by a liquid
dielectric. One of the electrodes is the "instrument" or "electrode," in this
case in tungsten alloy, while the other is the piece in which the hole must
be made. These holes have a diameter of between 0.1 and 0.3 mm, and
a depth—corresponding to the depth of the casing itself—of between 0.2
and 0.4 mm. The degree of tolerance set for this holes is in the order of a

micron, and, for this reason, it's very complicated to effectively measure their compliance in the production environment.

The overall investment in micro-drilling machines capable of satisfying the estimated production requirements at the beginning of this project had exceeded ten million euros over four years—just for the production of one component in the whole injector. Going forward, the working team decided that there was the need to design a lower cost technology that could meet the rigorous quality and performance requirements.

5.4.3 Getting Started: Scoping, Goal Setting, Partner Selection, and Planning

As the Pisa plant did not have sufficient resources to develop new technologies independently and in-house, the company decided to involve different partners with the necessary technical expertise and to use the Set-Based-Concurrent-Engineering process[6] to explore various alternatives before developing a specific technology solution. The big difficulty that the team were looking for solutions beyond the known boundaries of technical and economic feasibility. Consequently, the method for evaluating the alternatives ran up against a lack of objective data with which to confirm or refute the validity of initial hypotheses made both by Continental technicians and outside experts. We, therefore, drew up a full-scale plan of standardized tests in order to gather, over a reasonably brief period of time, objective elements to validate (or invalidate) the technical hypotheses as they were formulated. The project turned into quite a complex case of technological exploration and innovation involving fifteen different research partners

As cost was the primary goal, the first step was to define the unit of measurement to evaluate the various technology alternatives. Rather than considering the cost of every single component, a new *cost index* was defined. It was characterized by the relationship between the total estimated cost of the technological investment "connected" with the total estimated lifetime production cost.

The index was a ratio between the total estimated investment, including not just machinery but also the manpower to install it, quality control instruments, all infrastructural expenses, and technical support costs. As for the denominator, the calculation of the total estimated production cost took into account all the direct and indirect costs that would be incurred.

The team then set the goal of the project was to halve the cost index of the current technology within three years, without affecting the quality of the finished product. If successful, this would translate into savings of several millions of euros (actual figures cannot be shared due to confidentiality).

The team that was gathered included technicians from Pisa, product and assembling process experts coming from plants in US and Germany and integrated with Lenovys consultants.

In defining the scope of the project, three macro areas of research were considered:

1. *Evolution and improvement of the existing technology*: to obtain benefits in the short and mid-term.
2. *"Hybrid" technology, combining existing and new technologies*: to obtain benefits in the mid and mid-to-long term.
3. *Development of a completely new technology*: to obtain benefits in the mid-to-long term.

Various solutions were explored for each of the three areas using the principles of Set-Based Concurrent Engineering to lead the team to the best solution(s).

5.4.4 The First Steps: Analysis of the Current Situation and Competitive Benchmarking

Two types of initial screening were conducted—one internal and one external. Analyzing the current processes' capabilities (Figure 5.42) and the total costs, the internal screening resulted in short-term improvement actions, but also some useful ideas for the mid-to-long term development other technology solutions.

In particular, it yielded ideas for reducing the overall erosion time thus optimizing several process parameters. Analysis of the data and a profound understanding of the technical processes produced ideas useful for the evolution of the existing technology, such as introducing mechanisms capable of neutralizing various existing limits and giving rise to so-called hybrid solutions.

The analysis of the existing technologies on the market for producing micro apertures permitted a totally "out of the box" approach offering innovative ideas, despite the strict technical specification needed for the product. The technological concepts chosen to explore can be seen in Figure 5.43.

In order to see which partners to involve in the project, meetings were held several suppliers and research centers, each of which provided

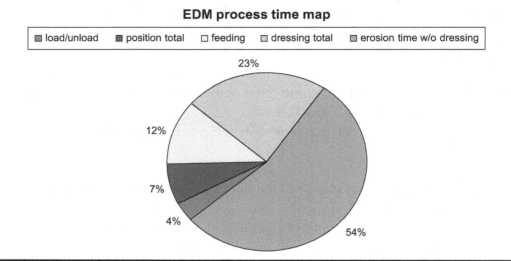

Figure 5.42 **Chart of process times for the EDM technology at the start of the project.**

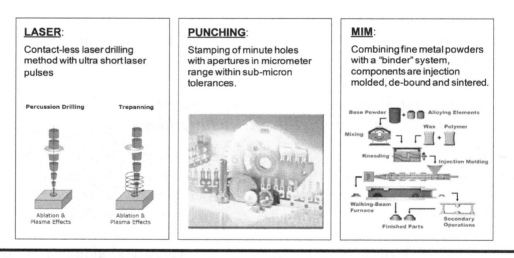

Figure 5.43 **Example of existing technologies for producing micro apertures.**

demonstrations of their potential technology and the results of pre-test activities before being "officially" admitted into extended test phase to collect specific quality and performance data for the given application.

5.4.5 Project Review System and Test Activities Standardization

The project was managed with the Project Review System, with particular care being taken to ensure a set pace and rhythm for the various project

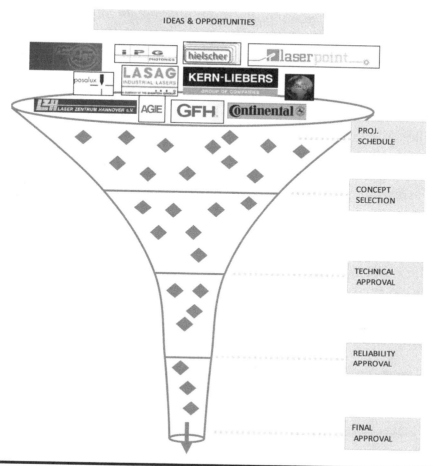

Figure 5.44 **Diagram of the general convergence process, with the identification of initial partners for the generation of alternative solutions.**

activities in order to allow a steady convergence to the final choice. A key deadline was fixed for each of the five phases (Figure 5.44), by which time the "salient features" of the project, the so-called key deliverables, were to be completed and documented. The activities required to achieve them were done by detailed planning charts drawn up directly by each partner responsible for the given deliverables. The progress status of each concept was followed using status A3's.

The project was divided into the following phases:

1. *Project scoping and scheduling.* Defining and agreeing the customer (performance, characteristics, and quality) and business (costs, restrictions, timing, and resources) goals.

2. *Exploration and selection of the different concept alternatives.* This is the phase that required the maximum technical effort to explore the proposed solutions including the testing and evaluation of prototypes developed during different convergent steps.

3. *Development of the technical and industrial concept.* After the selection of the solutions deemed potentially valid for mass production, the next step requires the development of the technological concept: plants, equipment, specifications, and manufacturing processes. For this kind of project three or four possible alternatives remain "on the table" during this phase.

4. *Assessment of the technical reliability of the solution.* Phase of application tests to evaluate the technology and the product in the customer configuration.

5. *Final technical approval.* Production of the technical specifications and of the other documents needed for the start of purchasing and industrialization phase.

The Project Review System used for the project is shown in Figure 5.45.

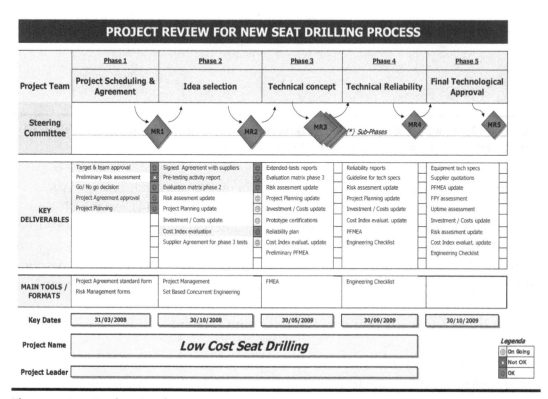

Figure 5.45   Project Review System excerpt.

One of the most difficult parts of the entire project was to establish objective technical parameters to evaluate the true value of the proposed ideas and solutions. Given the need to technically evaluate the quality of one technology as opposed to another, we immediately realized that we had to gather together and process an enormous amount of data. A standard methodology was introduced to manage the information flows from all the partners to provide standardized data in standard formats with the aim to compare effectively the different proposals. Without this standardization, it would have been impossible to objectively and consistently evaluate, in just four to six months, almost one hundred different tests made by fifteen partners. Some of the information that was standardized included:

1. Pre-test data used for the initial selection of technology/supplier
2. Prototypes and documentation used extended testing
3. Extended testing procedures and results
4. Technical validation and technical plant specifications

The testing activity, summed up in Figure 5.46, was standardized in order to avoid wasting time and money due to unforeseen eventualities and ambiguities in the operative process. Aspects such as the number of samples to deliver, the type of "template" to use, sender and delivery addresses, the list

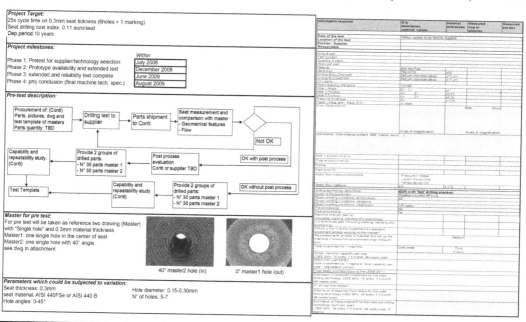

Figure 5.46   Chart of standard flows and formats for the test activities.

of data to be gathered for each test, the kind of master to employ, and so on, were all clearly laid out.

The preliminary standardization of the tests made it possible to collect and process large amounts of data without any great effort, because the initial work to define the flow eliminated much of the discontinuity and loss of time that typically arises during this phase. The standards pushed the Continental technicians to be very clear in their own minds about what to ask of the suppliers, but above all, it brought out in advance all the possible questions that the supplier would then have to find answers for in the technological preparation and execution of the various tests. It also helped to speed up and facilitate communication, given the objective language difficulties that inevitably arose in a team made up by German, French, Italian, American, Swiss, and English engineers. In this way, the technical meetings took place without the need to spend a lot of time re-discussing and re-aligning expectations. This made it possible to focus on key technical issues and risks rather than contractual deliverables.

5.4.6 Set-Based Concurrent Engineering put to the Test: The Evaluation Matrix

Even if the data collection for the evaluation of the single alternatives was standardized and accelerated, the screenings of alternatives were discussed in depth and reviewed using a standardized evaluation matrix. While apparently simple, it was actually very complex due to the need to explore twenty-nine different solutions, described by forty different parameters. Considering that thousands of casings were drilled and tested during the exploration phase, this meant that about five-thousand individual measurements were done in total. The matrix was developed with the collaboration of Continental engineers, who skillfully adopted the classic concept of the hierarchical multilevel evaluation matrix often used for comparing alternative solutions through the assessment of different characteristics, weights, and importance. In this case, we considered four different factors for each alternative:

1. Values from objective data: geometric measures, statistical dispersion of the measures, cycle times, number of defects, etc.
2. Values from objective facts: photographs obtained by means of an electron microscope for detecting the presence of burrs on the edges of the holes or of cracks, the extension of thermally modified areas, etc.

3. Values from objective total costs: official cost quotations, labor and technical assistance requirements, etc.
4. Values from subjective evaluations: technical risk assessments, feasibility estimates, supplier capability and flexibility, ease of access to know-how for solutions, and other strategic considerations.

A weight has been assigned to each characteristic, with a well-defined scale of evaluation in order to come up with an objective and standardized rating for each alternative. The result was an overall ranking that took into account all the factors. Figure 5.47 shows an example of a portion of the standard evaluation matrix that has been used for the project.

5.4.7 Trade-Off Curves

The evaluation carried out during the analysis enabled joint consideration of cost, quality, and several industrial performance variables. In order to more clearly picture and compare their relative impacts with regards to the various technical and economic variables, the key trade-offs were represented

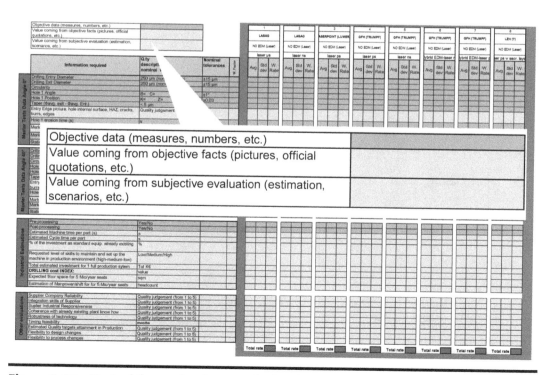

Figure 5.47   Part of the evaluation matrix for the twenty-nine alternative solutions.

by graphical means to assess the sensitivity of certain factors with respect to others. An example can be seen in Figure 5.48.

5.4.8 Chosen Solutions and Conclusions

Three solutions were ultimately chosen for the advanced testing phase. All of them met the criteria established at the beginning of the project: the first was the most innovative and promising in terms of economic benefits; the second was intermediate in terms of risk and benefits; and the third was industrially more conservative than the first two, albeit markedly more advanced in its development.

More analyses and development work were done in parallel for the 3 solutions. For example, in the diagram shown in Figure 5.49, you can see a microscope view of the quality of the micro-hole obtained by one of the chosen solutions.[7]

This research project shows how it is possible to find innovative solutions to a complex problem in a relatively brief period of time while coordinating a large number of resources, with the aim to achieve significant economic benefits using Lean principles in the conceptual phase. These Lean

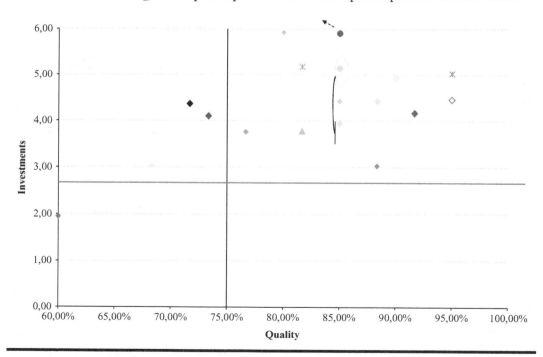

Figure 5.48   Example of trade-off curve for the comparative evaluation of the different solutions.

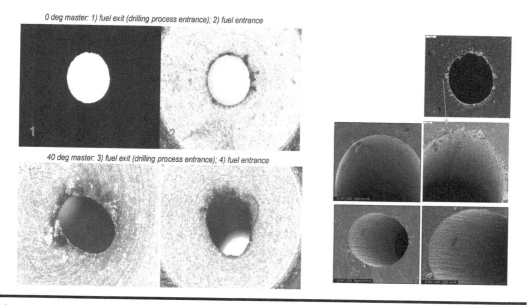

Figure 5.49 **Electron microscope photos of the holes obtained with one of the three chosen solutions.**

principles were the enablers to guide an "enlightened" management team and an extremely competent and highly motivated group of engineers to overcome challenges that seemed insurmountable at the time.

As of now, the Pisa plant appears to have weathered the recessionary storm that hit the European automotive industry in 2009–2011. Thus demonstrating that innovating in periods of cost-cutting crisis is not only possible, but it's also the best way to not only survive but to reach a position of industry leadership in one's sector.

5.5 PSA—Peugeot Citroen: Applying Set-Based Concurrent Engineering

5.5.1 Introduction

One of the key principles of Lean Product and Process development noted by Liker and Morgan (2006) is that of *"Front load the product development process to thoroughly explore alternative Solutions while there is Maximum Design Space."* One of the key methodologies to do this is the approach of *Set-Based Concurrent Engineering (SBCE)* that was first described by Dr. Al Ward.

There are really two different approaches to design. The traditional approach (Figure 5.50A), implemented by the vast majority of engineers, is the iterative model. The problem with this approach is that we only tend to look at a few concepts because of time, budget, resources (or all of the above). Consequently, we tend to down-select to one concept fairly quickly and will very likely have many iterations and changes during the development and industrialization phases before meeting the overall requirements. With the Set-Based approach (Figure 5.50B) described by Dr. Al Ward, we explore the design space more thoroughly by generating many feasible alternatives at the subsystem/component level, we evaluate the concepts relative to risks and goals and we combine those subsystem/components alternatives to evaluate different system-level options and gradually to converge to the optimal system-level solution. That optimal concept is then developed, validated, and industrialized in a shorter period of time with less rework.

While many companies do spend time generating alternatives, very few spend sufficient time to systematically explore alternatives in the early stages while the design is still fluid and it can be best optimized. There are several reasons for this including costs (it is often mentioned that it might seem a waste to invest on a project that is not yet approved or for which we are not sure it will go to market someday), time pressures, and lack of clarity in the voice of the customer. However, as we will see in the following case study, the Set-Based approach can be done with only a slight increase in resources upfront while saving much more time in the latter phases of a project.

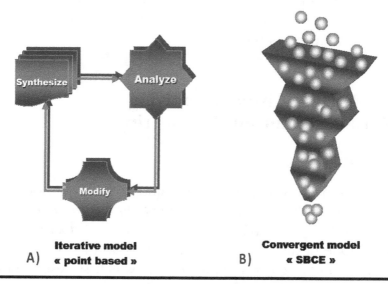

Figure 5.50 (A) Iterative model and (B) Set-Based Concurrent Engineering model.

PSA Peugeot Citroen started their Lean Product Development journey in July 2007. In their first year, it became clear more front-loading, exploration, and evaluation of alternatives was necessary to develop more robust products in a timely manner. While exploring multiple design alternatives was not new to PSA, the process of exploring, evaluating, and optimizing design choices was not always efficient leading to late changes and tight deadlines.

While some groups at PSA already claimed to be "Set-Based," several in the company were not so sure. In the spirit of Lean, one engine team working on the development of a brand-new generation of engines decided to give a try using the more systematic approach of Set-Based Concurrent Engineering and to see how it would work at PSA and see its potential benefits compared to how they had done projects in the past.

PSA PEUGEOT CITROËN

5.5.2 SBCE Approach

5.5.2.1 Set-Based Concurrent Engineering—Scoping: What Is Value-Added? Where Do We Need to Search?

Set-Based Concurrent Engineering obviously has to be done in the early phases of the project while the design is still fluid. To begin, the team needed to have a clear understanding of the voice of the customer regarding the product's performance. They also needed to clarify the voice of the business with regards to cost and project timing. By knowing the voice of customers (VoC) and the voice of business (VoB), they were in a better place to know what ranges they had open to them to explore and what key trade-offs would need to be considered during the convergence phase.

Based on the findings, the team realized that they needed to explore around five specific functional areas of the engine in order to meet the customer and business needs. It is important to note that rarely will you need to explore all facets of a given product design. Part of early scoping is to determine which parts of the design can we re-use (or slightly modify) and which parts do we truly need to find new innovative solutions to meet the customer's needs.

Experts for each of these functional areas participated in the project to ensure that the design space was thoroughly explored, and that past learnings could be leveraged in evaluating alternatives.

5.5.2.2 Set-Based Concurrent Engineering—Initialization Workshop

While the convergent process, when done well, will usually take several months, it is recommended that teams starting out on their Lean journey with SBCE begin with an initialization workshop. The goals of the workshop are:

■ Train the team in the SBCE methodology.
■ Orient the team to begin exploring in the correct design space.
■ Begin the convergence process so that all team members are aligned and converging in the same direction.
■ Create an agreed-upon convergence plan to meet the overall project timing.

Most initialization workshops last two to five days depending on the scope and complexity of the product. In the case of this engine project, the workshop was done over three days.

5.5.2.2.1 Phase 1: Clarify the Voice of the Customer

From the preliminary scoping, the chief engineer should provide the team with the key needs of their customer. In the spirit of Lean, keep it simple. The Voice of Customer should be kept to a small number of key criteria they will be used later to evaluate. If too many "voices" are present, it will be difficult for the team to effectively evaluate alternatives and meet the key needs of the customer. As the Greek proverb says: "When two roosters sing at cockcrow, the sunrise might be delayed."

The customer needs typically include key performance characteristics, quality requirements, and cost targets. Ideally, the targets should be expressed in ranges in order to give the team the maximum area of design space.

5.5.2.2.2 Phase 2: Exploration of Alternatives

In this phase, the team is divided into subgroups by their respective disciplines. The subgroups, search for alternatives from various perspectives (technical, industrial, styling, etc) that:

■ meet the customer needs;
■ are feasible from the point of view of the technical discipline.

In traditional brainstorming, we would have the entire cross-functional team do a group brainstorming. However, experience has shown that it is better in the beginning of the exploration phase that the engineers do some independent studies of what is possible from their perspective. It has been shown that this approach is the best to accelerate the time to explore alternatives and helps by opening up the opportunity to learn from looking at a whole set of possible alternatives proposed by all groups simultaneously.

Each alternative is documented on an A3 (Figure 5.51) that includes: a description of the concept, a sketch (if relevant, but highly useful), and the relative pros and cons. In the case of the engine project, five teams generated a total of 130 concepts that could potentially meet the customer needs and found that seventy-one of these concepts were technically feasible to present to their peers.

5.5.2.2.3 Phase 3: Presentation of Alternatives and Feedback

Each subgroup presented their alternatives to their peers for feedback. The other subgroups asked any questions to clarify the concepts being presented and then provided feedback on its feasibility relative to their design choices. The feedback was posted on the wall on a Venn-type diagram (Figure 5.52). A scribe also documented all the alternatives and feedback in a spreadsheet.

It is important to note that the team did not "throw away" any solutions. Rather, keeping solutions that have been eliminated in a designated repository (e.g. Books of Knowledge), as they may be applicable to future projects. Going through the SBCE process in itself increases teams' overall knowledge of the design space that will obviously be useful for further projects.

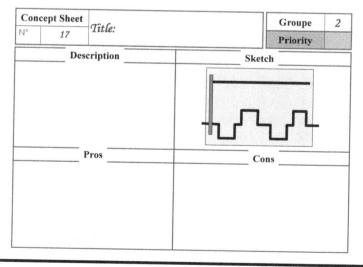

Figure 5.51   Example A3 template for concepts.

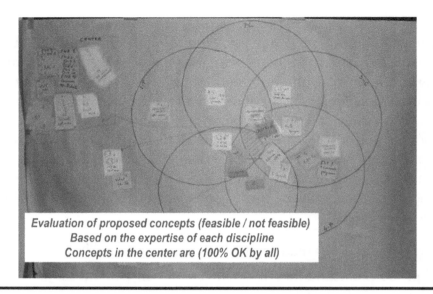

Evaluation of proposed concepts (feasible / not feasible)
Based on the expertise of each discipline
Concepts in the center are (100% OK by all)

Figure 5.52   First convergence of feasible alternatives (due to drawing constraints, the center area here, was located in the upper left part of diagram).

5.5.2.2.4 Phase 4: Quantification of Remaining Alternatives

The team members then returned to their subgroups to better quantify the remaining alternatives. The quantification (actual numbers are not displayed for proprietary reasons) was based on the following criteria:

Voice of Customer needs which included:

■ CO_2 emission level
■ Fuel efficiency
■ Cost.

At this point, other constraints from a technical and business perspective were also introduced into the analysis. These included:

■ Mass
■ Packaging
■ Meet project timing.

The above customer needs and constraints were the basis for the teams to begin taking into account the key trade-offs in the design alternatives.

Based on the analysis at this point, the five subgroups had converged to a total of twenty-six alternatives as shown in Figure 5.53.

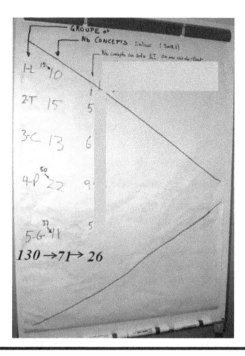

Figure 5.53　Convergence after subgroup analyses.

As we can see in the figure above, some teams had gradually converged and still had several alternatives whereas other groups had rapidly converged into only one alternative. At this point of the process, it became clear that some groups were down-selecting too quickly and without sufficient data to support it. One of the key principles of SBCE is to keep the alternative in the set until there is factual data to support it being removed from the set of alternatives—"Innocent until proven guilty."

5.5.2.2.5　Phase 5: Additional Brainstorming and Review "Risky" Alternatives that Should Re-enter the Set

Based on the analysis in phase 4, it is recommended that subgroups step back at this stage to brainstorm additional alternatives and/or review the alternatives that were not "in the center" but close to the center of the Venn diagram. (i.e. those alternatives where only one or two groups had some reservations). The subgroups should review innovative yet riskier solutions that have high potential:

■ To meet or exceed customer needs
■ Have risks that can be mitigated
■ Can be explored in the timing of the project.

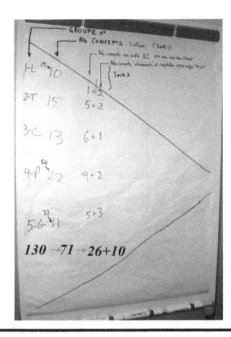

Figure 5.54 Convergence + re-entry of risky yet innovative solutions.

The subgroup should negotiate with subgroup(s) that had reservations on the proposed concept to:

■ Identify/quantify concern
■ Propose risk mitigation(s) (as a key success factor for future activity) or modify the concept
■ Estimate timing.

The subgroups can then collectively determine which alternatives should re-enter the set of alternatives to carry forward.

In the case of the PSA engine project, the subgroups identified a total of ten "innovative" solutions (Figure 5.54) that had potential worthy of keeping them in the set a while longer.

5.5.2.2.6 Phase 6: Identify Backup Solution

At this stage, subgroups began identifying their backup solution. The backup is the alternative that is the low-risk alternative where the team has a high degree of confidence that it will work within the overall system even if it may lack some of the requirements. The backup solution is essentially the "80% solution." In some cases, it may even be the existing component or subsystem. The backup is introduced as a safety net that allows the teams to simultaneously and confidently pursue both radically innovative solutions and a more conservative solution to mitigate the risk of potential engineering failure.

5.5.2.2.7 Phase 7: Create Schedule and Action Plans to Complete the Convergence Phase

At this point, the team had narrowed down the alternatives as best they could in the initialization workshop. Now they needed to look at how they would analyze and evaluate alternatives through the remainder of the project. To do this requires the following:

1. Note the potential risks associated with each alternative.
2. Identify what *minimum* actions would be needed to prove (or invalidate) the feasibility of each alternative. Who will do them? When can we expect to know the results?
3. Managing the convergence by evaluating the value of actions (i.e. balancing the need to know or the need to learn further, with the need to decide based on the project timing).
4. Create the convergence plan that aligns with the overall project plan. The convergence plan at a minimum should include:
   a. Integration events—when will we integrate the various remaining alternatives to see their overall system-level feasibility?
   b. Final decisions (cut-off dates)—when will we need to make the final choice for each subgroup?

Figure 5.55 provides an illustration of a convergence plan.

5.5.2.3 Convergence Phase

As was mentioned, the workshop is only the beginning of the convergence phase. In the convergence phase itself, there are several activities that the project manager (system integrator) must do to guide the design to the optimal solution.

First week after the workshop:

1. Communication to all affected members of the team and key stakeholders who were not part of the workshop. The communications should include decisions made, concepts still in play, action plans, and timing for convergence.

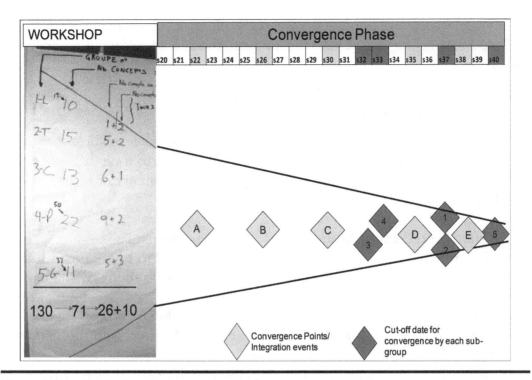

Figure 5.55   Example of a convergence plan.

2. First meeting with subgroup team leaders to confirm/expand action plans and timing.

Weekly meetings:
System integrator should meet with the team on a regular cadence to:

1. Follow up on action plans.
2. Facilitate scheduled integration events.
3. Ensure decisions are made at the right time to ensure that they meet the cut-off dates established by each group.

The integration events are critical to making sure that the teams evaluate the combination of alternatives so that decisions can be made at the right time.

5.5.3 *Conclusions*

During their Lean journey applying Set-Based Concurrent Engineering, the teams at PSA learned that there were several elements that were important to making the convergence phase effective. The key success factors include:

1. All disciplines respect decisions made by the team.
2. Resource planning (people and budget) to front-load the exploration.
3. Alternatives stay in the set until there is data to support eliminating it (i.e. keep the funnel open as long as possible).
4. Avoid going back to second-guess or re-explore solutions already eliminated.
5. Document all solutions that have been explored during the project in a designated repository (e.g. Books of Knowledge) as they may be applicable to future projects.
6. Decisions are made when specified in the convergence plan (not later or earlier).

The engine team who went through the SBCE process saw several benefits of using the process including:

- The ability to explore and evaluate more solutions more rapidly.
- Improved collaboration between functional groups.
- A better and faster consensus on decisions made.
- Limited late changes.

As a corollary to the case study, during the convergence phase, the team had an unexpected change to the project requirements that came about from the government regulatory requirements. While this did cause the engine team to change the design direction on some subsystems, the system integrator said it was it was great that they had used SBCE. Why?

> *"Had we simply done our traditional approach of looking at a few solutions and picked one to design early, we would have spent a lot of time iterating to find a new feasible solution. With SBCE we had thoroughly explored the design space, we knew exactly which solutions we had already examined that were at one time not feasible which now needed to re-enter the set so we did not have a lot of perturbation to our development plan."*

Since the case study presented above, the PSA team has used the SBCE approach on several other projects. They have also begun to incorporate the methodology into their core product development process. However, they are still learning and refining the methodology to fit their various product groups. As the engine project shows, the SBCE approach is a strong Lean methodology that can help teams improve the strength and speed of their product development process.

Acknowledgments

Special thank you to the PSA teams for sharing their experiences on SBCE. In particular, thank you to Olivier Soulié from the PSA R & D Excellence System for providing interesting insights and collaboration in providing content for the case study.

5.6 Lamborghini

5.6.1 Applied Research and Bold Product Innovation

In collaboration with Luciano De Oto[8]

The history of Lamborghini is an interlocking chain of challenges and innovation.

But what does being innovative really mean?

Sometimes it means starting from existing products and trying to improve them, as company founder Ferruccio Lamborghini did in the famous clutch story. Before going too far, let's step back for a minute and look at the company's history. At the end of the 1940s, having served as a repair mechanic in the air force in the Second World War, Ferruccio Lamborghini embarked on an entrepreneurial career as a tractor manufacturer. He bought up surplus military vehicles and turned them into agricultural machines. In 1948, he founded Lamborghini Trattori, which, in the 1950s and 60s, became one of the largest agricultural machinery manufacturers in Italy.

In 1961, Ferruccio bought a Ferrari 250 GT for his second wife, but the car had a very rigid clutch. He then bought a second Ferrari, a 250 GT2 Plus, the bodywork of which was also designed by Pininfarina, but this too had a stiff clutch. So he dismantled the clutch in his workshop, only to find that it was the same type as the ones used for his tractors. Bitterly disappointed, he went to see Enzo Ferrari, an old friend, and said:

> I pay you all this money, only to find I have a tractor clutch fitted in the car?" And that was the start of their rivalry, because Enzo

Ferrari answered: "You go off and make tractors and leave me to take care of the sports cars.

This is also when his desire to innovate started. He got cracking straight away, because the 350 GT, the first model of the newly established "House of the Bull," had many innovative features and was superior to the Ferraris of the time. Presented at the Turin Auto Show of 1963, it was the first of many memorable Lamborghini models to come. Located since the beginning in Santa'Agata Bolognese, Italy, and owned since 1998 by Audi, Volkswagen Group, in 2016 Lamborghini reached for its first time the record revenue of 906 million euro, with 3.547 sold vehicles achieving its sixth consecutive increasing year.

Today, after many successes, Lamborghini has set itself a fresh challenge and embarked on another journey of innovation. It wants to be the world's most avant-garde car manufacturer in the integral application of carbon fiber for the manufacturing of automobiles (Figure 5.56). Why? The key parameter of super sports cars is the weight-to-power ratio, and so, given the emissions regulations that place a limit on how much power can be increased, it is necessary to work on reducing weight. The extensive use of carbon fiber, also at a structural level, has already put Lamborghini into the lead, and it wants to continue distinguishing itself with respect to the competition. It is, then, a crucial technology for the super sports cars of the future, increasingly light, lower fuel consumption, and low CO_2 emissions.

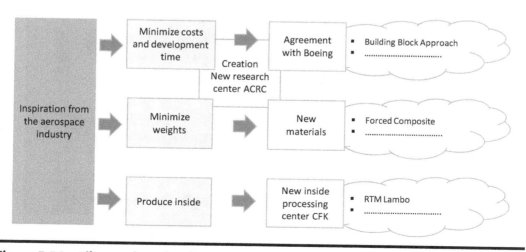

Figure 5.56 Fiber carbon development program at Lamborghini.

5.6.2 The Sesto Elemento, a Laboratory of Excellence

The Research and Development center has always been one of the company's most active departments: new technologies are being studied all the time, technologies designed to guarantee and improve the performance characteristics of the cars and, at the same time, to meet the required environmental standards. In 2008, a laboratory was set up in Seattle, where research is currently underway into carbon fiber-based technologies. The project is being run in conjunction with two prestigious partners, the University of Washington and Boeing.

Lamborghini's engineers and technicians actually began to explore composite materials in 1983, with the first applications on some Countach components. Since then, the know-how within the company has grown steadily, leading to the establishment of the Sesto Elemento technological laboratory (Figure 5.57).

The Sesto Elemento's name is a reference to the atomic number of carbon, in recognition of the car's extensive use of carbon fiber. Presented at the Paris Auto Show in 2010, just twenty Sesto Elemento vehicles have been produced and sold, used exclusively on racetracks for evaluation purposes. Reported prices range from US$2.2 million to US$2.9 million. At the time, the Sesto Elemento was the most expensive Lamborghini ever created.

Figure 5.57 Luciano De Oto, in the center, with members of the Sesto Elemento team.

Figure 5.58   Rendering of the Lamborghini Sesto Elemento.

The Sesto Elemento (Figure 5.58) is a *Technological Demonstrator and* represents the future of super sports cars, in line with the Lamborghini philosophy that handling and acceleration are increasingly important, and will become even more so in the years to come, on a par with a stylish design.

An exceptional power-to-weight ratio of just 1.75 kg per HP permits unequalled performance levels: from a standing start, the Sesto Elemento can reach 100 km/hour (62mph) in just 2.5 seconds.

These values are made possible thanks to an innovative structure made entirely of carbon fiber, which uses technology co-developed by an American supplier and with Callaway, the world's biggest golf club manufacturer. The new patented material, called Forged Composite, possesses a number of innovative characteristics: it has excellent structural properties, and so can be used to construct high load-bearing components. It is also revolutionary in terms of the production process, as it can be molded in a little less than three hundred seconds, a much shorter time than that employed for standard lamination processes for composite materials.

Above all, however, it offers a huge advantage: weight. Through this technology it is possible to obtain a material that has the same structural properties as aluminum in a much shorter production time (Figure 5.59).

Having achieved great savings on the hours of production, the current focus is on reducing the cost of the raw material, because the price of carbon fiber is by no means comparable to that of aluminum. The great

Figure 5.59   3D CAD view of the Forged Composite "tub" (occupant cell) of the Sesto Elemento.

advantage of carbon fiber, and the reason why it can be considered revolutionary in auto manufacturing, is that it is possible to significantly reduce manufacturing time compared to traditional metallic structures, given that Forged Composite can be molded in less than five minutes.

5.6.3 Frontal Impact Absorption

The material is not the only innovation. The Sesto Elemento also employs a new concept for absorbing the forces released in a frontal impact, different from those of a traditional aluminum or steel chassis. The geometric properties of the composite can be exploited due to a greater specific energy absorption.

While for metallic materials the section that reacts better to compression is generally a closed section, this is not the case for composite materials. Indeed, closed sections are the ones that perform worst. In the quest for knowledge, a number of sinusoidal geometries have been studied to further reduce weight while maintaining the desired energy absorption capacity (Figure 5.60).

Also new is the concept for fixing the front frame to the "tub." It derives from our learnings from the aerospace industry, and it has been introduced for the first time into the sports car industry. Normally, drilling a hole in a carbon fiber frame produces delamination effects that are hard to control during the product's life cycle. In this case, given the material's very low sensitivity to cutting, a way was found to pierce it and to use aerospace rivets, the same ones used on the Boeing 787, rather than typical metal inserts.

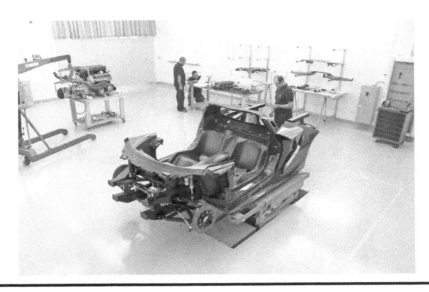

Figure 5.60   The Sesto Elemento chassis under construction.

5.6.4 *Aventador: The Industrialization of the Product in Carbon Fiber*

The challenge of industrializing the production of a chassis in carbon fiber was inspired by Lamborghini's thirty years of experience in the use of composite materials, but also by Audi's drive toward the construction of light chassis. In fact, Lamborghini has been part of the VW Group since 1998, and the German manufacturer's propensity for using light materials in the structure of car chassis has given impetus to the development of a new production process. The craft operations required of the skilled workers were thus optimized in relation to an automatization of the working of the carbon fiber, the end result being to produce a monocoque complete with roof and struts. One consequence of the new way of making the carbon shell lies in the style of the Aventador, developed in 2011 based on the Sesto Elemento.

The two projects have a fundamentally different philosophy: one is for a select few—about twenty cars in all, for VIP customers; the other one, the Aventador, occupies a lower product band, albeit at the top end of the range for its segment.

The Aventador project is distinguished by taut lines and deep tornado lines on the sides, and is not subject to the severe limitations associated with the processes for working the composite. An example of this is the lines of the roof, which have sharp edges that do not produce problems in the manufacturing phase (Figure 5.61).

Figure 5.61   The new Lamborghini Aventador.

Thanks to important partnerships with companies that have worked successfully with these materials for years, such as Boeing and Callaway Golf, the process of producing the composite has reached a level at which it can be supported and managed in the company itself.

That is why, although the use of carbon is not new in the automotive industry, it can confidently be stated that a great step forward has been taken in the evolution of the manufacturing technique.

In particular, the agreements signed between Lamborghini and Boeing in recent years has enabled the company to benefit from concepts such as the Building Block Approach (BBA), and to learn new ways of doing things, and to gain preferential access and to raw material suppliers. This has permitted the industrialization of a highly complex process capable of creating the Aventador's monocoque, which weighs just 147.5 kg and can boast a torsional rigidity coefficient of 35,000 Newton meters per degree (Figure 5.62).

Figure 5.62   The carbon fiber monocoque.

The BBA is a development process elaborated by Boeing and adapted to the auto industry by Lamborghini built with the aim to calculate the quantity of material, the arrangement of fibers, and various other parameters on the basis of project requirements. The process is only possible with the use of composite materials because both forms and resistances can be molded. This has made it possible to obtain an object—the monocoque—that offered perfect safety and dynamics from the very first prototype, unlike what used to happen in the past, when a "crash" development of a steel composite component required corrective measures in the form of "patches," which inevitably added weight to the structure and affected the dynamic performance.

5.6.5 *Building Block Approach*

The BBA approach consists of the progressive alignment between test activities and the simulation model, starting with the basic material samples and working through to a model on a 1:1 scale, gradually increasing its geometric complexity (Figure 5.63).

The advantage that can be gained is a validation and certification phase limited to a single test (level 5), in that the simulation model is 100% reliable. This process was reused by Lamborghini for the monocoque of the Aventador (Figure 5.64).

In Lamborghini's BBA pyramid, each of the five levels is a "gate" to get through after having completed all the required activities (Figure 5.65).

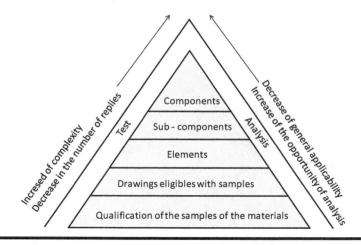

Figure 5.63   Diagram illustrating Boeing's Building Block Approach (BBA).

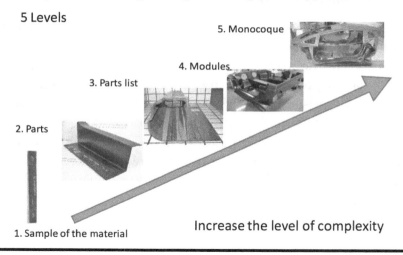

Figure 5.64   Lamborghini's adaptation of the BBA.

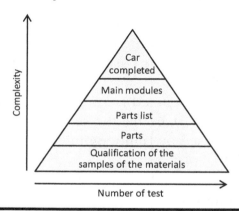

Figure 5.65   Methodological steps of the BBA approach.

1. The goal is to generate the model of the material with the "admissibilities" for traction, compression, and cut, and represents the real (not nominal) processes of production, including the effects of damage/yield.
2. The aim is to calibrate the model with greater geometric complexity. The material modeling parameters are regulated in accordance with experiments.
3. Validate the modeling of the materials: the scale model is assembled at this stage.
4. Evaluate performance and the absorption of energy of the monocoque's structure on the lateral bracket. Supplies data for calibrating the crash model.
5. Performance of a dynamic crash test on a 1:1 scale vehicle.

The number of tests is reduced as we climb the pyramid saving time and cost.

In fact, when the test was performed on a 1:1 scale, the simulation model was so accurate that it proved to be 100% reliable, and the test was passed on the first attempt. This made possible to make great savings (cost and time) in the development phase relative to the traditional method, used by competitors, which tends to involve doing the crash test, failing it, applying patches, redoing the test, further failure, and so on. The result of these traditional continual additions is an increase in weight. By contrast, in the Lamborghini approach, you start with a base weight, which then continues to fall as the development process evolves.

5.6.6 *Advanced Composite Research Center*

Another important element to increasing innovation was the opening of an in-house Advanced Composite Research Center (ACRC), which studies the development of technologies and their optimization on the costs and production volumes basis. The center's work runs in parallel with studies carried out by Boeing and university research financed by Lamborghini. One very important issue regarding composites is repaired. This is managed entirely by the ACRC, which guarantees and certifies the quality of repair work by using techniques derived from the aerospace industry. As Boeing does with its planes, specialized technicians known as "flying doctors" go directly to dealers. They have the necessary skills to repair damage to the monocoques, and to restore the vehicle to its original state (Figure 5.66).

Figure 5.66　A flying doctor in action.

5.6.7 *Innovative Processes*

The lower section of the Lamborghini Aventador's monocoque is produced using RTM (Resin Transfer Molding) Lambo technology, which involves manual preforming of the fiber which then comes into contact with resin injected at low pressure, while the upper and perimeter sections are made with Pre-Peg technology; this involves the use of fiber soaked in epoxy resin. These lines are flanked by the foam line, which works on the foams that are used to fill cavities in order to increase the torsional inertia of the structure. Great attention was also given to positioning and installing aluminum flanges in the monocoque; these support the front and rear sub-frames, on which the suspension, engine, and secondary components operate (Figure 5.67).

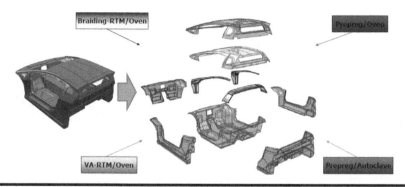

Figure 5.67　Material composition of the monocoque.

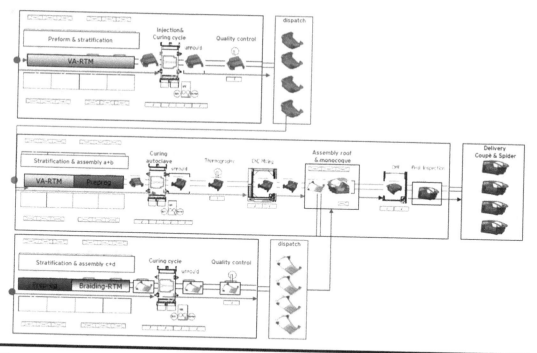

Figure 5.68   Flow diagram of the new Lamborghini CFK department.

The processes were designed together with the product, and this synergy gave rise to the new production center (CFK) for composite materials (Figure 5.68). Talking about the production and industrialization processes, the introduction of this technology was also made possible by reducing the time required to produce the monocoques. At present, it takes 130 working hours to produce a monocoque, which is perfectly in line with the need to build an average of 4.5 cars a day, with annual production that may in any case vary on the basis of orders between 700 and 2000 vehicles a year. Rapid progress is currently being made toward achieving maximum production speed, optimizing manufacturing and assembly processes, and reducing waste.

5.6.8 *RTM Lambo*

While the composites traditionally used in the luxury sports car industry have always been aerospace-derived presoaked fibers with autoclave polymerization, processes that do not involve the use of the autoclave, like the Resin Transfer Molding (RTM) technique, are now considered more efficient in terms of cost and production, with performance and quality remaining

Step 1 – Positioning of Dry Fibers, Foam & Vacuum Bag

Step 2 – Preforming

Step 3 – Closing of mould

Step 4 – Heating, RTM-Light injection and Thermal cycle

Figure 5.69   Photos of the RTM Lambo process.

essentially the same. To satisfy all the requirements of the RTM process, the resin needs to have a very low viscosity, an adequate pot-life,[9] and a good fiber impregnation capacity. In addition, it must be able to deliver the mechanical properties necessary for guaranteeing the resistance and torsional rigidity of the monocoque.

This is the new patented RTM Lambo process (Figure 5.69).

In order to increase the performance of the Aventador monocoque, sections containing epoxy foam were introduced in order to obtain the desired geometries without adding unnecessary layers of carbon fiber.

5.6.9 Conclusions

In the last two years, Automobili Lamborghini S.P.A. has registered eleven patents, clear proof of the great changes introduced thanks to the humble approach taken in relations with the aerospace industry, the main source of inspiration (partnering with Boeing).

In order to innovate at Lamborghini, great attention is paid to the following aspects:

- Development processes (time and cost reductions)
- Manufacturing processes for enhanced flexibility (setting up a new department)
- Product (use of new materials, unique styling studio)

- People (consolidation of a collaborative attitude at all levels, acquisition of necessary know-how, and establishment of a new research center and creation of long-term relationships with the University of Washington)
- Tools (application of the BBA and introduction of new calculation systems)
- Protection of know-how through the strategic decision to keep the whole development process and the production of composite materials in-house

All those elements are the basis for the on-going challenge of finding new technical solutions to earn ever-greater customer satisfaction, ensuring at the same time a reduction in production costs. Special thanks also goes to the support offered by the Lean coaching and consultancy of Lenovys that helped us apply Lean processes and tools that enabled the innovations we discussed above.

5.7 The Natuzzi Case—Relaunching a Company Starting from Its Products

With the contribution of Gianluigi Bielli and Lorenzo Lucchesi

5.7.1 The Company and Its History

The Natuzzi Group, founded in 1959 by Pasquale Natuzzi, is an Italian industrial group specialized in the production and sale of sofas, armchairs, furniture and furnishing accessories for residential use. The Natuzzi SPA Holding has been listed on Wall Street since 1993. The family Natuzzi still holds over 61% of the shares today. With 90% of production exported to 123 markets, Natuzzi holds the largest market shares in EMEA with 45.2% and in the Americas with 41.8%.

The Group makes its products inside its horizontally integrated production sites in Italy, China, Brazil, and Romania. Natuzzi controls 92% of raw materials and semi-finished products, and 82% of services.

The distribution network has been developed around 390 Natuzzi single-brand shops. The turnover as of December 31, 2016 recorded €457 million. Natuzzi Group employs 5171 people (2016).

Its commercial offices are located all over the world, and some of them are in fact unique constructions, like the one in Figure 5.70, which is the commercial headquarters in High Point, North Carolina, designed by architect Mario Bellini, where there is also one of the largest and most important

Figure 5.70 Natuzzi Commercial Headquarters in High Point, North Carolina.

shows in the furniture sector, during which all new models are presented annually.

The founder and current owner has dedicated his life to the construction of a dream that has come true. At the age of fifteen, Pasquale Natuzzi joined as an apprentice the workshop of an upholsterer friend of his and, in 1959, he started his own businesses by opening the first craft workshop for the production of sofas and armchairs, which developed into the current multinational corporation. The keys to success are linked both to his technical ability and to his stubbornness as an entrepreneur. Thanks to them, his first great intuition came to life, turning out to be an excellent example of radical high-impact innovation: *the democratization of the leather sofa*. Until a few years before, the leather sofa was, in fact, a product reserved for an elite clientele. It is thanks to Pasquale Natuzzi the leather sofa has been made financially accessible to everyone, revolutionizing the product's architecture and its manufacturing process. With the introduction of a manufacturing technique known as "hooding the sofa," he managed to drastically reduce the production cost and, above all, to manufacture on an industrial scale a product that until then had been mainly hand-crafted. Before this technique, an artisan placed the leather or fabric covering directly on the rigid frame, then broke and modeled it, working the sofa directly on the frame, with very long times and very high costs. Pasquale Natuzzi's innovation has been to completely distinguish the structural part, which is technically called "stem," from the covering, which is cut, sewn, and then assembled in one stroke: this has meant that the times were reduced noticeably, cutting down costs. Thanks to this enlightening discovery, and to products characterized by an extremely attractive design for those times, Pasquale started collaborations with large stores (Macy's and other large retail chains) that allowed him to successfully enter the difficult North American market and reach the goal of stock market listing in 1993. In October 2008, Pasquale Natuzzi was inducted into the American Furniture Hall of Fame for the contribution to the growth and development of the furniture industry in the United States. Natuzzi is the first non-American to have received this recognition.

5.7.2 Today's Context and Challenges

The current context presents such an industrial and economic complexity that the company's competitiveness on the market is challenged daily. In addition to the real price war that is in progress—due to the proliferation of numerous national and international competitors in every market segment—there is an impressive growth in the industrial complexity necessary to remain in this kind of business. By reading some figures, one easily gets the idea of such complexity, and in particular of the Natuzzi world:

■ About 1,600,000 "sitting places" produced every year
■ A new project every two days, around 120–130 new models per year
■ Five-hundred models in production
■ Twelve different versions for each model (ex. the armchair, the "2-seater," the "3-seater," the corner, the "recliner," the bed)
■ Each version in thirty types of leather, each of which in ten colors, or twenty types of fabric, each of which in ten colors
■ One-thousand different codes for sofa feet
■ Six wooden finishes
■ Five metal finishes
■ Five types of "comfort."

One needs to know that "comfort," that is, the morphological configuration of the sofa to obtain a certain comfort of sitting, changes according to the market. For example, you can distinguish "comfort" in two categories: the "seat in" and the "seat on," the first represents the typical American comfort, "I sit inside" and *"I want to sink,"* the second represents the typical comfort of Northern Europe (Germany, Sweden), "I sit on top" and *"I want stiff sitting."* In Italy, there are both types of comfort are common. There are also comforts that are linked to national regulations: in order to be sold in over 120 countries in the world, the products must respect all the existing regulations. For example, if you want to sell a sofa in the UK, expanded polyurethane, the dominant part of the sofa's upholstery, must comply with that country's fire-proof regulations.

One of the most important challenges to be overcome, the object of this case study, has been the reduction of the Design Lead Time. In fact, the average amount of launches every two days of a new model coexisted with an average time to market of four to five months. So, this caused problems every time something was changed during the development of the product launched five months earlier, such as changes in specifications, new requests from retailers, new production constraints, etc. In a context that is now used to obtaining new products in a very short time, sometimes even to deal with sudden customer requests, obviously, this performance was not acceptable.

5.7.3 Project Setting and Starting

The purpose of the project carried out was to introduce the principles of Lean Product and Process Development in the R & D department of the Natuzzi Group (consisting of more than one hundred people divided into seven departments with forty different roles) to achieve the following three main objectives:

- Reduction of the development time of a new product from the initial brief to the start of production.
- Increased productivity of the department in terms of products developed per man hours employed.
- Reduction of the product cost according to the logic of the full product cost (materials, components, and production).

We started with specific training to convey the approach and the main methods necessary to correctly tackle this project. This phase was important not only for the sake of technical alignment, but above all for the alignment and the "social" involvement, which must not be neglected or left to chance in any project—even less so for projects of this complexity—if we want to achieve the results, and in the shortest time possible.

After the methodological alignment phase and the definition of the "reason for action" of the project, the complex mapping of the current state was performed (Figure 5.71) which revealed over one hundred critical issues throughout the process and an estimate of the average lead time between fifteen and twenty working weeks depending on the type of product.

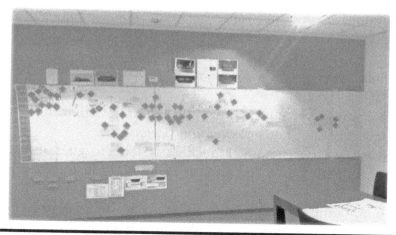

Figure 5.71   Mapping of the current state of the Natuzzi Group R & D processes.

The main critical issues identified in the corporate R & D system are summarized below, broken down by the various departments:

Value Area

- Difficulties in synchronizing Marketing and other Product Development functions (for example, the market requires products that are not developed by the prototype section, and products that remain unsold are developed).
- Not always an optimal correlation between the quality of the components used and the performances of the product, with specifications often aligned to the best brand without reason (waste of resources and materials).

R & D Process Area

- Frequent emergencies that produce continuous deviations and changes to the process.
- Need to strengthen methods to promote the standardization of components and the use of existing modules in the development of new sofas.
- Weakness of processes and design systems for creating industrial platforms and the reduction of complexity.

R & D People Department

- Absence of a transversal coordination figure from the beginning to the end of the development (e.g. Chief Engineer).

■ Duplications, rework, and waste between prototyping, testing and costs, and production sampling phases.

R & D Tools Area

■ Need to improve the effectiveness of planning, visualization, and synchronization of the status of ongoing projects.
■ Need to introduce structured Checklist systems to guarantee industrial feasibility, quality, costs, and compliance with industrial restrictions.

At this point, being guided by the objectives to be achieved, the principles of Lean Product and Process Development were introduced to plan the future state of the process, so as to overcome the criticalities encountered in the current state.

The operational phase, due to the complexity of the department to be transformed and the number of people directly and indirectly involved in the process, was very delicate and full of pitfalls. We started from grouping the 101 critical issues in twenty-one intervention areas, subsequently classified on an impact/effort matrix (Figure 5.72) to be tackled with the right priorities and based on available resources.

Once the priority projects were identified—some "quick wins" (top left) and other more complex, but necessary ones (bottom left)—for each of them a customer team was set up, supported by one of our consultants, with the final goal of making the planned future state operational.

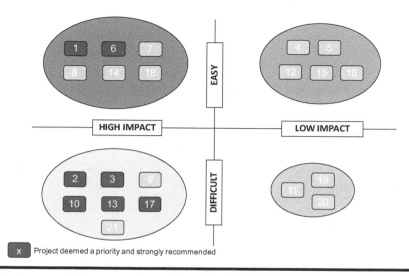

Figure 5.72   Impact/Effort matrix used to choose project priorities.

5.7.4 *The New Product Development Process*

The New Products Development process was revised with the introduction, where possible, of the principles of the Lean Product and Process Development described in this book. Below are some of the main guidelines that have been applied for implementing the future state:

- *Frontloading*: structured moments of debate and decision were introduced (product committees-creativity committee, etc.) in order to align people as far as possible and filter the products to be launched into the development process.
- *Modular product architecture*: a range plan was developed and real industrial platforms from which to start the entire development process were defined.
- *Process standardization*: the development of the new models was managed through the Project Review System tool seen in Chapter 2 of the book and the Engineering Checklist.
- *Pull System*: a Pull synchronization system of activities has been introduced, with a pragmatic Kanban of fine scheduling, regulated by a Visual Planning tool.
- *Capacity control*: a system for leveling and correctly dimensioning the workloads of the individual R & D departments was introduced.
- *Design to Cost and Design for Manufacturing*: a huge effort has been made to introduce the key principles and, above all, to obtain measurable benefits over a few months.

To make the key steps of the new process tangible and easily visible by everybody, as well as to make decision-making easy by considering the whole process and all the design constraints, the Visual Planning tool was developed (Figure 5.73). This tool has constituted the unique framework on which to base most of the other process improvement projects, a kind of common ground that is easy to share with all one hundred people in the department and the rest of the organization.

Following the guidelines of this concept, namely the sequencing of the phases, the limited capacity based on the available resources, the pull system, and the immediate visualization of the progress, the first prototype on paper was created and affixed in the corridor accessing the area common to all offices.

The board showed at the top the timeline of the various trade shows for which the products had to be presented, on the left was the panel of

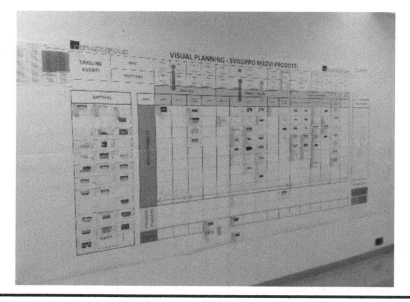

Figure 5.73   Visual Planning and Kanban system in R & D activities.

all the products (tags) that were waiting to be included in the development process; at the center, the progress of each product (tag) through the various sequential phases in which the new product development process was divided following the map of the future state; at the bottom, the products that presented some problems and needed an intervention and/or decision; and finally, on the right, the products completed during the year.

The complexity determined by the many different phases of the process, the large number of people involved with different functions, managerial and operational, the high number of shows to attend at different times throughout the year, the wide variety of products in phase of development, are critical issues that became clear and immediately available to all the people directly or indirectly involved in the process itself.

In a short time, the area in front of the board has become the preferred place to conduct all meetings, from operational to strategic management ones. After the end of the project carried out with Lenovys, the customer digitalized the Visual Planning and the Kanban system, allowing it to be visible also to people not physically present in the R & D area.

Another critical area of the process successfully dealt with was that of the continuous iterations that made the products in progress go back and forth between the phases of the process, due to the information necessary for the following phases being incorrect or not available. This also is a critical issue that is encountered very often in the product development processes, which leads to high waste in terms of quality of the products developed, of time used by the staff, as well as the obvious extension of throughput times.

In this case, using the structure divided in phases of the Visual Planning, the Project Review System was developed, to be associated with each product in development. For each of the development phases, we have carefully identified the *deliverables* to be released, considering that each downstream phase acts as a customer of the upstream phase and listing all the information required step by step, who must produce them, and when they must be produced. To complete the operation of the system, the deliverables contained in the Project Review System have been used as a mandatory checklist in order to be able to consider a single phase as finished and advance the product (the tag) to the next phase of the process on the same Visual Planning board. No product can advance in the process without the information necessary for the subsequent steps; on one hand, this leads to identifying and solving problems in time (preventing them from moving forward, with the inevitable consequence of making them more difficult and more expensive to solve), and, on the other, it prevents the project from blocking and returning to the previous phases, provoking continuous "Stop and Go" and out-of-control problems of various kinds (if, for example, an information present in the project Review System in phase 2 is not available, and is obtained later when the project is in phase 5, the decisions made in phases 3 and 4 will be based on incomplete information, almost certainly not optimal, and very often wrong).

5.7.5 Product Architecture and Platforms

One of the project features that had the greatest industrial impact was the effort that was carried out to implement the industrial product platforms based on a modular approach.

The objective was threefold: to build modularity, to make it sustainable over time (it is not enough to implement it, it must be maintained, too) and to regulate its growth by managing the demand for new models in this field.

This part of the intervention was conducted with the modularity approach (see the technical details in the Appendix of this book) that takes into account both the structure of the entire product range and the constraints imposed by the production flow: innovation in terms of product architecture must emerge from the best combination of the two points of view: that of the "product" and that of the "production process" (Figure 5.74).

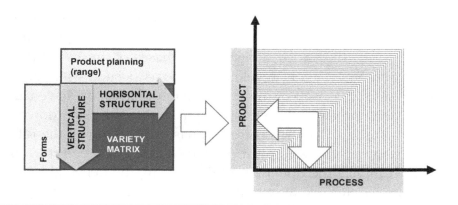

Figure 5.74 Modularity framework.

The modular approach to the "product" is based on the concept that multiple models, previously generally designed in succession and separately from the others, must be designed after being planned simultaneously. The application of this concept is made by defining what is now often called "modular architecture of the entire product range" or "Variety Matrix."

There are two reference archetypes to define the product variety matrix:

- the vertical structure
- the horizontal structure

The vertical structure divides the product into basic modules; the horizontal structure considers the product as a range of models.

The focus of this project was to produce the largest number of models with the lowest number of components.

For the part of "production process" it was necessary to take into account the innovation previously applied by the *Natuzzi* Group, adopting the concept of the "moving line" from the automotive sector, namely, a continuous and sequential path in which the sofa is manufactured in every detail, from the cutting of the leather to the packaging. While previously the upholsterer made his sofa from beginning to end—a sofa that may weigh up to 120 kg—with the new concept of the moving line the sofa is divided into its main parts: left armrest, right armrest, backrest, and seat (minimum four parts), and each part is assigned to an upholsterer. With this production concept, the product moves and goes through different workstations where the operators make the individual parts of the sofa. No longer separate compartments, production islands, but a continuous process in which teamwork makes work faster and more varied, but above all cheaper and therefore occupationally favorable.

The first part of the project to introduce the industrial platforms focused on the implementation of a pilot project starting from the commercial platforms, or rather the range of models on sale which would remain unvaried in the future or which would be changed according to market requirements. Therefore, an attempt was made to construct a first industrial platform composed of similar models for the construction logistics of the product and the manufacturing structure (Figure 5.75).

After the development of the first industrial platform, the volumes and their stability over time were verified. Subsequently, a variety reduction plan was applied to the identified models, with a consequent reduction in the number of codes and an increase in the common component indices, which led to encouraging results. Initial results of the implementation of the first pilot project to apply the principles of modularity and platforms (Figure 5.76), and were then far exceeded in the subsequent industrial platforms that were implemented.

An example of the component reduction technique is shown in Figure 5.77, with a case in which the wooden frame of the sofas is standardized.

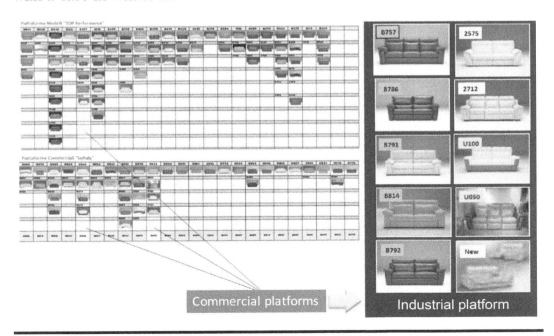

Figure 5.75   Development of an industrial platform starting from various commercial platforms.

	Before	After	Delta
No. of Models	6	6	0%
No. of Codes	118	69	−42%
Commonality index	34%	55%	21%

Figure 5.76   Summary table of the first pilot of modularity implementation.

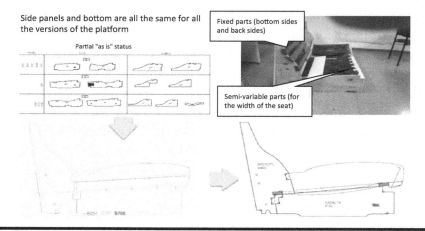

Figure 5.77   Example of technique for reducing components in the pilot industrial platform.

Once the pilot phase was completed, the results were expanded with the following steps:

1. Standardization and "lightening" of the commercial ranges by convergence on industrial platforms.
2. Standardizing the construction of industrial platforms with the help of "rules."
3. Monitoring and managing the lifespan and evolution of industrial platforms with "visual cards."
4. Managing the times for the introduction of new models, ranges and industrial platforms (also in "visual" mode) to avoid conflicts and conjunction with ordinary new product development activities.

The Natuzzi industrial platform is a logical grouping constructed according to predefined rules (see Figure 5.78) of models and product versions, independent of the commercial ranges and brands.

1. Dimensions
2. Style

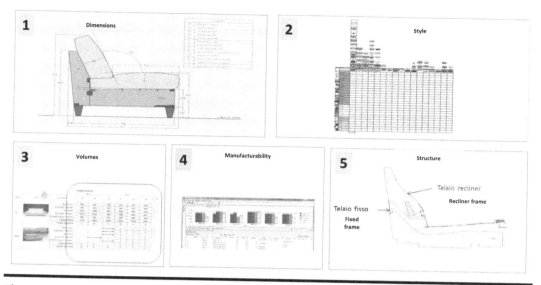

Figure 5.78 **Rules for the construction of industrial platforms.**

3. Volumes
4. Manufacturability
5. Structure.

The distinctive elements are:

1. The *dimensional* features of the product i.e. the seat height (H1), the total depth (P1), the seat width (L1), the seating angle (A1), and the seat inclination (A2), while the other dimensional characteristics are dependent from the entry "style."
2. The *style* for which seventeen "groups" to be observed were identified.
3. The *sales volumes* taken from the range plan. A platform, consisting one or more models, in order to be initiated must have a minimum sales forecast in order to feed a moving line at least for a shift.
4. The "*manufacturability*" derived from the division into components: bottom, backrest, and armrest. As far as possible, we tried to make the components equivalent in terms of number and type of pieces. The decision was made not to fall below the defined parameters of the percentage of common elements and to reduce the number of codes and total pieces to a minimum. The sewing did not play a role in the conditioning of the platforms.
5. The *structure* for which today the rule is that of fixed, variable and semi-variable parts (see example in Figure 5.79).

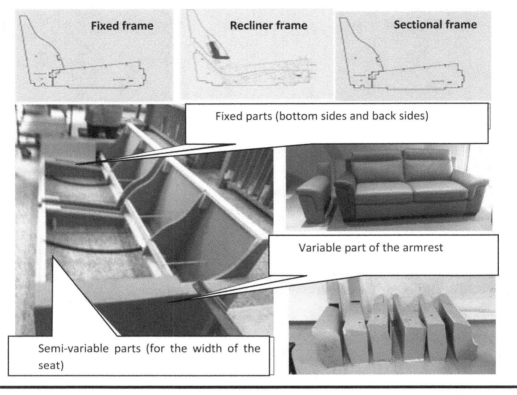

Figure 5.79 Example of an industrial platform structure based on the combination options of the parts.

The models, to be part of a platform, must respect the logical/numeric values defined for each element at the same time.

5.7.6 Operational Management of Industrial Platforms

The new platform system has been integrated into the development process starting from the introduction into the range plan and from the definition of the new designer briefs up to the production of the prototype. In fact, the constraints of the platforms must move as far upstream as possible in the R & D process in order to avoid deviations in the course of the various decisions to be taken downstream in the design process and implementation phases; as an indirect consequence the process phases even further downstream—such as industrialization and production—gain the advantage of optimizing and standardizing part of the work, thus saving precious time and energy, which can be used to face the many challenges that every new product inevitably poses.

The industrial platforms are archived and managed through the "cards" or forms and their implementation or enrichment of models/versions takes place during the process of developing new products in the phases listed below:

- Brief coordination
- Acceptance brief
- Concept.

The production checklist is as follows:

1. Analysis of the proposed model.
2. Comparison with the parameters of existing platforms, not with the intention of creating new platforms but of "forcing" the logic(for example see note on the heights on the next page).
3. If positive:
   - immediately implement the (common) structure;
   - rapidly proceed to prototyping.
4. If negative (which means that there is really no possibility of using existing platforms):
   - Check if the platform is sustainable (volumes of the proposed range plan).
   - If sustainable, proceed with the implementation (checking the new structure with the ideas of technological innovation "on the shelf").
   - If not sustainable, find other alternatives or implement the concept (out of standard production) to test the market.

The platform boards (in "A3" format, see example in Figure 5.80) must be compiled by Product Development after the concept phase, in the following way:

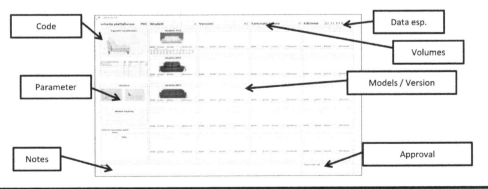

Figure 5.80   Example of a standard platform card.

■ New card
■ Update of previous card (update volumes).

In the absence of enrichment requests, the cards must be updated every year, aligning them with the volumes required by the range plan. If the updates show a worsening of the parameters, the platform itself must be reviewed.

The management of the first phase of the platforms aims to consolidate their definition, and to reduce the number from the "first" creation:

■ "Open" platforms to accommodate new products
■ "Closed" platforms will be eliminated over time.

5.7.7 Design to Cost: Design for Manufacturing and Assembly

Through the extended analysis carried out by teams from various functional departments, an in-depth investigation of Design to Cost and Design for Manufacturing and Assembly has been conducted in search of all the opportunities to reduce the total product costs: revision of materials, geometry, functional optimization, standardization of components, unification, reduction of the number of components, supplier changes, etc. In this case, we have adopted an operating technique that I call "Tear Down," that is, progressively stripping the product in search of wasted values which represent opportunities for cost reduction.

Hundreds of costs reduction or simplification proposals have been generated (see example in Figure 5.81); each of them has been evaluated at an economic level and assessed at an industrial and commercial feasibility level. From the early stages of evaluation, the joint commitment of all the company departments necessary to complete the assessment was fundamental. Unlike previous similar experiences of the company, in this project we have taken extreme care regarding the management of the process steps following the creation of ideas for improvement. In fact, five different monitoring phases have been defined in order to follow the evolution of individual ideas thoroughly:

■ The potential evaluation phase of the proposal
■ The economic, industrial and commercial validation phase of the proposal
■ The prototyping phase
■ The production launch phase
■ The final calculating and accounting stage.

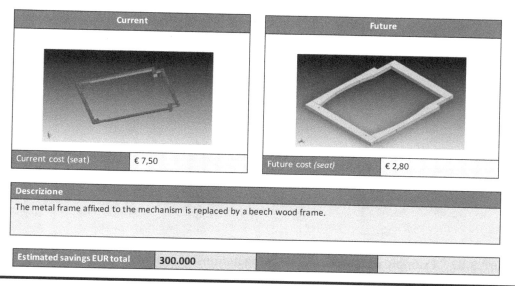

Figure 5.81 Example of a standard form for cost reduction proposals.

Of the hundreds of proposals generated, seventy-five were validated and actually brought to series production and this led to both an important reduction of waste in the components, and an optimization of design choices and consequently resulted in a consistent average reduction in the cost of components used (−5%) and an even more marked decrease in the cost of production (−15%). The choices were then formalized in a series of Engineering Checklists ("design rules") to avoid that in the future we would return to designing and manufacturing components without taking the enormous work of optimization carried out into account (Figure 5.82).

5.7.8 *Implementation Phase of the New Principles*

In order to better focus the energy available and to accelerate in the implementation phase of what has been seen so far, a task force has been created, consisting of professionals covering the entire product development process. Furthermore, an area dedicated to this activity was created where the project leader, the designers, the analysts, and the prototypes could work separately from the others, reproducing workshop conditions in which they normally worked on a small scale, with all the necessary equipment.

The 120 most significant models were chosen (considering the Pareto of revenues) to be re-engineered and assigned to the task force experts committed to inserting them as soon as possible into the new respective

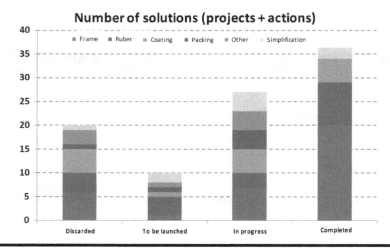

Figure 5.82   Example of monitoring ongoing actions to reduce product costs.

industrial platforms (hence the name given to the team "Task Force Top 120" team) to start up the new operations as soon as possible and reach the required targets (the overall range covers more than five-hundred models).

The project manager monitored the state of transformation of the models every day—to make them linked to the defined platforms—and the reduction of their full cost, divided into various types, through the representation of the data that were updated by everyone on the task force in the Obeya (Figure 5.83).

A fundamental step was the setup of the Obeya System, comprising of the following:

■ A room (the Obeya) where the activities (from the design to the construction of the prototype) could be developed, and in which a permanent multidisciplinary task force operated.
■ A visual system for monitoring activities, from planning to cost reduction.
■ A series of routines (daily meetings, etc.) that, once appropriately introduced, formed the habits of the members of the task force, guaranteeing focus and results.

5.7.9 Results

The revision of the entire product development process, including organizational changes and the introduction of new tools, has led to a significant reduction of the Lead.

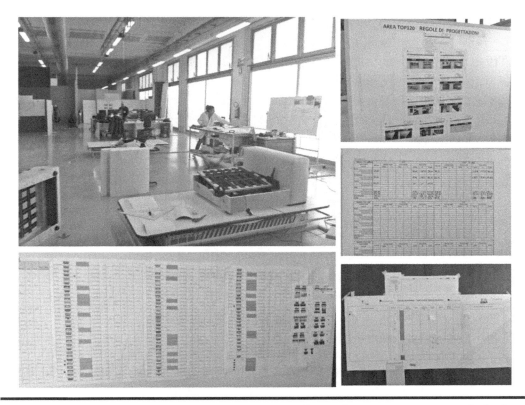

Figure 5.83   Scenes of daily life in the Obeya of the Task Force Top 120, anti-clockwise, are a view of Obeya, the Visual Planning of activities, the product/process setting for each model, target and cost figures, the design rules (engineering checklist).

- After the first six months of the project: from over sixty to forty-eight days.
- After twelve months: from forty-eight to thirty-seven days.
- During 2017 there were special cases, such as seven days on simpler, private label models, and about twenty days on the more complex Natuzzi Italia models.

Another important goal was the reduction of changes and iterations along the process:

- A reduction of around 70% of the errors identified at the end of the project.
- A reduction in the number of hours necessary for the development of a product thanks to the clarity of information and the elimination of non-value-added operations.

■ An increase in capacity of around 15%.

Through the re-engineering of the first 120 sofa models, the path continued independently, and with the complete renewal of the entire Natuzzi range according to the new rules introduced, further results were obtained:

■ Savings of around 4% on materials, with a saving of over € 5 million.
■ A reduction of over 10% of the cost of sales (COGS).
■ Introduction of eighty design rules and fifty-two platforms that industrially represent the thousands of commercial models for sale.

However, probably the greatest result obtained, beyond the numerical evidence, was overcoming one of the most difficult periods in the company history, returning to believe in their own means, their vision and in products, guided by the historical founder of the company, Pasquale Natuzzi.

5.7.10 Lessons Learned

There are so many ideas and lessons learned in this project that are useful both to the Natuzzi Group for its future projects and to all readers of this book. I will try to summarize the main ones:

■ Always involve the top management from the beginning to avoid costly backtracking during the project. The involvement of top management must, however, be done using management language and not technical language, through effective communication, and clarifying the correlations between technical factors and strategic factors for the company.
■ Manage the change well by means of appropriate activities involving people, immediately identifying potential obstacles and managing them by prevention.
■ Choose team leaders well. It will be them to successfully complete the project. Do not be influenced by other people who tell you who to appoint but choose based on direct knowledge and that of direct superiors.
■ Attention to the correct identification of results and measurement from the earliest stages. Remember that there will always be someone ready to dispute matters, even when the results are good, saying they could have been even better, so be aware of all eventualities. Just imagine what can happen if you do not have any tangible index or result to show.

- Attention to excessive self-reference especially in the creative sector. Creativity in the company must be organized, managed by processes and aligned to make everything work.
- Beware of the rules, because very often I heard things like *"The platforms or checklists or visual planning are stifling me, you're blocking my creativity."* The rules strengthen the systems; they don't stifle anything. Lack of rules weakens the corporate systems.
- The results obtained are not the direct consequence of a formal and rigid application of a method. That is never enough. Unfortunately, I have often seen companies in which the staff developed the *"copy and paste"* syndrome regarding the Lean tools, considered to be foreign bodies that do not become the company's assets, and therefore lose their effectiveness. The implementation of the Lean method and tools must always be accompanied by the social aspect, the deep involvement of people, the growth of human energy in the company and a degree of customization essential for their effective applicability in that reality in which they are inserted.

5.7.11 Next Steps

Despite the remarkable progress that the company has made in recent years, new challenges are visible on the horizon. The first concerns the capitalization of the work done in order not to fall behind compared to the new techniques introduced: from modularity and platforms to design to cost, from pull systems of R & D management to the correct sizing of departments, from the daily use of the Project Review System and Engineering Checklist to avoid reworking, unnecessary iterations, Stop and Go, loss of standardization.

Another challenging element is represented by the raising of the bar of competitiveness, with new and stringent cost targets required to remain on the market while continuing to guarantee products of undisputed quality. In this strand of challenge, the search for the highest quality undoubtedly must be considered in all phases of production and supply chain, as at this point, no type of defect is acceptable anymore. A real focus on absolutely zero errors. In this regard, it will be fundamental to push more and more toward the joint design of the product and the production process, thanks to the adoption of the principles of Lean Accounting, while continuing with all downstream production phases with undiminished energy.

The last challenge, from my point of view, is represented by the consolidation and full exploitation of all forms of digitalization of R & D activities; activities started during this project and destined to gain ever more importance and relevance in the coming years.

Resources

https://www.lenovys.com/en/case-history/laika/
https://www.lenovys.com/en/case-history/lamborghini/
https://www.lenovys.com/en/case-history/sacmi-ceramica/
https://www.lenovys.com/en/case-history/sacmi-closures/

Notes

1. Data taken from the Sacmi Annual Report 2016, refer to: www.sacmi.com.
2. Sacmi Annual Report 2010, consultable at www.sacmi.com.
3. Data taken from the 2010 Annual Report, on line at www.sacmi.it.
4. Taken from the Sacmi Group's Lean Transformation Program newsletter of July 2011.
5. Report available on line at www.sacmi.it
6. For more about Set-Based Concurrent Engineering, see Section 2.3.
7. By courtesy of Continental Automotive Italia S.p.A.
8. Luciano De Oto joined Automobili Lamborghini S.p.A. in 2001. In 2006, he became responsible for the design and development of the external and internal parts of all Lamborghini products. In 2007, he was the Project Leader for the Gallardo Superleggera, and, in 2010, he was manager for the Sesto Elemento BIW Engineering. Before joining Lamborghini, Luciano worked for Ferrari and Minardi in Formula One. Currently he runs the division dealing with the development of all the components made from advanced composite materials.
9. Pot-life is the period of time in which a mix in a concentrated mass of 200 g can be used at 20°C before it begins to harden.

Conclusion: The Secrets to Being a Lean, Innovative, and Winning Company

The Importance of Really Investing in the Company Fighting against the Procrastination

A journey of a thousand miles begins with a single step.

Lao Tzu

When is the right moment to embrace the change? When should the Lean transformation of your company be faced? Will it be worth it? I knew the CEO of an Italian company who hesitated for months about whether or not to "do something Lean." He confessed his doubts to me about investing money and time in consultancy and in staff training, and not seeing any significant return. He also went to visit various companies that have begun to implement change, each one with different consultants and different methods. And he was almost proud to tell me about the things he had seen that, in his opinion, were not going well, and what he did not like. He forgot, however, that every company is always a case apart, and that a Lean journey consists of falls, of picking yourself up and of small successes, which then lead to the learning and acquisition of a bundle of technical and social competencies capable of making the difference. He has still not made up his mind, and unfortunately, the performance of his company is distinctly lackluster. Is this entrepreneur saving? Or has he already missed out on opportunities? Or is he putting off until who knows when some possible savings that could be made in his company?

Perhaps none of all this. But let me give you another example.

The Cost of Procrastination

I have always been fascinated by what a good and well-known investor friend of mine once told me. With illuminating calm, he explained how to calculate the real cost of putting off a small investment decision. The magic of compound interest is such that if I were to put aside one euro a day, and I learned how to exploit my savings at an annual rate of 10%, repeating this operation for fifty-eight years, I would accumulate a million euros.

If, instead of one euro, I put aside two euros, the number of years required to accumulate a million euros would fall from fifty-one to fifty-eight years. And if I put aside three euros, forty-seven years would suffice. In the United States, these kinds of investors are known as "bread and butter" investors.

Well, after having made sure I had understood this basic concept, I set about quantifying the cost of procrastination.

Let's suppose that I was able to regularly save two-hundred euros a month for the next twenty years, with an annual return of 20%, a rate lower than what an investor would, on average, like to see if he or she invested in a serious and successful company investment. I would obtain capital amounting to 540,000 euro after twenty years. Now let's suppose that I started one year late: doing the sums again, for nineteen years instead of twenty, I would find myself with about 440,000 euros instead of 540,000, that is to say, approximately 100,000 euros less. This is the cost of procrastination: 100,000 euros in a year for not having started the investment plan now. But there is more than that: the cost of putting off investment is very high: every day of delay would cost me almost three hundred euros. In fact, dividing 100,000 by 365, I would find myself with loss of earnings amounting to over 273 euros for every day of delay.

If we were to apply the calculation of the cost of procrastinating about an investment, however simplified and rough-and-ready, to what happens in our companies, we would come to realize how many real opportunities we lose if we delay investing in the growth of our resources, in the growth of our entire company. Why does this happen? Because there is little propensity to attribute value to the intangible assets of our companies. If, from an economic and financial point of view, it is very easy to calculate the asset value of buildings, means of production, the number of "heads" in a company, stock, and so on, it is much more difficult to estimate the value of knowledge, of available human capital, and of the genuine know-how present in a firm.

How much is the autonomous capacity to solve a problem more quickly than someone else worth? Or the ability to learn from one's mistakes more quickly than others? And the capacity to spot areas of waste in a company and eliminate them? And to develop new products faster than competitors do? Although these are hard to quantify from a purely accounting point of view, these are just some of the abilities that can determine the success or otherwise of a company.

Today, people really can increase the assets of a company, enabling it to achieve objectives that would be unthinkable following a short-term perspective, and without considering the real value of certain characteristics that are apparently intangible but which have very tangible consequences. So, starting on a Lean journey today is like putting off a small investment every day that can lead to acquiring a much bigger value over the years. The situation of many excellent companies has shown that the virtuous path of continual, long-term growth brings advantages over both the long and short-term.

The reverse is not true.

What Does It Mean to Invest in a Company Today?

Unlike what has traditionally been done, investing in a company should no longer be seen just as the acquisition of capital goods and resources capable of ensuring the transformation of materials and information so productive and economical as to guarantee a return on investment superior to the cost incurred. Today, the word "investment" involves the most precious of all available resources: time. Ours and that of everyone working in a company.

The old saying "time is money" still holds good today, but it is even more valid in relation to the greatest waste that we run the risk of every day:

> The greatest waste in the world is the difference between what we are, and what we could become.

Ben Herbster

Not knowing which risks we are running and which opportunities we are missing is a form of waste similar to the procrastination about the investment that I have just told you about.

In contrast to some years ago, company assessment sessions can now be carried out very rapidly. In the space of just a few days, it is possible to map the real situation of the company's chief processes, to identify the risks and opportunities, and to economically quantify the effects of introducing appropriate countermeasures.

It is no longer necessary to resort to expensive and long company assessments which ended up—and still do if the method of analysis is not chosen well—with an embarrassingly large quantity of slides, then turned into anti-ecological heaps of paper and rivers of words in order to propose solutions for how knows what. Basically, the idea was "I'll tell you what to do, and you get on and do it. I'm leaving now."

In order to carry out these rapid assessments, it is necessary to have skills and experience built up during many other evaluations that are methodologically similar but never the same in terms of content or the individual processes dealt with from one company to the next. The ability to immediately get to grips with the issue at hand and provide concrete evidence of what could be obtained is now more valuable than ever.

This type of analysis should never last more than a few days, conducted together with a team of experts. Longer analyses would undoubtedly cost more and tend, in my view, to create the risk of once again bearing out the Pareto principle, otherwise known as the eighty-twenty rule: What is the 20% of factors that gives me 80% of the results?

There is no need to get lost in the meanderings of the useless.

How to Achieve a Winning Company

> Always dream and shoot higher than you know you can do. Don't bother just to be better than your contemporaries or predecessors. Try to be better than yourself.
>
> **William Faulkner**

Enthusiasm for the Products We Offer

The secret of a company capable of prospering over time lies in its capacity to systematically conceive of new products that "excite" customers, to produce them in the most efficient way possible, and to get them onto the market quickly. We have seen how many opportunities there are for improving the products and services that are developed. We have also seen that the best way to obtain winning products depends essentially on the construction of solid processes and the development of winning people who never stop learning.

It is possible to make real innovations without inventing anything, but by transforming the many weak signals we receive all the time both from within our companies and from outside, above all from our customers. Being enthusiastic about the products we develop, manufacture, and sell means knowing how to step into the shoes of those who use them, and achieving a profound understanding of how they are used and experienced, the problems that exist "in the field," and what opportunities there may be for their future use. All of this can be turned into a systematic process, where a combination of creativity and discipline creates a happy marriage of technical, social, and relational aspects. In this systematic process, there is of course space for the essential elements associated with the development of a winning product.

Love Simplicity

If asked for a phrase that captures the spirit of the Lean philosophy, the one I would choose is "Keep it simple." Simple, essential, brief, and documented. In this book, we have examined many examples of summary documents fundamental to projects run in companies, for example, the Concept Paper or the matrix for evaluating the different concepts that are explored. We have also seen the importance of all the other forms of communication, and to what extent these can make a specific and effective impact, with numbers and facts, in any part of the development process. Consider, for instance, the standards employed or the A3 techniques, written documents that communicate important decisions with a desire to be succinct and to learn continually from experience.

Winning Convictions

We have seen how much weight the social dimension has in development processes, and how much it can really influence the results of a business: from the ways in which we hold our meetings, to how we manage working relations within the company; from the correct management of continual learning to focusing on the prevention of conflicts or problems in the future. And if we talk about the social factor, we must also focus on the individual person that is the center of this process, and about how the "individual beliefs" can influence the spirit of a group in one direction or another. How much time do we spend on our own or in a group trying to sort out problems that were simply underestimated in the early phases of a project? What is the effective impact of the belief that the best way to obtain results is the "just do it" approach, rather than devoting much more time than usual to thinking about and planning things before swinging into action? What is the effective impact of the powerful orientation toward achieving results at all costs, rather than taking care to build the processes through which we will achieve results? All of these questions have precise answers, but it will be our beliefs about them that determine whether we discover them or not.

Fall in Love with Problems

We tend to hide problems, to run from and minimize them, hoping that they will not get worse, rather than learning from them in order to implement the continual innovation of products, processes, and people. Continuous improvement is a sustainable and enduring strategy for progress at both an individual and company level. It is also markedly less expensive than many other strategies. However, there is a catch: it only works if we accept the need to discover the opportunities that lie behind the many problems facing us every day.

The Right Process Always Leads to the Right Results

When this set of elements begins to become established in a business, I have always noted that an aggressively result-oriented approach gives way to a reflective attention toward the rules of the game, with the realization that the right process always leads to the right results in less time overall and with less stress. First of all, it can be replicated by ourselves and others over time, with similar results. By contrast, we have seen that the absence of stable and solid processes can lead to a certain unpredictability in the results, for this reason, things may work out well or badly depending on the various factors that have influenced our activities and projects each time.

Experts in Assistance Rather than Control

In order to run businesses capable of introducing Lean innovation, some traditional forms of management may be inadequate in many ways and could limit the innovative drive within a company. Relying on authority and "vertical" delegation to run groups and organizations is no longer sufficient to deal with the powerful need to spread responsibilities more widely in order to solve cross-functional and horizontal problems. Managers today are being called upon more and more to involve people and transmit a sense of responsibility to them, making them increasingly able to solve problems that may lie outside their specific sphere of action. In these cases, the role of the manager shifts from being an expert in control to that of being an expert in assisting and watching over processes and the responsible activation of individuals.

Have Faith in Experiments

Another aspect of traditional management that may limit the force of Lean innovation is, paradoxically, an excessive "faith" in planning as a tool for obtaining the right results. Often, we delude ourselves that good results are equivalent to implementing a good plan. Together we have seen that plans are important, but even more so are the processes with which we act. In many cases, it is wise to go back to the basics, that is to say, considering all planning processes as genuine scientific experiments, in which we draw up a plan, put it into practice, check the results, respond to unforeseen factors, and start again, following the old but still valid Deming cycle: plan, do, check, act.

Go Slowly to Arrive First

A final, but by no means less important, limitation of traditional management is "moving fast." Jumping straight to solutions and results gives us the impression of going faster, but in reality leads to a systematic slowing down later on, what with errors, problems, and repetitions, as a result of which we end up being much slower. In Lean innovation, starting off slowly is always a valid principle. This means beginning with a perfect understanding of the problem to solve or the need to satisfy, analyzing and defining many different possible countermeasures or solutions, exploring them in parallel without having to choose in a rush, and converging slowly toward the final solution, often with higher costs at the beginning, but actually with lower costs, less time spent, and happier customers by the time the project is complete.

Sometimes we feel almost "frightened" by the size of the mountain to climb. *But instead of stopping, we must always try to understand what the first step might be for us, and do it as well as we can.* Because only after having done it will we be able to clearly see the next step to take. Months, or perhaps even years later, we will find that we have scaled mountains we never thought could be climbed.

Appendix: Modularity: The Way to Reduce the Total Product Costs While Drastically Increasing the Industrial Flexibility

Gianluigi Bielli[1]

Modular Development

Over the course of time, modularity has had different meanings and been applied in various ways. For example, the notion of the module was first employed widely in classical architecture. Just think of the ancient temples, based on reconfigurable modules assembled in different ways in order to produce very different end results. Or take the works of many Renaissance artists: their proportionate construction of forms was achieved through an art based on a scientific knowledge of standard, modular components.

In the 20th century, with the phenomenon of industrialization, modularity became a "tool" that responded to specific requirements associated with the mass production of components. With the advent of the third millennium, mass customization has become the chief characteristic of the market (Figure A.1), with modularity being a source of innovation offering the most efficient answer to the joint requirements of rapid response, product flexibility, and low cost.

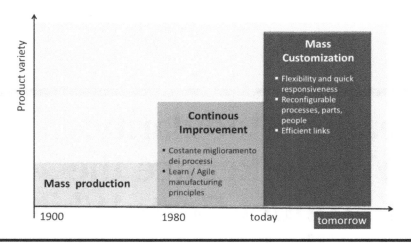

Figure A.1   From mass production to mass customization. (Ramani, K., Cunningham, R., Devanthan, S., Subramaniam, J., Patwardhan, H., 2004.)

Mass Customization

To be successful, the two objectives to pursue simultaneously in today's competitive world are continual differentiation of the product/service in order to meet the needs of customers, and the continuous reduction of total product costs(materials, processes, distribution).

An effective strategic response to these challenging objectives is product modularity, that is to say, the breaking down of a product into standardized parts (modules).[2] The great advantage of this is that it is possible to obtain cost benefits and differentiation at the same time.

From this point of view, product and process modularity is one of the cornerstones of mass customization.[3] A number of typical features of mass production are employed in a different way: standardization and economies of scale are used principally in relation to the hidden parts of the product, while customization is achieved through exterior design and other more visible components of the product.[4]

The auto industry, which has always set trends by virtue of the characteristics of its products and its customers, exemplifies the progress from common platforms to interchangeable modules (Figure A.2).

The differences in price between models in the same family are no longer the result of substantive differences in value and content, but are now more "driven" by marketing policies designed to maximize the image of a brand. This is done, in part, through a careful selection of modules (for example engines, chassis, bumpers) to be used on one brand or another.

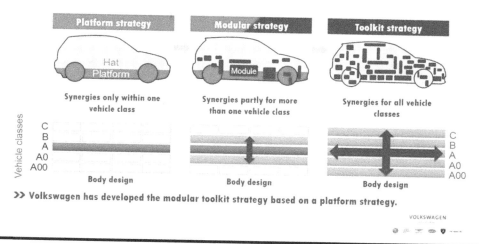

Figure A.2   The evolution of the Volkswagen Group modular assembly toolkit.
(Source Volkswagen Group.)

Together with Fiat, Volkswagen was one of the first car manufacturers to grasp how fundamental the synergy between models and brands for the future of the industry. For these two companies, they estimate saving an overall cost of approximately 20% and the number of design and development hours by approximately 30%.

Based on these activities at Volkswagen and Fiat Chrysler Automobiles, the proportion of costs devoted to modules common to many models would rise from 60% to 70%, while the proportion devoted to specific components of each model would drop from 40% to 30%.

The aerospace industry has also relied on modularity to contain costs, amongst other things. One example is the development of the Joint Strike Fighter program, the goal of which was to produce a plane that could replace different models used by various air forces (United States, Britain, Italy, Holland, Canada, Japan, Israel, Turkey, Australia, Norway, and Denmark). The program was set up to replace many different planes while keeping development, production, and operational costs low. This goal was pursued by building three variants of a single plane through the use of shared components (Figure A.3):

■ F-35A: conventional take-off and landing variant (CTOL)
■ F-35B: short take-off and vertical landing variant (STOVL)
■ F-35C: carrier variant (CV).

The F-35A is the smallest and lightest, and is the basic model; the main difference of F-35B from the base version is that it has an engine with an

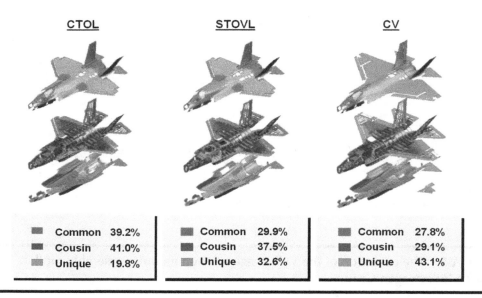

Figure A.3   Chart comparing common parts between each of the three F35 variants. (Source Lockheed Martin.)

exhaust nozzle that can be directed downward, and a lift fan with mobile lower fins that could be oriented 15°–30° forward or backward from the vertical position. The fins are installed behind the cockpit, in the place of the in-flight refueling system, which is in the plane's nose, and of the cannon. The F-35C differs from the basic version in that it uses a different engine, has greater internal fuel capacity, and has larger wings and tail control surfaces.

Coming to Terms with Costs and Time

The previous considerations suggest the need for a different and alternative view about costs that can be broken down into three categories:[5]

- Functional costs (F)
- Variable costs (V)
- Control or management costs (C).

In other words, total costs = F costs + V costs + C costs.

F costs are those for the parts required to satisfy the necessary specifications, and the processing or assembly of those parts; they derive from the specific functions and structures of the products.

V costs vary according to the production volumes of each product or production process and stem from the types of parts and of production processes. C costs are those incurred in checking the parts and the manufacturing; they are calculated on the basis of the total number of parts, production processes, and control points. An indication of the breakdown of V, F, and C costs in relation to the mass production of, for instance, cars and consumer electronics, is given in the histogram of Figure A.4.[6]

On the other hand, build to order industries, for example, those specializing in the production of heavy electromechanical equipment, have an F cost of 40%–60%, a V cost of 20%–30%, and a C cost of around 30%–40% of the total.

The requirements of mass customization lead to a rise in costs, because of the need for a greater number of components (F), the increase in the number of production processes (V costs), and the increase in the control functions and other indirect tasks (C costs).

The common conviction is that a product modularity strategy leads to cost savings for the manufacturer and a reduction in the price for the customer.

In the short term, investments in modular architecture can lead to an increase in the costs borne by the manufacturer, due to added costs in research, design, and testing activities.[7]

However, in the long term, cost savings connected to the projects could can be significant. Figure A.5 shows the breakdown of the actual costs of a complex electromechanical product in the food sector emphasizing that the application of modularity not only reduces costs but also reduces the

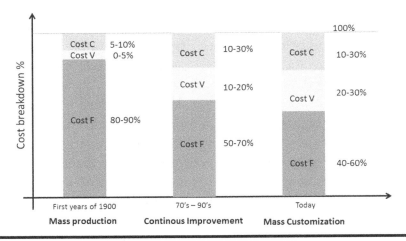

Figure A.4   Trend of the incidence of V, F, and C costs.

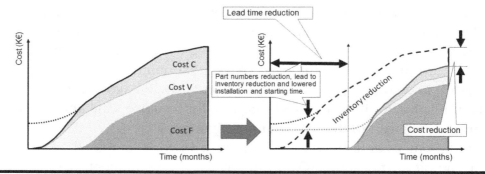

Figure A.5   Effect of modularity on the reduction of costs and lead time.

product development lead time. Companies often struggle with this phenomenon, because their traditional accounting systems do not necessarily capture the true savings. As discussed earlier in this book, understanding and quantifying the savings along the entire Value Stream using Lean Accounting[8] techniques can assist in seeing the true benefits of modularity.

According to many published reports, most businesses invest the resources freed up by modularization to support new product development projects to provide customers new features and products rather than cutting prices. In other words, modularity can help to get more value-added products to the marketplace with the same number of people.

Basic Characteristics of Modular Development

In the development of new products, dimensional and functional coordination on modular designs represents the practical link between the overall project, the production of components, and final assembly. The products may be of a single specific type (closed-cycle industrialization) or belong to different categories (open-cycle industrialization).

In the first case, non-configurable products are offered to the customer; these are internally managed with a number of standard modules that are reused on various models. In the second case, after having introduced the modular architecture, customers can configure the products during the purchasing phase. For example, open platforms are produced with standard interfaces that can be used to make finished products combined with products from other suppliers.

In particular, the adoption of a modular system tends to ensure the union of components at the geometric level. This characteristic ensures their compatibility, from both dimensional and functional points of view, with other components. From this perspective, the main capabilities that the module must provide for the manufacturing and assembly can be summed up as follows:

■ Interchangeability: the need to give the designer maximum freedom in choosing between "comparable" products.
■ Reduction of product variety: offer a sufficiently wide but not unlimited range of models, the goal being to rationalize production (and significantly extend the market, particularly if the module is internationally accepted).
■ Reduction of process variety: facilitates standardized assembly and permits economy of scale by reducing production time.

Interchangeability between different modules is an indispensable condition for a modular product. Interchangeability can come in two forms:

■ Class "I" interchangeability, obtainable without further work (design or manufacturing).
■ Class "R" interchangeability, obtainable with additional work (minor design or process changes).

Interchangeability is normally managed throughout the manufacturing cycle:

■ As designed, and therefore assured at the design phase as a morphological correspondence and with tolerances for the planned pairing.
■ As built, through the realization of reference masters for industrialization (Gold Master, Silver Master, etc.), either physical or electronic.
■ As delivered, thanks to checking of manufactured items with appropriate Acceptance Gauges, which may be physical or computer-based.

The management of interchangeability is one of the most important steps in modular product development. One suitable tool is the interface matrix; the one illustrated in Figure A.6, in the form of a relationship chart for a vacuum, shows some types of connections. For example, in this case, the "G" ("I" and "R" class geometries) and "E" (energetic/functional) are cited, and there could be others.

The interface coding can be expanded upon with indications regarding the mechanical tolerance and other significant parameters, besides the level of importance/criticality of the pairing.

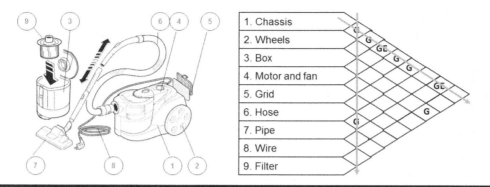

Figure A.6   Interface matrix for vacuum cleaner modules.

The arrows indicate the two optimum solutions: the vertical one regards combined assembly, and the diagonal one illustrates platform assembly (in this case the chassis is the platform); any connection outside such zones should be avoided.

The reduction of product and process variety must be managed separately: the architecture of a single modular product is one situation; the architecture of a whole range of modular products is another story. Today's markets are increasingly demanding the second one.

Modular Architecture of the Single Product

Product architecture can be defined as "the way in which the features of the product are associated with the physical components."[9]

The architecture may be integral, where each function of the product is associated with more than one component, or modular, when each function of the product is linked to just one component. The latter are normally distinguished as follows:

■ Slot architecture, where each component has a different interface from the others.
■ Bus architecture, where there is a common bus to which all the components connect with the same type of interface.
■ Sectional architecture, where all the interfaces are identical, and there is not a base component to which the others connect.

In order to create a modular architecture for a single product, it is necessary to determine how to divide the product into how many modules.

Various methods are available to guide the process of establishing the number of modules. They include the following:

- Heuristic method
- Modular Function Deployment (MFD)
- Design Structure Matrix (DSM).

The heuristic method consists of two phases. In the first phase, the product architecture is represented through the use of the function structure method,[10] represented as a flow of material, energy, or information inside the functions (or components). In the second phase, empirical rules are applied to identify the modules.

- Rule 1: dominant flow, that is to say, if it passes through a series of functions (or components), these should form a module.
- Rule 2: branching flow, that is, chains of parallel functions (or modules) downstream of a flow that branches, should form a module.
- Rule 3: conversion/transmission, in the sense that a conversion function (or component) or a conversion and transmission pair (or chain) should form a module.

Modular Function Development (MFD) is a modularization method consisting of the following steps:

- Identify customer needs and the product functions capable of satisfying them by applying the principles of Quality Function Deployment (QFD) and tools such as the Kano matrix.
- Define the technical solutions able to perform the requested functions, starting with a functional breakdown of the product and then evaluating the possible alternatives with the application of the methodological steps belonging to Value Analysis (VA)/Value Engineering (VE).
- Define the modules on the basis of the impact of the functions (or components) on the twelve predefined modularity drivers, and consequently define the dominant functions and construct the modules around them. In an optimum situation, the number of modules should be the square root of the number of parts or the number of assembly operations.

The Design Structure Matrix (DSM) is an objective method for suggesting the possible grouping of functions (components) into modules. It is based on a "grouping" algorithm. In the matrix intersections, the relative dependencies between the components or functions are indicated and prioritized.

Modular Architecture of the Whole Product Range

The modular approach is based on the concept that multiple models, which in the past were generally designed in succession and separately from each other, should be designed after having been planned simultaneously.

This concept is applied by defining what has now widely come to be known as the "modular architecture of the whole product range," or "Variety Matrix" (Figure A.7).

There are two reference archetypes to define the product variety matrix:

- Vertical structure
- Horizontal structure.

The vertical structure classifies the product into base modules; the horizontal structure considers the product as a range of models.

A range of military vehicles designed with a toolkit logic offers a simple illustration of the concept (Figure A.8). In the top section of the figure, there is the product range (four finished products); beneath these are the established modules, ten in all; and finally, at the bottom, there is an illustration of the modular architecture of the product range.

To construct the matrix, the bill of materials of the different reference models (Figure A.9) is used. A choice will be made between the technical or the production bill of materials. Special attention needs to be given

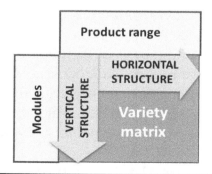

Figure A.7   Modular architecture of the product range.

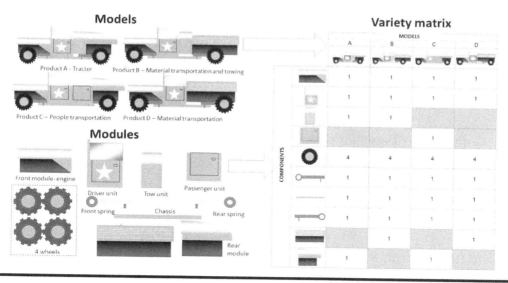

Figure A.8   Example of product range elements and modular architecture.

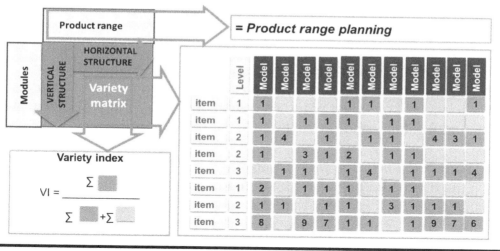

Figure A.9   Variety matrix structure.

to homogeneity when unifying the individual bills of materials in order to facilitate analysis of the commonalities.

Reduction of Variety in the Domain of the Product Range

The Variety Reduction Program (VRP) was developed in 1975 by Akira Koutade and Toshio Suzue from the Japan Management Association.

The aim was to drastically reduce the costs derived from product innovation and diversification requirements. The VRP is the most important complementary tool for modular design, and its goal is to reduce the variety of modules (and of components) required by the product range.

Five techniques are fundamental to this approach:

1. Comparison between fixed parts and variable parts
2. Combination
3. Multifunctionality and integration
4. Range
5. Series.

The first technique involves the comparison first of the fixed modules and the variable modules, and then of the fixed parts and variable parts that are their components. This is done in order to determine the numerical values and the configuration of the structure of the models, to establish the production process routing, and to define the equipment needs.

This means creating a different set of products so as to combine the fixed parts that form the base of the product groups with the variable parts that form the base of the individual models. Defining the parts adjusts the products to the diversification of the specifications; at the same time, there is a rationalization of the fixed parts. The technique is also employed to ensure maximum flexibility and productivity in the manufacturing processes.

■ Fixed parts: first, the product groups are examined, to identify those parts that could be shared by different products; then the corresponding production processes are determined, trying to ensure that each fixed part corresponds to a process or a small number of processes. Efforts are also made to automatize, mechanize, and simplify such processes.

■ Variable parts (and semi-variable ones, where possible): these are the parts used in a distinctive way for particular types of product. They are essentially produced manually, but there is the possibility to automatize and mechanize the control of operations.

The goal of the second technique is to simplify the set of products and to eliminate the gap between product requirements and characteristics, creating a combination of interchangeable parts and modules suited to the diversification of product models, with three possible methods:

1. Use base elements plus additional elements, to establish first of all the basic parts of the products and production processes, separating out the structural parts from the additional ones. Various combinations of additional parts are then formed to create a variety of finished products.
2. Combine identical modules, thus establishing which modules are identical; the products are then built primarily by varying the number of these modules.
3. Combine independent modules; to build the products different types of modules are used, each of which has been designed to perform specific functions.

The third technique, multifunctionality and integration, is to reduce the number of component parts and the number of production processes utilized to process them. This gives rise to a series of alternative physical structures realizable with the smallest possible number of parts.

The fourth technique—range—is mainly employed when the objects of examination are dimensions, numerical values, and specifications. The goal is to ascertain a range or interval within which a specific requirement can be applied, minimizing the type of parts performing a particular function.

The fifth technique ensures that the variable parts is in compliance with a "series" of performance and measurement values. By pinpointing these basic principles for ordering the values, it is possible to reduce the proliferation factors of useless parts.

Product Range Planning

The product range planning is used to build an industrial plan based on the full range of the models to be developed in the next three to five years. For each of these models are defined: the market phase-in and phase-out dates, the costs, and the profits so far as all the relevant information needed to build the plan.

All current and future products of the company are shown in the plan.

It is drawn up using the format of Figure A.10.

The data are drawn from the Concept Papers of the related single products or product families. You can see a real example in Figure A.11.

It is typically updated quarterly rolling with the consolidation of the sold units in the quarter and with the addition of a further quarter to maintain the fixed horizon of at least three years. All the data will be updated quarterly: volumes, costs, and profits of all models in the plan.

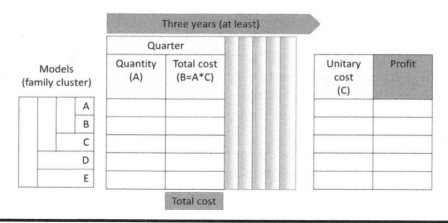

Figure A.10   Product range planning (format).

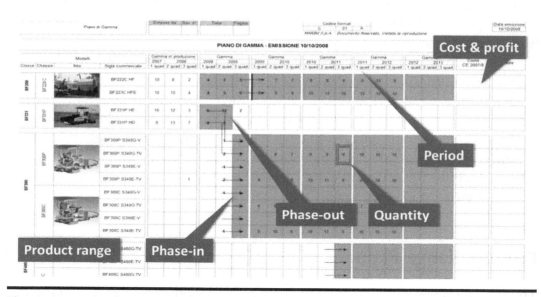

Figure A.11   Product range planning (example).

Coincident Product and Process Modularity

The application of what has been outlined thus far leads to the construction of a mushroom-shaped product architecture (Figure A.12), creating a variety of options at the very first levels of the bill of materials.

It must be noted, however, that the range variety also has a parallel course with regards to the production process. The concept of "modularity in production," especially from a mass customization perspective[11] should also be considered. The variety funnel (Figure A.13) can be used to

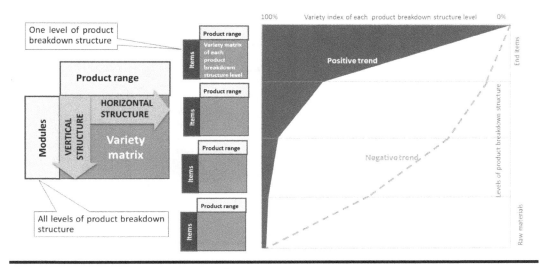

Figure A.12   Mushroom concept of range.

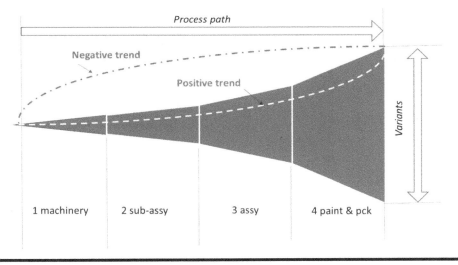

Figure A.13   Manufacture variety funnel. (Hines, P., Silvi, R., Bartolini, M., 2003, p. 79.)

understand how much variety impacts the efficiency and effectiveness of the production Value Stream.

Through greater organizational autonomy, a group of focused and accountable module owners working on their modules will enhance the quality level of their modules, their rate of development, and their continual innovation, with a visible impact on the whole system/product.[12]

In addition, a greater involvement on the part of production units/cells dedicated to specific processes or components will help to accelerate the time-to-market and the rate of innovative development of the modules and

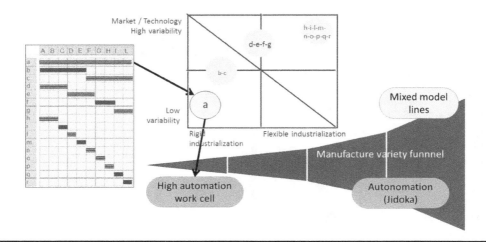

Figure A.14   Variety versus industrialization.

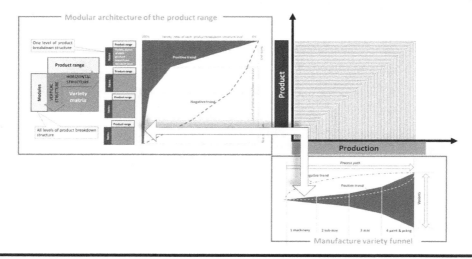

Figure A.15   Alignment of variety distribution.

their associated processes. Finally, Systems Integrators play an important role, especially in the design phase of the product, facilitating interorganizational coordination between the different people contributing to the module design and those involved in the production processes. Figure A.14 illustrates the relative trade-offs between product variety and industrialization.

A modular development strategy must clearly take place early in the Kentou phase, and the innovation must emerge from the best combination of both the product and the process point of view (Figure A.15).

The industrial vision for product families developed with this method is to build basic shared modules that can be produced in specific cells, and to

have very short flexible assembly lines designed to make a variety of finished products to respond quickly to specific customer orders. Known as
mixed-model lines, they must be designed so all the models in the range
can be assembled, often without interruption, bearing in mind the following
characteristics:[13]

- Ability to react to demand
- Quick set-up times from one product to the next
- Ability to appropriately sequence the products to assemble
- Management of component flows
- Management of parallel stations.

Figure A.16 illustrates a solution adopted by one of our clients,
Husqvarna, for the assembly of grass mowers. The solution is based on two
continuous-type lines, in order to eliminate the waiting required with the
four previous synchronous lines. The flow racks permit supplying components from just one side and are designed to accept all the models without
any adaptation.

Using prepared subgroups(kits) to reduce the differences between the
simple and the complex models helped to achieve better line balance and

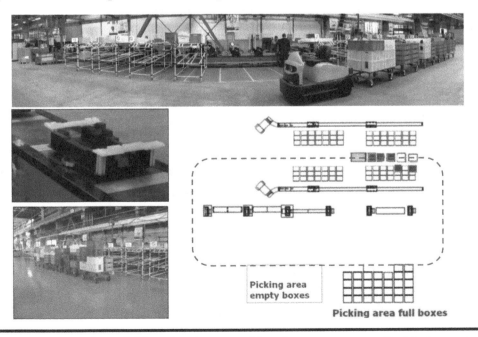

**Figure A.16   Mixed-model line for the assembly of grass mowers. (By kind courtesy of
Husqvarna Outdoor Products Italia S.p.A.)**

a simple distribution system using a tugger transport system. Resupplying is by means of small standard quantities for all components. Using these approaches, the facility was able to reduce the model-change time to essentially zero.

Value Stream Mapping for Production

One basic and simple tool for developing a modular process is the Value Stream Mapping; considered one of the most important—if not the most important—tools in the Lean world, as this book has already frequently demonstrated.

The idea is to produce a simple drawing, outlining the information flow in the top half of a sheet of paper and the material flow in the bottom half, and highlighting the interactions between the two flows. The value added flow time and total flow time are then recorded at the bottom (see Figure A.17), where the added value flow time is 9.5 minutes out of a total of 23.62 days.

The representation of the Current State differs from traditional schemes for studying industrial organization by facilitating the mental process for creating a Future State in a relatively brief period of time.

Improvements are achieved by eliminating all the activities with no value added and reducing the ones that have no value added but are necessary.

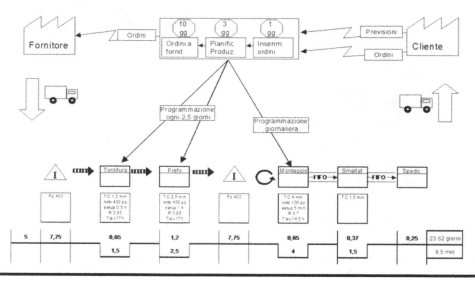

Figure A.17   Value Stream Map.

From the modularity point of view, there are three aspects of the Lean approach that make it possible to achieve the Future State:

■ The supermarket
■ The pacemaker
■ The FIFO (First In First Out) line.

To reduce throughput time, the Toyota Production System vision is that the upstream process only produces what the downstream customer consumes. This is similar to the principle used for restocking shelves in a supermarket. This makes it possible to always have components, and to rapidly replenish the amount "pulled" by the customer. Setting up a pull supermarket of this kind involves the planning of production in just one point of the Value Stream, the pacemaker process, so named because it controls the pace of all the upstream processes. Downstream of the pacemaker, the flow continues with a FIFO logic.

Coming back to our module discussion. The proliferation of variants should occur in the same point, in order to have in the supermarket a common base of product component modules. Customization then takes place in the remaining part of the flow as shown in Figure A.18.

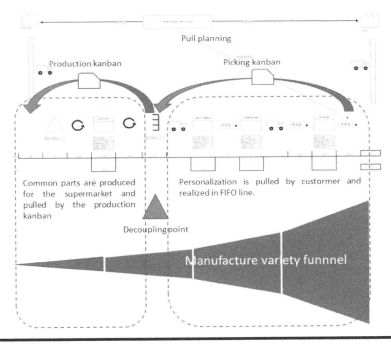

Figure A.18   Highlighting of the modular process on the Value Stream Map.

Steps for the Modular Development of a Product Range

Innovation based on the modular development of a product family, as described in the previous sections, can be summarized in the chart shown in Figure A.19. The module strategy should be an integral part of Lean Product and Process Development (LPPD) described in this book.

We can summarize the general process at a glance as follows.

We start from the Concept Paper, derived from the research of innovation, and from product range planning integrated in the document.

According to the information contained inside the document, we build variety matrix and the mushroom of the product range to keep aligned with the manufacturing variety funnel.

The vertical structure of the variety matrix we get with the split into modules of the product under development by the following steps: Kentou (Set-Based Concurrent Engineering), basic design, detailed design, industrialization, etc.

In the framework of the modular methodology, the key issue is the effective collaboration of all those involved in the product design and the production process design.

The product architecture is constructed so as to identify the widest possible product range (Figure A.20), in order to grasp opportunities and respond to threats throughout the product's life cycle, without the need for systemic redesigns. It also needs to be aligned to the Concept Paper.

Applying Modularity in the Service Sector

Modularity may be adopted for intangible products and product families. In such cases, the product domain and the process domain overlap, merging into a single service platform.[14]

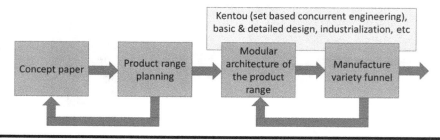

Figure A.19   Steps for the modular development of a product range.

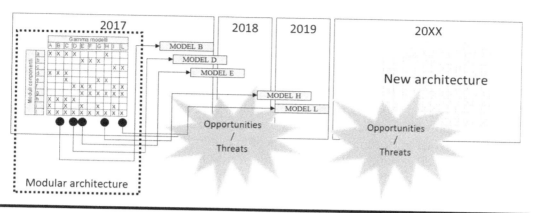

Figure A.20   Rolling logic of the modular development of a product family.

Modularity and the adoption of a platform approach enable service companies not only to compete in the market with efficiency, quality, and production flexibility, but also to continually and readily "create" new markets.

Designing a shared product structure in the same ways as those described for physical products, comparable to an "open" modularity, leads to the effective and efficient generation of a variety of services.[15]

The conceptual model for the modular service platform is first of all an organizational structure not entirely visible to the customer. The client has the perception of receiving a customized service when the service provider has actually adopted production standardization.

Mass customization is implemented by creating standardized service modules for market segments, for example in logistical services, and combining them in various ways to enable the company to satisfy different market demands. In any case, the customization of the service takes place at the point of delivery (paper, electronic, email, etc.).

This is becoming a widespread trend in many service companies, where the differentiation of the final service to the customer is obtained by skillfully putting together standard modules and processes, assembling them in different ways to create a unique product for the end customer. Examples of these can be seen in financial services (credit cards, bank accounts), insurance (policies with various add-on features) and restaurants (menus with common ingredients recombined to make a variety of entrees).

As we have seen, a well thought out module strategy for products (and services) can dramatically reduce costs while also reducing time to market. It also can provide customers more product choices to fit their individual needs and grow sales. While challenging to implement at first, the long-term benefits are clearly worth the effort.

Notes

1. Co-founder and partner of Lenovys, Gianluigi Belli has wide experience in the areas of product development, industrialization, and production. After working for some large mechanical and aeronautical companies, he moved into consultancy, working together with leading Italian and international companies. In a career spanning over twenty years, he has successfully completed innumerable projects with important firms in almost every industrial sector.
2. Baldwin, C.B., Clark, K.B., 1997, pp. 84–93; Calcagno, M., 1999, pp. 201–240; Langlois, R.N., 1999.
3. Zipkin, P., 2001; Sanchez, R., Heene, A., 2001.
4. Lanzara, R., Giuliani, E., 2001.
5. Bianchi, F., Koudate, A., Shimizu, T., 1996.
6. Bianchi, F., 2002.
7. Garud, R., Kumaraswamy, A., 1995, pp. 93–110.
8. see Maskell B. and BMA Inc. Team, *Lean Business Management System*, Cherry Hill, NJ, USA: BMA Publishing, September 1, 2007.
9. Ulrich K., 1995.
10. Pahl G., Beitz W., 1988.
11. Baldwin C.B., Clark K.B., 1997; Mikkola J.H., 2003, pp. 439–454.
12. Benassi M., Tunisini A., 2000.
13. See also Mansouri S.A., "A Multi-Objective Genetic Algorithm for Mixed-Model Sequencing on JIT Assembly Lines," *International Journal of Operational Research,* 167, 2004, pp. 696–716.
14. Ulrich and Robertson (Ulrich K., Robertson D., 1998, p. 21) define the service platform as a collection of resources shared between a variety of products.
15. Gallinaro S., 2009.

Glossary

The glossary contains the more specialist terms used in this book. For a more in-depth treatment, or for terms not included in this glossary, further resources are available at www.lenovys.com.

5S: Working tool and method for obtaining an organized, tidy workplace with everything that is strictly necessary. The term refer to the first letters of the five, transliterated Japanese words summing up the five phases of the method: sort, setting in order, sweeping, standardizing, and sustaining.

A3 Report: Problem-solving and coaching practice developed by Toyota. It consists of getting a given problem, the analysis, the corrective measures, and the action plan down onto a single sheet of A3 paper, often making use of graphs and illustrations. It is one of the main tools for making communication more effective and for teaching the practice of problem-solving.

Added value activities: Activities with a value for which the customer is willing to pay. In production, added value activities are mechanical jobs and processes. In deciding whether an activity creates value or not, it is fundamental to consider how the end customer perceives it, the value that the client associates with a given activity, and value that he or she is willing to pay for that activity.

Andon (= lantern): Term used to refer to a visual system that highlights the state of a process and it points out when there is an anomaly. Typical examples are the luminous boards often found in workshops or production departments in order to make clearly visible various kinds of information about the state of the system or the production process.

Balanced scorecard: Performance measuring technique that considers four aspects: client satisfaction, internal productivity, innovation and continual improvement, and the financial aspect.

Benchmarking: Technique for comparing one's performance with that of one's competitors, determining the existing gap and the reasons for it, and using the information to improve the performance itself. The focus of benchmarking may be strategy, a process, a method, an operation, and so on.

Brainstorming: Group technique designed to generate as many ideas as possible with the aim to investigate many aspects without the subsequent critical analysis.

Cause-effect diagram: Also known as the "Ishikawa diagram," after the engineer who developed it, or the "fishbone diagram," because the complete diagram resembles the skeleton of a fish. It is used for the analysis of root causes during problem-solving, so as to explore and illustrate the main causes and sub-causes that yield a given effect (the problem).

Cell: Group of workstations ordered according to the sequence of the operations of a process for continual flow production.

Checklist: Tool used to ensure that all the important phases or actions in an operation have been done. Checklists contain elements that are important for or relevant to a given problem or situation.

Commonality index: Measure of a sub-assembly's potential to realize multiple finished products.

Concept Paper: Document that contains all the useful information for developing a new product: goals, team, market analysis, cost targets, basic trade-off curves, etc. Once approved, the Concept Paper becomes the reference document for all the members of the product and process development team.

Continuous improvement: Continuous improvement of products, services, or processes through small incremental improvements and gradual steps forward.

Corrective action: Implementation of actions to reduce or eliminate a problem that has arisen.

Cost drivers: Elements that have a significant impact on the cost of the product.

Cost of non-quality: Cost associated with the supply of poor-quality products or services. There are four categories of such costs: internal malfunctioning costs (associated with defects found before the customer receives the product or service), external malfunctioning costs (associated with defects found after the customer receives the product or service), control costs (sustained in order to determine the degree of compliance with quality requirements), and prevention costs (sustained to keep to a minimum the costs of malfunctioning and control).

Cross-functional team: Team made up of people from all the company departments: marketing, production, technical office, R & D, administration, purchasing, quality, sales, etc.

Customer need: The customer's product or service need, to be satisfied irrespective of the type of technology used.

Design review: Milestone in a product development process, when a project is assessed in relation to its targets, so as to evaluate the result of previous activities and identify problems that may have emerged before moving on to new activities.

Engineering checklist: Set of checklists supplied to project designers with the aim of avoiding previously made errors, using the best methods available, facilitating the standardization of parts, facilitating the revision of a design, etc.

Evaluation matrix: Methodology used to compare different design alternatives in an objective way, taking account of all the project goals at the same time.

FMEA—Failure Mode and Effects Analysis: Method for discovering and analyzing every potential failure mode of a system or sub-system, determining its effect on other sub-elements and on the functionality of the element produced.

FMECA—Failure Mode, Effects, and Criticality Analysis: Like the FMEA, but including criticality analysis as well; this is done to correlate the probability of occurrence of the various failure modes with the severity of their consequences.

Fundoshi scheduling: Detailed scheduling of all the activities involved in every single part or component of the product. It is a fundamental tool for Pull Planning in projects.

Genchi Genbutsu: "Go and see for yourself": this is part of the Toyota Production System, where the emphasis is placed on the importance of gathering information personally and directly in the field, so as to avoid errors in design and evaluation in general.

Hansei (reflection): A practice of continuous improvement. It involves looking back, objectively evaluating results achieved, and thinking about how a technical or organizational process can be improved.

Hoshin Kanri: A fundamental tool in Lean Leadership, which focuses on the "management of objectives." The main goal is to align the vision and the objectives of the group. It is used to subdivide high-level company objectives into objectives at operative level, enabling everyone to grasp their contribution to the overall project.

Impact Innovation: The management framework developed by Lenovys in order to enhance the capacity to generate innovation in the company. It is composed of five elements: Innovation Strategy, that focus on the customer problems to be solved through product and services; Impact Design, the focus on the right way to develop winning product and service; Impact Review, the focus on the way to go faster and successfully on the market; Innovation Governance, that focus on the company systems to manage the innovation projects in the company; and Innovation Enablers, that focus on the way to get advantage by using at the right time the right internal and external levers.

Jidoka: *Jidoka* can be described as "automation with a human touch," and it consists of the automatizing of mechanical processes so that machines are able to detect the production of defective parts and shut down immediately until the operator intervenes. In this way, the defect is not replicated over time. It is a quality control process used in the Toyota Production System, which applies the following four principles: find the abnormality and then stop, fix, and correct the condition, investigating the causes of the error and implementing a countermeasure.

Just in time: Production methodology introduced by the Toyota Motor Company, whereby each workstation receives the materials it requires from the upstream station exactly when, and in the quantity in which, they are needed.

KAI—Key Activity Indicators: Measures that quantify the level of activities underway prior to the definite performance indicators (e.g., the number of anomalies detected, the number of improvement teams closed down).

Kaikaku: Radical change.

Kaizen: Literally, "change for the better." This is a Japanese term that expresses the idea of continuous and overall improvement in order to achieve ever higher standards, creating increasing value with less waste and less effort.

Kanban: Japanese word meaning "signboard" or "chart." This is a method of communication for unblocking the movement of material when a one-piece flow is not possible. It is also a signal of the necessity for the upstream process to produce material for the ones that follow it.

Kentou: Phase of creativity at the beginning of the product development process. Various different conceptual alternatives are generated.

KozoKeikaku (K4): Document that brings together all the various individual study drawings of the components. It is the design plan of the overall vehicle, containing all the critical issues for the assembly and the vehicle's system requirements.

KPI—Key Performance Indicators: The key performance measures of a company or process.

Lead time: Time taken from the placement of an order by the customer through to its delivery. In manufacturing, it is the time from when the primary materials arrive to when the finished items rolls off the production line.

Lean Leadership: Model of leadership based on the Toyota Way principles in which the management supports the organization by creating clear objectives, providing tools and knowledge, and removing barriers that prevent satisfaction of customer needs, with zero waste in the whole organization.

Lean Lifestyle®: The management framework developed by Lenovys in order to implement the Lean Thinking as a Lifestyle. The ultimate goal of the Lean Lifestyle® is to get more value with less stress and waste of people energy, bringing at the same time well-being and high performance in the company. It is composed of five sections: Personal Excellence, Energy, People Development, Vision, and Lifestyle Excellence.

Lean Production: Production strategy that, compared with traditional mass production, permits a more sparing use of resources. The focus is on the elimination of waste and of the activities in the process that do not have added value.

LPPD: Lean Product & Process Development.

Make or buy: Tool for comparing the cost and strategic risks with the benefits of creating a product or service in-house rather than buying it from an outside supplier.

MDT—Module Development Team: Development team responsible for a subsystem of the vehicle, which reports to the Chief Engineers Team.

Mizen Boushi: Design process to achieve quality by making every possible effort to design intrinsics in the process of devising countermeasures for possible problems.

Modularity: An approach to project design that breaks down a product into smaller systems (modules) that can be created independently and reused in different products. The main benefits of this project technique derive from the possibility of creating broad product ranges starting from a small number of standard components. This offers advantages in terms of production costs, flexibility, and response time.

Muda: Waste activities that do not add value for the customer.

Mura: Waste resulting from fluctuations, variability, and a lack of leveling.

Muri: Waste generated by the overloading of a production resource or of a person.

Nemawashi: Process that lays the foundations for the making of decisions by slowly building consensus and giving deep consideration to all the options. Such decisions can then be taken rapidly.

Obeya room: Large room in which the Chief Engineer and all the members of the project team work together. Simple visual management tools are used to display on the walls of the room the state of progress of each sector with respect to the project targets.

OPL—One Point Lesson: Document summing up, in a simple, visual manner, key information for training in relation to a specific, crucial point.

Pareto diagram: Graphic technique for quantifying the impact of each problem by means of a common measure (occurrence, severity, downtime generated, etc.), so that efforts can be concentrated on solving the "few vital things," ignoring the "many things of little importance." By working on the 20% of most important things, it is usually possible to impact on 80% of the total problem.

PDCA: An acronym for Plan-Do-Check-Act, this is the model underlying the continuous improvement process. It consists of four phases: planning, execution of the program, testing and checking of results, and action to make the achieved results definitive. Also known as the Deming cycle or wheel.

PDVSM—Product Development Value Stream Mapping: Method for mapping the activities performed by all the working groups involved in a product development project. Its purpose is to gain a shared vision of risks and opportunities in a simple, visual manner.

Poka Yoke: Mistake proofing system. This design technique makes it practically impossible to produce a defective piece, even by an untrained operator. In other words, it is a process/tool built in such a way as not to permit the generation of defects (for example, a square pin and a round hole).

Quality Function Deployment: Structured method whereby customer requirements are transformed into appropriate technical requirements for each phase of the product development and production. The QFD process can also be described as "listening to what the customer is saying."

Reliability: The probability that a product will work for a certain period of time in the conditions defined within the technical specifications.

Reworking: Work with no value added that is necessary to correct a defect or an error that has occurred during the process.

Ringi System: Way of achieving a consensus on new ideas that are typical of Japanese firms. It is based on wide-ranging consultation between managers at different levels. The ideas start from the lowest levels and work their way upward when they are approved by the level management. Final approval is given by the top management.

Risk Assessment: Quantitative and qualitative assessment of the risks associated with a project/idea and a known threat. The risk is quantified by calculating the size of the loss and the probability of that loss occurring.

SBCE—Set-Based Concurrent Engineering: Expression referring to the practice of taking many design alternatives into consideration from the outset, moving them forward, selecting them on the basis of emerging restrictions, and maintaining a range of solutions coherent with the final product.

Sensei: Japanese term meaning "teacher." A *sensei* is a person with a profound knowledge of the Lean system, who teaches its principles in a business. The figure is akin to that of a coach or mentor, external or internal, who teaches by example and by working alongside others.

SMED—Single Minute Exchange of Die: Method for changing rapidly from one product to another in the same production process, in order to reduce batch sizes and therefore waste.

Standardized work: Document that combines the elements of a particular job into the most effective and waste-free sequence in order to obtain the maximum level of efficiency in a process.

Takt Time: Relationship between the time available for delivering the products and the volume of products to deliver in the given time period. Takt Time represents the "rhythm of demand," and hence "consequently" the delivery rate of the Lean business. As a consequence, it determines the speed at which the flow will proceed, in that it establishes every how often a product must move from one phase to another of the production flow, so that production and consumption are synchronized.

Throughput time: Time required by a product to proceed from the concept to the launch, from order to shipment or delivery of the material into the hands of the customer. It includes both the processing time and the queue time.

Value Stream Mapping: Identification and graphic representation of all the activities performed along the value stream relating to a product or family of products.

Variety matrix: Matrix that analyzes the percentages of commonality between the components/modules and the total of the models/versions of a product range.

VRP—Variety Reduction Program: Methodology enabling the reduction of overall costs by rationalizing the variety of products and processes in the design phase.

WIP—Work In Process: Items or information that are in the course of being processed in one of the various steps.

Bibliography

Allen T.J. and Fusfeld A.R., *Research Laboratory Architecture and the Structuring of Communications*, Cambridge, MA: MIT Press, 1974.

Attali J., *Survivre aux crises*, Paris: Fayard, 2009.

Badia E., *Zara and Her Sisters: The Story of the World's Largest Clothing Retailer*, London: Palgrave Macmillan, 2009.

Baldwin C.B. and Clark K.B., "Managing in the age of modularity," *Harvard Business Review*, 75 (5), 1997.

Benassi M. and Tunisini A., *Esperienze modulari nella produzione*, Padua: CEDAM, 2000.

Bianchi F., *Dal cliente al profitto*, Milan: Franco Angeli, 2002.

Bianchi F., Koudate A. and Shimizu T., *Dall'idea al cliente*, Milan: Il Sole 24 Ore Libri, 1996.

Brown B.B. and Anthony S., "How P&G tripled its innovation success rate," *Harvard Business Review*, June 2011.

Calcagno M., "Nuove logiche di progettazione: architetture modulari e strategie multiprogetto," *Finanza, Marketing e Produzione*, September 1999.

Covey S.R., *First Things First*, New York: Touchstone, 1997.

Crenshaw D., *The Myth of Multitasking: How Doing It All Gets Nothing Done*, San Francisco, CA: Jpssey Bass Wiley, 2009.

Cusumano M. and Nobeoka K., *Thinking Beyond Lean*, New York: The Free Press, 1998.

Ericsson A. and Gunnar E., *Controlling Design Variants: Modular Product Platform*, Southfield, MI: SME, 1999.

Fleischer M. and Liker, J.K., *Concurrent Engineering Effectiveness: Integrating Product Development Across Organizations*, Munich: Hanser-Gardner, 1997.

Gallinaro S., "La modularità nello sviluppo e nella produzione dei servizi," *Impresa Progetto* (DITEA online magazine), 1, 2009.

Garud R. and Kumaraswamy A., "Technological and organizational designs to achieve economies of substitution," *Strategic Management Journal*, 16, 1995.

Godin S., *Linchpin: Are You Indispensable?*, New York: Portfolio, 2011.

Goleman D., *Working with Emotional Intelligence*, New York: Bantam, 2000.

Hines P., Silvi R. and Bartolini M., *From Lean To Profit*, Milan: Franco Angeli, 2003.

Hölttä-Otto K., *Modular Product Platform Design*, Helsinki: Helsinki University of Technology, 2005.

Hopp W. and Spearman M., *Factory Physics*, New York: McGraw-Hill/Irwin Series Operations and Decision Sciences, 2007.

Isaacson W., *Steve Jobs*, New York: Simon&Schuster, 2011.

Jay E., *The Steve Jobs Way: iLeadership for a New Generation*, New York: Carroll & Graf, 2011.

Kahney L., *Inside Steve's brain*, New York: Portfolio, 2008.

Kennedy M.N., *Product Development for the Lean Enterprise*, Richmond, VA: The Oaklea Press, 2003.

Kim W.C. and Mauborgne R., *Blue Ocean Strategy*, Cambridge, MA: Harvard Business Review Press, 2005.

Koch R., *The 80/20 Principle: The Secret to Achieving More with Less*, New York: Crown Business, 1998.

Kramer S.J. and Amabile T.M., "The power of small wins," *Harvard Business Review*, May 2011.

Kohdate A. and Suzue T., *Variety Reduction Program*, Cambridge, MA: Productivity Press, 1990.

Langlois R.N., "Modularity in technology, organization and society, working paper," University of Connecticut, 1999.

Lanzara R. and Giuliani E., "Mass customization ed evoluzione progettuale del prodotto: un riesame teorico-empirico," *Finanza, Marketing e Produzione*, 20, 2001.

Lean Product Development Benchmark Report, Boston, MA: Aberdeen Group, 2007.

Liker J.K., *Becoming Lean: Inside Stories of U.S. Manufacturers*, Porltand, OR: Productivity Press, 1997.

Liker J.K., *The Toyota Way: Fourteen Management Secrets from the World's Greatest Manufacturer*, New York: McGraw-Hill, 2004.

Liker J.K., *The Toyota Way Fieldbook*, New York: McGraw-Hill, 2006.

Liker J.K., *Toyota Culture: The Heart and Soul of the Toyota Way*, New York: McGraw-Hill, 2008.

Liker J.K., *Toyota Under Fire: Lessons for Turning Crisis into Opportunity*, New York: McGraw-Hill, 2011.

Liker J.K. and Convis G., *The Toyota Way to Lean Leadership*, New York: McGraw-Hill, 2011.

Liker J.K. and Meier D., *Toyota Talent: Developing your People; The Toyota Way*, New York: McGraw-Hill, 2007.

Liker J.K., Ettlie J.E., and Campbell J.C., *Engineered in Japan: Japanese Technology Management Practices*, New York: Oxford University Press, 1995.

Loehr J. and Schwartz T., *The Power of Full Engagement*, New York: Simon & Schuster Paperbacks, 2005.

Mikkola J.H., "Modularity, component out-sourcing and inter-firm learning," *R&D Management*, 33 (4), 2003.

Morgan J. and Liker J.K., *The Toyota Product Development System: Integrating People, Process, and Technology*, New York: Productivity Press, 2006.

Pahl G. and Beitz W., *Engineering Design. A Systematic Approach*, London: Springer, 1988.

Pessoa M.V., *Lean Advancement Initiative*, Cambridge, MA: Massachusetts Institute of Technology, 2008.

Phelps E.S. and Tilman L.M., "Wanted: A first national bank of innovation," *Harvard Business Review*, January 2010.

Ramani K., Cunningham R., Devanathan S., Subramaniam J., and Patwardhan H., *Technology Review of Mass Customization, International Conference on Economic, Technical and Organisational Aspects of Product Configuration Systems*, Copenhagen, June 2004.

Richtel M., "As gadgets take over, focus falters," *The New York Times*, June 14, 2010.

Rosso R., *Be Stupid*, Milan: Rizzoli, 2011.

Rother M., *Learning to See: Value Stream Mapping to Add Value and Eliminate MUDA*, Cambridge, MA: Lean Enterprise Institute, 1999.

Rother M. and Harris R., *Creating Continuous Flow*, Cambridge, MA: Lean Enterprise Institute, 2001.

Sanchez R. and Heene A., *The New Strategic Management. Organization, Competition and Competence*, New York: John Wiley & Sons, 2001.

Schonberger R.J., *World Class Manufacturing*, New York: Free Press, 2008.

Stenebo J., *The Truth about Ikea*, London: Gibson Square Books, 2010.

Stone R.B., Wood K.L., and Crawford R.H., "A heuristic method for identifying modules for product architecture," *Design Studies*, 21, 2000.

Taiichi O., *Toyota Production System: Beyond Large-Scale Production*, Portland, OR: Productivity Press, 1988.

Ulrich K., "The role of product architecture in the manufacturing firm," *Research Policy*, 24, 1995.

Ulrich K. and Eppinger S.D., *Product Design and Development*, New York: McGraw-Hill, 2004.

Ulrich K. and Robertson D., "Planning for product platform," *Sloan Management Review*, Summer 1998.

Walton M., *Strategies for Lean Product Development*, MIT Working Paper Series, Lean Aerospace Initiative, 1999.

Ward A.C., *Lean Product and Process Development*, Cambridge, MA: Lean Enterprise Institute, 2007.

Womack J.P. and Jones D.T., *Lean Thinking*, New York: Free Press, 1998.

Womack J.P., Jones D.T., and Roos D., *The Machine That Changed the World: The Story of Lean Production*, New York: Harper Perennial, 1990.

Zipkin P., "The limits of mass customization," *Sloan Management Review*, 2001.

Index